SPSS Categories® 8.0

For more information about SPSS® software products, please write or call

Marketing Department
SPSS Inc.
444 North Michigan Avenue
Chicago, IL 60611
Tel: (312) 329-2400
Fax: (312) 329-3668

SPSS Categories® 8.0
Copyright © 1998 by SPSS Inc.
All rights reserved.
Printed in the United States of America.

1 2 3 4 5 6 7 8 9 0   01 00 99 98

ISBN 1-56827-211-1

Preface

SPSS 8.0 is a powerful software package for data management and analysis. The Categories option is an add-on enhancement that provides a comprehensive set of procedures for optimal scaling. The procedures in Categories must be used with the SPSS Base system and are completely integrated into that system.

The Categories option includes:

- Optimal scaling techniques that cover two-way correspondence tables, multiway contingency tables, and comparisons of sets of variables of mixed measurement levels.

- A variety of high-resolution graphic plots for easy interpretation of optimal scaling results.

About This Manual

This manual is divided into two sections. The first section documents the graphical user interface and provides examples of the statistical techniques available. In addition, this section offers advice on interpreting the output. The second part of the manual is a Syntax Reference section that provides complete command syntax for all of the commands included in the Categories option. Most features of the system can be accessed through the dialog box interface, but some functionality can be accessed only through command syntax.

This manual contains two indexes: a subject index and a syntax index. The subject index covers both sections of the manual. The syntax index applies only to the Syntax Reference section.

Acknowledgments

The optimal scaling procedures and their SPSS implementation were developed by the Data Theory Group in the Faculty of Social and Behavioral Sciences at Leiden University, the Netherlands. We would like to thank the Leiden group for their expertise and advice in the development and documentation of the optimal scaling techniques included in SPSS Categories.

Willem Heiser, Jacqueline Meulman, Gerda van den Berg, and Patrick Groenen were involved with the 1990 versions of the HOMALS, PRINCALS, and OVERALS procedures. Jacqueline Meulman, Peter Neufeglise, and Anita van der Kooij were responsible for the development of the new CATREG and CORRESPONDENCE procedures.

Compatibility

The SPSS system is designed to operate on many computer systems. See the materials that came with your system for specific information on minimum and recommended requirements.

Customer Service

If you have any questions concerning your shipment or account, contact your local office, listed on page v. Please have your serial number ready for identification when calling.

Training Seminars

SPSS Inc. provides both public and onsite training seminars. All seminars feature hands-on workshops. Seminars will be offered in major cities on a regular basis. For more information on these seminars, call your local office, listed on page v.

Technical Support

The services of SPSS Technical Support are available to registered customers. Customers may contact Technical Support for assistance in using SPSS products or for installation help for one of the supported hardware environments. To reach Technical Support, see the SPSS home page on the World Wide Web at *http://www.spss.com*, or call your local office, listed on page v. Be prepared to identify yourself, your organization, and the serial number of your system.

Tell Us Your Thoughts

Your comments are important. Please send us a letter and let us know about your experiences with SPSS products. We especially like to hear about new and interesting applications using the SPSS system. Write to SPSS Inc. Marketing Department, Attn.: Director of Product Planning, 444 N. Michigan Avenue, Chicago, IL 60611.

Contacting SPSS

If you would like to be on our mailing list, contact one of our offices, listed on page v, or visit our WWW site at *http://www.spss.com*. We will send you a copy of our newsletter and let you know about SPSS Inc. activities in your area.

SPSS Inc.
Chicago, Illinois, U.S.A.
Tel: 1.312.329.2400
Fax: 1.312.329.3668
Customer Service:
1.800.521.1337
Sales:
1.800.543.2185
sales@spss.com
Training:
1.800.543.6607
Technical Support:
1.312.329.3410
support@spss.com

SPSS Federal Systems
Arlington, Virginia, U.S.A.
Tel: 1.703.527.6777
Fax: 1.703.527.6866

SPSS Argentina srl
Buenos Aires, Argentina
Tel: +541.816.4086
Fax: +541.814.5030

SPSS Asia Pacific Pte. Ltd.
Singapore, Singapore
Tel: +65.3922.738
Fax: +65.3922.739

SPSS Australasia Pty. Ltd.
Sydney, Australia
Tel: +61.2.9954.5660
Fax: +61.2.9954.5616

SPSS Belgium
Heverlee, Belgium
Tel: +32.162.389.82
Fax: +32.1620.0888

SPSS Benelux BV
Gorinchem, The Netherlands
Tel: +31.183.636711
Fax: +31.183.635839

**SPSS Central and
Eastern Europe**
Woking, Surrey, U.K.
Tel: +44.(0)1483.719200
Fax: +44.(0)1483.719290

SPSS East Mediterranea and Africa
Herzlia, Israel
Tel: +972.9.526700
Fax: +972.9.526715

SPSS Finland Oy
Sinikalliontie, Finland
Tel: +358.9.524.801
Fax: +358.9.524.854

SPSS France SARL
Boulogne, France
Tel: +33.1.4699.9670
Fax: +33.1.4684.0180

SPSS Germany
Munich, Germany
Tel: +49.89.4890740
Fax: +49.89.4483115

SPSS Hellas SA
Athens, Greece
Tel: +30.1.7251925
Fax: +30.1.7249124

SPSS Hispanoportuguesa S.L.
Madrid, Spain
Tel: +34.91.447.3700
Fax: +34.91.448.6692

SPSS Ireland
Dublin, Ireland
Tel: +353.1.66.13788
Fax: +353.1.661.5200

SPSS Israel Ltd.
Herzlia, Israel
Tel: +972.9.526700
Fax: +972.9.526715

SPSS Italia srl
Bologna, Italy
Tel: +39.51.252573
Fax: +39.51.253285

SPSS Japan Inc.
Tokyo, Japan
Tel: +81.3.5466.5511
Fax: +81.3.5466.5621

SPSS Korea
Seoul, Korea
Tel: +82.2.552.9415
Fax: +82.2.539.0136

SPSS Latin America
Chicago, Illinois, U.S.A.
Tel: 1.312.494.3226
Fax: 1.312. 494.3227

SPSS Malaysia Sdn Bhd
Selangor, Malaysia
Tel: +603.704.5877
Fax: +603.704.5790

SPSS Mexico SA de CV
Mexico DF, Mexico
Tel: +52.5.575.3091
Fax: +52.5.575.2527

**SPSS Middle East and
South Asia**
Dubai, UAE
Tel: +971.4.525536
Fax: +971.4.524669

SPSS Scandinavia AB
Stockholm, Sweden
Tel: +46.8.102610
Fax: +46.8.102550

SPSS Schweiz AG
Zurich, Switzerland
Tel: +41.1.201.0930
Fax: +41.1.201.0921

SPSS Singapore Pte. Ltd.
Singapore, Singapore
Tel: +65.2991238
Fax: +65.2990849

SPSS South Africa
Johannesburg, South Africa
Tel: +27.11.7067015
Fax: +27.11.7067091

SPSS Taiwan Corp.
Taipei, Republic of China
Tel: +886.2.5771100
Fax: +886.2.5701717

SPSS UK Ltd.
Woking, Surrey, U.K.
Tel: +44.1483.719200
Fax: +44.1483.719290

Contents

1   **Introduction to SPSS Optimal Scaling Procedures for Categorical Data   1**

Why Use Optimal Scaling?   1

Optimal Scaling Use   2

Optimal Scaling Level and Measurement Level   3
    Transformation Plots   5
    Category Codes   7

Categorical Regression with Optimal Scaling   9

Nonlinear Principal Components Analysis   10

Nonlinear Canonical Correlation Analysis   11

Correspondence Analysis   12

Homogeneity Analysis   14

Displays with More Than Two Dimensions   15
    Three-dimensional Scatterplots   16
    Scatterplot Matrices   17

Identifying Point Labels on Charts   18

Aspect Ratio in Optimal Scaling Charts   19

2   **Regression with Optimal Scaling (CATREG)   21**

To Obtain a Regression with Optimal Scaling   22
    Define Range and Scale in CATREG   23
    To Define the Range and Scale in CATREG   23
    Regression with Optimal Scaling Options   24
    Regression with Optimal Scaling Transformation Plots   25
    To Obtain Transformation Plots in CATREG   25
    CATREG Command Additional Features   26

3 Nonlinear Principal Components Analysis (PRINCALS) 27

To Obtain a Nonlinear Principal Components Analysis 28
Define Range and Scale in PRINCALS 29
To Define an Optimal Scaling Range and Scale in PRINCALS 30
Define Range in PRINCALS 31
To Define an Optimal Scaling Range in PRINCALS 31
Nonlinear Principal Components Analysis Options 31
PRINCALS Command Additional Features 32

4 Nonlinear Canonical Correlation Analysis (OVERALS) 35

To Obtain a Nonlinear Canonical Correlation Analysis 36
Define Range and Scale in OVERALS 38
To Define an Optimal Scaling Range and Scale in OVERALS 38
Define Range in OVERALS 39
To Define an Optimal Scaling Range in OVERALS 39
Nonlinear Canonical Correlation Analysis Options 40
OVERALS Command Additional Features 41

5 Correspondence Analysis 43

To Obtain a Correspondence Analysis 44
Define Row Range in Correspondence Analysis 45
To Define a Row Range in Correspondence Analysis 45
Define Column Range in Correspondence Analysis 46
To Define a Column Range in Correspondence Analysis 47
Correspondence Analysis Model 48
Correspondence Analysis Statistics 49
Correspondence Analysis Plots 51
CORRESPONDENCE Command Additional Features 52

6 Homogeneity Analysis (HOMALS) 53

To Obtain a Homogeneity Analysis 54
Define Range in Homogeneity Analysis 56
To Define an Optimal Scaling Range in Homogeneity Analysis 56
Homogeneity Analysis Options 56
HOMALS Command Additional Features 57

7 Regression with Optimal Scaling Examples 59

An Example: Carpet Cleaner Data 59
Standard Linear Regression 60
Optimal Scaling 62

Another Example: Ozone Data 72
Categorizing Variables 73
Selection of Transformation Type 74
Optimality of the Quantifications 79
Effects of Transformations 80

8 Nonlinear Principal Components Analysis Examples 83

Basic Terminology 83

Optimal Scaling Level 84
Selecting the Optimal Scaling Level 85

Example 1 86
Number of Dimensions 87
Quantifications 88
Object Scores 89
Component Loadings 90
Additional Dimensions 91

Example 2 93
Numerical Variables 94
Ordinal Variables 96
Transformation Plots 97

9 Nonlinear Canonical Correlation Analysis Examples 101

Basic Terminology 101

Optimal Scaling Level 102

An Example 102
Examining the Data 103
Accounting for Similarity between Sets 104
Component Loadings 108
Transformation Plots 109
Single versus Multiple Category Coordinates 111
Centroids and Projected Centroids 112

An Alternative Analysis   115

General Suggestions   118

10 Correspondence Analysis Examples   119

Example 1   120
  Profiles and Distances   124
  Inertia   126
  Row and Column Scores   126
  Supplementary Profiles   127
  Dimensionality   129
  Contributions   130
  Normalization   133
  Permutations of the Correspondence Table   135
  Confidence Statistics   136

Example 2   137
  Dimensionality   138
  Contributions   139
  Principal Normalization   140
  Symmetrical Normalization   142

Example 3   143
  Row and Column Scores   144

11 Homogeneity Analysis Examples   145

An Example   145
  Multiple Dimensions   146
  Object Scores   147
  Discrimination Measures   148
  Category Quantifications   150
  A More Detailed Look at Object Scores   152
  Omission of Outliers   154

Syntax Reference

Introduction 159

ANACOR 162

CATREG 176

CORRESPONDENCE 185

HOMALS 197

OVERALS 206

PRINCALS 216

Bibliography   227

Subject Index   231

Syntax Index   237

Introduction to SPSS Optimal Scaling Procedures for Categorical Data

SPSS Categories contains five related procedures for performing optimal scaling—Categorical Regression, Nonlinear Principal Components Analysis, Nonlinear Canonical Correlation Analysis, Correspondence Analysis, and Homogeneity Analysis.[1] This chapter describes what each procedure does, the situations in which each procedure is most appropriate, relationships among the procedures, and relationships of these procedures to "classical" statistical procedures.

Why Use Optimal Scaling?

Categorical data are often found in marketing research, survey research, and research in the social and behavioral sciences. In fact, many researchers deal almost exclusively with categorical data. Categorical data are typically summarized in contingency tables. Analysis of tabular data requires a set of statistical models different from the usual correlation- and regression-based approaches used for quantitative data.

Traditional analysis of two-way tables consists of displaying cell counts along with one or more sets of percentages. If the data in the table represent a sample, the chi-square statistic might be computed along with one or more measures of association. Multiway tables are handled with some difficulty, since your view of the data is influenced by which variable is the row variable, which variable is the column variable, and which variables are control variables. Traditional methods don't work well for three or more variables because all statistics that might be produced are conditional statistics which do not in general capture the interrelationships among the variables.

Statisticians have developed loglinear models as a comprehensive way for dealing with two-way and multiway tables. **Loglinear models** is an umbrella term for several different models: models for the log-frequency counts in a two-way or multiway table, logit models for log-odds when one categorical variable is dependent and there are one or more categorical predictor variables, association models for the log-odds ratios in two-way tables, and many other special-purpose models.

Loglinear models have a number of advantages. They are comprehensive models that apply to tables of arbitrary complexity. They provide goodness-of-fit statistics, so

1. These procedures and their SPSS implementation were developed by the Data Theory Group, Faculty of Social and Behavioral Sciences, Leiden University, the Netherlands.

that model-building can be undertaken until a suitable model is found. They provide parameter estimates and standard errors.

However, loglinear models have a number of drawbacks. If the sample size is too small, the chi-square statistic on which the models are based is suspect. If the sample size is too large, it is difficult to arrive at a parsimonious model, and it can be difficult to discriminate between competing models that appear to fit the data. As the number of variables and the number of values per variable go up, models with more parameters are needed, and in practice, researchers have had some difficulty interpreting the parameter estimates.

Optimal scaling is a technique that can be used instead of—or as a complement to—loglinear models. Optimal scaling extends traditional loglinear analyses by incorporating variables at mixed levels. Nonlinear relationships are described by relaxing the metric assumptions of the variables. Rather than interpreting parameter estimates, interpretation is often based on graphical displays in which similar variables or categories are positioned close to each other.

The simplest form of optimal scaling is correspondence analysis for a two-way table. If the two-way table portrays two variables that are associated (not independent), correspondence analysis assigns scores to the categories of the row and column variables in such a way as to account for as much of the association between the two variables as possible. Depending on the dimensionality of the table, correspondence analysis assigns one or more sets of scores to each variable. Conventionally, row and column categories are displayed in two-dimensional plots defined by pairs of these scores. Using correspondence analysis and the plots it produces, you can learn the following: within a variable, categories that are similar or different; within a variable, categories that might be collapsed; across variables, categories that go together; what category a user-missing category most resembles; and what the optimal correlation is between the row and the column variable.

Optimal Scaling Use

The techniques embodied in four of these procedures (Correspondence Analysis, Homogeneity Analysis, Nonlinear Principal Components Analysis, and Nonlinear Canonical Correlation Analysis) fall into the general area of multivariate data analysis known as **dimension reduction**. That is, as much as possible, relationships between variables are represented in a few dimensions, say two or three. This enables you to describe structures or patterns in the relationships between variables that would be too difficult to fathom in their original richness and complexity. In market research applications, these techniques can be a form of **perceptual mapping**. A major advantage of these procedures is that they accommodate data with different levels of optimal scaling.

The final procedure, Categorical Regression, describes the relationship between a categorical response variable and a combination of categorical predictor variables. The categories are quantified such that the squared multiple correlation between the response and the combination of predictors is a maximum. The influence of each predictor variable on the response variable is described by the corresponding regression weight. As in the other procedures, data can be analyzed with different levels of optimal scaling.

Following are brief guidelines for each of the five procedures:

- Use Categorical Regression to predict the values of a categorical dependent variable from a combination of categorical independent variables.

- Use Nonlinear Principal Components Analysis to account for patterns of variation in a single set of variables of mixed optimal scaling levels.

- Use Nonlinear Canonical Correlation Analysis to assess the extent to which two or more sets of variables of mixed optimal scaling levels are correlated.

- Use Correspondence Analysis to analyze two-way contingency tables or data that can be expressed as a two-way table, such as brand preference or sociometric choice data.

- Use Homogeneity Analysis to analyze a categorical multivariate data matrix when you are willing to make no stronger assumption than that all variables are analyzed at the nominal level.

Optimal Scaling Level and Measurement Level

In standard statistical analysis, level of measurement is a fixed property attached to each variable in the analysis. The measurement level guides the choice of an appropriate technique. In Categories, the optimal scaling level is usually regarded as a user-specified option. By adjusting the specified level of optimal scaling for some variables in the analysis, you may be able to uncover hidden nonlinear relationships.

For our purposes, there are three levels in optimal scaling:

- The **nominal** level implies that a variable's values represent unordered categories. Examples of variables that might be nominal are region, zip code area, religious affiliation, and multiple choice categories.

- The **ordinal** level implies that a variable's values represent ordered categories. Examples include attitude scales representing degree of satisfaction or confidence, and preference rating scores.

- The **numerical** (interval) level implies that a variable's values represent ordered categories with a meaningful metric, so that distance comparisons between categories are appropriate. Univariate examples include age in years and income in thousands of dollars.

For example, suppose the variables *race*, *class*, and *age* are coded as shown in Table 1.1.

Table 1.1   Coding scheme for race, class, and age

Race		Class		Age	
1	white	1	lower	20	twenty years old
2	black	2	working	22	twenty-two years old
3	other	3	middle	25	twenty-five years old
		4	upper	27	twenty-seven years old

The values shown represent the categories of each variable. *Race* would be a nominal variable. There are three categories of *race*, with no intrinsic ordering. The values 1 through 3 simply represent the three categories; the coding scheme is completely arbitrary. Class, on the other hand, could be assumed to be an ordinal variable. The original categories form a progession from lower class to upper class. Larger codes represent a higher class. However, only the order information is known—nothing can be said about the distance between adjacent categories. In contrast, *Age* could be assumed to be a numerical variable. In the case of *age*, the distances between the values are intrinsically meaningful. The distance between 20 and 22 is the same as the distance between 25 and 27, while the distance between 22 and 25 is greater than either of these.

The fact that a variable is intrinsically numerical does not mean that a relationship with another numerical variable has to be linear. Two numerical variables can have a nonlinear relationship. For example, age in years and hours spent at work can both be measured at the numerical level, but since both children and retirees spend little or no time at work, the linear correlation between these two variables will probably be low. Optimal scaling can detect nonlinear relationships and produce maximum correlations between the variables.

The five optimal scaling procedures extend the classical statistical techniques of principal components, canonical correlation, and regression analysis to accommodate variables of mixed optimal scaling levels. If the optimal scaling level for all variables in the analysis is chosen as numerical (assuming relationships between the variables be linear), then standard correlation-based statistical procedures in SPSS should be used and there is no need to turn to optimal scaling procedures. However, if variables in the analysis have different optimal scaling levels, or if nonlinearities in the relationships between some pairs of variables are suspected, then the appropriate associated optimal scaling procedure in SPSS Categories should be used.

In optimal scaling, the level for each variable is specified by the user. By varying the specified optimal scaling level of variables in the analysis, you can search for solutions that fit the data well. Optimal scaling will also reveal nonlinear relationships. This is done in exploratory fashion, in contrast to standard hypothesis testing in the context of distributional assumptions such as normality and linearity of regression of the original variables.

The output for optimal scaling analysis includes a set of **optimal quantifications** for the categories of each variable. The optimal scale values are assigned to categories of each variable based on the optimizing criterion of the procedure in use. Unlike the original labels of the nominal or ordinal variables in the analysis, these scale values have metric properties, so these techniques are often described as a form of quantification of qualitative data, which also includes techniques such as nonmetric multidimensional scaling (available in the SPSS ALSCAL procedure). The category quantifications of each variable can be plotted, and their juxtaposition on the same plot is useful for revealing patterns of association between the variables.

The level of optimal scaling determines the optimality properties of the quantifications. For nominal variables, the optimal quantifications are unrestricted. For ordinal variables, the scale values will be ordered in the same manner as the original categories. For numerical variables, the quantifications will not only be ordered, but the difference between any two will be proportional to the difference between the corresponding original categories. Different nonlinear relationships between variables are explored by analyzing the same variable at many different levels in a series of optimal scaling analyses.

Transformation Plots

The different levels at which each variable can be scaled impose different restrictions on the quantifications. Transformation plots illustrate the relationship between the quantifications and the original categories resulting from the selected optimal scaling level. For example, a linear transformation plot results when a variable is treated as numerical. Variables treated as ordinal result in a nondecreasing transformation plot. Transformation plots for variables treated nominally which are U-shaped (or the reverse) display a quadratic relationship. Nominal variables could also yield transformation plots without apparent trends by changing the order of the categories completely. Figure 1.1 displays a sample transformation plot.

Transformation plots are particularly suited to determining how well the selected optimal scaling level performs. If several categories receive similar quantifications, collapsing these categories into one category may be warranted. Alternatively, if a variable treated as nominal receives quantifications that display an increasing trend, an ordinal transformation may result in a similar fit. If that trend is linear, numerical treatment may be appropriate. However, if collapsing categories or changing scaling levels is warranted, the analysis will not change significantly.

Figure 1.1   Transformation plot of price (numerical)

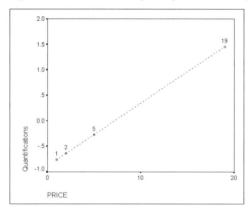

Although PRINCALS and HOMALS do not currently offer the transformation plot in Figure 1.1 as an option, creating this plot is a straightforward procedure. For each variable, create a new variable containing the values (and labels) of the categories. Create a new variable containing the quantifications for that variable from the Categories analysis. For variables treated as nominal or ordinal, use the Line facility with the data in the chart representing the values of individual cases. Use the quantifications for the line in the chart and use the categories to label the chart. For variables treated as numerical, use the Scatterplot facility to plot the quantifications against the categories.

Scatterplot is preferred to Line for numerical variables because the former preserves the differences between the categories. Compare Figure 1.1 and Figure 1.2. The quantifications and the original categories are identical for the two plots. However, the scatterplot (Figure 1.1) clearly displays the linear restriction on the quantifications.

Because the Line chart (Figure 1.2) ignores the category differences and spaces all observed categories equally along the horizontal axis, the line appears curved.

Figure 1.2   Line chart of price (numerical)

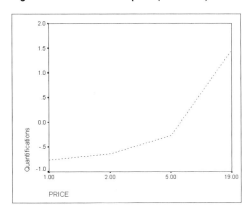

Category Codes

All of the optimal scaling procedures require coding categorical variables using integers. The choice of which integers to use is completely determined by the user. However, some coding schemes may yield unwanted output or incomplete analyses. Possible coding schemes for *Class* are displayed in Table 1.2.

Table 1.2   Alternative Coding Schemes for Class

	Scheme			
Category	**A**	**B**	**C**	**D**
lower	1	1	5	1
working	2	2	6	5
middle	3	3	7	3
upper	4	10	8	7

The range of every variable used in any of the Categories procedures must be defined. Any value outside this range is treated as a missing value. The minimum category value is always 1. The maximum category value is supplied by the user. This value is not the *number* of categories for a variable; it is the *largest* category value. For example, in Table 1.2, scheme A has a maximum category of 4 and scheme B has a maximum category value of 10, yet both schemes code the same four categories.

The variable range determines which categories will be omitted from the analysis. Any categories with codes outside the defined range are omitted from the analysis. This is a simple method for omitting categories, but can result in unwanted analyses. An incorrectly defined maximum category can omit *valid* categories from the analysis. For example, for scheme B, defining the maximum category value to be 4 indicates that *Class* has categories coded from 1 to 4; the *upper* category is treated as missing. Because no category has actually been coded *4*, the fourth category in the analysis contains no cases. If you wanted to omit all upper class categories, this analysis would be appropriate. However, if upper class is to be included, the maximum category must be defined as 10 and missing values must be coded with values above 10 or below 1.

For variables treated as nominal or ordinal, the range of the categories does not affect the results. For nominal variables, only the label and not the value associated with that label is important. For ordinal variables, the order of the categories is preserved in the quantifications; the category values themselves are not important. All coding schemes resulting in the same category ordering will have identical results. For example, the first three schemes in Table 1.2 are functionally equivalent if *Class* is analyzed at an ordinal level. The order of the categories is identical in these schemes. Scheme D, on the other hand, inverts the second and third categories and will yield different results than the other schemes.

Although many coding schemes for a variable are functionally equivalent, schemes with small differences between codes are preferred because the codes have an impact on the amount of output produced by a procedure. All categories coded with values between 1 and the user-defined maximum are valid. If any of these categories are empty, the corresponding quantifications will be either system missing or zero, depending on the procedure. Although neither of these assignments affect the analyses, output is produced for these categories. Thus, for scheme B, *Class* has six categories that receive system missing values. For scheme C, there are four categories receiving system missing indicators. In contrast, for scheme A there are no system missing quantifications. Using consecutive integers as codes for variables treated as nominal or ordinal results in much less output without affecting the results.

Coding schemes for variables treated as numerical are more restricted than the ordinal case. For these variables, the differences between consecutive categories are important. Table 1.3 displays three coding schemes for *Age*.

Table 1.3   Alternative Coding Schemes for Age

Category	Scheme		
	A	B	C
20	20	1	1
22	22	3	2
25	25	6	3
27	27	8	4

Any recoding of numerical variables must preserve the differences between the catego-ries. Using the original values is one method for ensuring preservation of differences. However, this can result in many categories having system missing indicators. For ex-ample, scheme A in Table 1.3 employs the original observed values. For all Categories procedures except for Correspondence Analysis, the maximum category value is 27 and the minimum category value is set to 1. The first 19 categories are empty and receive system missing indicators. The output can quickly become rather cumbersome if the maximum category is much greater than 1 and there are many empty categories between 1 and the maximum.

To reduce the amount of output, recoding can be done. However, in the numerical case, the Automatic Recode facility should not be used. Coding to consecutive integers results in differences of 1 between all consecutive categories and as a result, all quanti-fications will be equally spaced. The metric characteristics deemed important when treating a variable as numerical are destroyed by recoding to consecutive integers. For example, Scheme C in Table 1.3 corresponds to automatically recoding *Age*. The differ-ence between categories *22* and *25* has changed from three to one and the quantifications will reflect the latter difference.

An alternative recoding scheme which preserves the differences between categories is to subtract the smallest category value from every category and add one to each differ-ence. Scheme B results from this transformation. The smallest category value, 20, has been subtracted from each category, and 1 was added to each result. The transformed codes have a minimum of 1 and all differences are identical to the original data. The max-imum category value is now eight and the zero quantifications before the first nonzero quantification are all eliminated. Yet the nonzero quantifications corresponding to each category resulting from scheme B are identical to the quantifications from scheme A.

Categorical Regression with Optimal Scaling

CATREG is an acronym for *cat*egorical *reg*ression with optimal scaling. The goal of re-gression analysis is to predict a response variable from a set of predictor variables. The standard approach requires continuous variables and entails deriving weights for the pre-dictor variables such that the squared correlation between the response and the weighted combination of predictors is a maximum. For any given change in a predictor, the sign of the corresponding weight indicates whether the predicted response increases or de-creases. The size of the weight indicates the amount of change in the predicted response for a one-unit increase in the predictor.

If some of the variables are not continuous, alternative analyses are available. If the response is continuous and the predictors are categorical, analysis of variance is often employed. If the response is categorical and the predictors are continuous, logistic regression or discriminant analysis may be appropriate. If the response and the predic-tors are both categorical, loglinear models are often used.

Categorical regression with optimal scaling extends the standard approaches of regression and loglinear modeling by quantifying categorical variables. Scale values are assigned to each category of every variable such that these values are optimal with respect to the regression. The technique maximizes the squared correlation between the transformed response and the weighted combination of transformed predictors.

One advantage of the optimal scaling approach over standard regression analysis is in dealing with nonlinear relationships between variables. If, for example, a predictor has both high and low values associated with one value of the response, standard linear regression will not perform very well. The predictor receives only one weight, and one weight cannot reflect the same amount of change in the predicted response for both large and small predictor values. However, in CATREG, nonlinear transformations of the variables are employed. The predictor described earlier could be treated as nominal, receiving large quantifications for both large and small observed values. Thus, both values affect the predicted response in the same manner.

In addition to revealing nonlinear relationships between variables, nonlinear transformations of the predictors usually reduce the dependencies among the predictors. If you compare the eigenvalues of the correlation matrix for the predictors with the eigenvalues of the correlation matrix for the optimally scaled predictors, the latter set will usually be less variable than the former. In other words, in CATREG, optimal scaling makes the larger eigenvalues of the predictor correlation matrix smaller and the smaller eigenvalues larger.

Categorical regression with optimal scoring is equivalent to optimal scaling canonical correlation analysis (OVERALS) with two sets, one of which contains only one variable. In the latter technique, similarity of sets is derived by comparing each set to an unknown variable that lies somewhere between all of the sets. In categorical regression, similarity of the transformed response and the linear combination of transformed predictors is assessed directly.

Nonlinear Principal Components Analysis

PRINCALS is an acronym for *prin*cipal *c*omponents analysis via *a*lternating *l*east *s*quares. Standard principal components analysis is a statistical technique that linearly transforms an original set of variables into a substantially smaller set of uncorrelated variables that represents as much of the information in the original set as possible. The goal of principal components analysis is to reduce the dimensionality of the original data set while accounting for as much of the variation as possible in the original set of variables. Objects in the analysis receive component scores. Plots of the component scores reveal patterns among the objects in the analysis and can reveal unusual objects in the data. Standard principal components analysis assumes that all variables in the analysis are measured at the numerical level and that relationships between pairs of variables are linear.

Nonlinear principal components, also known as optimal scaling principal components, extends this methodology so that you can perform principal components analysis with any mix of nominal, ordinal, and numerical scaling levels. The aim is still to account for as much variation in the data as possible, given the specified dimensionality of the analysis. For nominal and ordinal variables, the program computes optimal scale values for the categories.

An important application of PRINCALS is to examine preference data, in which respondents rank or rate a number of items with respect to preference. In the usual SPSS data configuration, rows are individuals, columns are measurements for the items, and the scores across rows are preference scores (on a 0 to 10 scale, for example), making the data row-conditional. For preference data, you may want to treat the individuals as variables. Using the TRANSPOSE procedure, you can transpose the data. The raters become the variables, and all variables are declared ordinal. There is no objection against using more variables than objects in PRINCALS.

More generally, an optimal scaling principal components analysis of a set of ordinal scales is an alternative to computing the correlations between the scales and analyzing them using a standard principal components or factor analysis approach. Research has shown that naive use of the usual Pearson correlation coefficient as a measure of association for ordinal data can lead to nontrivial bias in estimation of the correlations.

If all variables are declared numerical, PRINCALS produces an analysis equivalent to standard principal components analysis using factor analysis. Both procedures have their own benefits.

If all variables are declared multiple nominal, PRINCALS produces an analysis equivalent to a homogeneity analysis run on the same variables. Thus, optimal scaling principal components analysis can be seen as a type of homogeneity analysis in which some of the variables are declared ordinal or numerical.

Nonlinear Canonical Correlation Analysis

Nonlinear canonical correlation analysis (OVERALS), or canonical correlation analysis with optimal scaling, is the most general of the five procedures in the optimal scaling family. This procedure performs nonlinear canonical correlation analysis on two or more sets of variables.

The goal of canonical correlation analysis is to analyze the relationships between sets of variables instead of between the variables themselves, as in principal components analysis. In standard canonical correlation analysis, there are two sets of numerical variables. For example, one set of variables might be demographic background items on a set of respondents, while a second set of variables might be responses to a set of attitude items. Standard canonical correlation analysis is a statistical technique that finds a linear combination of one set of variables and a linear combination of a second set of variables that are maximally correlated. Given this set of linear combinations, canonical correlation analysis can find subsequent independent sets of linear combinations, referred to as canonical variables, up to a maximum number equal to the number of variables in the smaller set.

Optimal scaling canonical correlation analysis extends the standard analysis in several ways. First, there can be two or more sets of variables, so you are not restricted to two sets of variables, as is true in most popular implementations of canonical correlation analysis. Second, the scaling levels in the analysis can be any mix of nominal, ordinal, and numerical. Third, optimal scaling canonical correlation analysis determines the similarity among the sets by simultaneously comparing the canonical variables from each set to a compromise set of scores assigned to the objects.

If there are two sets of variables in the analysis and all variables are defined to be numerical, optimal scaling canonical correlation analysis is equivalent to a standard canonical correlation analysis. Although SPSS does not have a canonical correlation analysis procedure, many of the relevant statistics can be obtained from multivariate analysis of variance.

If there are two or more sets of variables with only one variable per set, optimal scaling canonical correlation analysis is equivalent to optimal scaling principal components analysis. If all variables in a one-variable-per-set analysis are multiple nominal, optimal scaling canonical correlation analysis is equivalent to homogeneity analysis. If there are two sets of variables, one of which contains only one variable, optimal scaling canonical correlation analysis is equivalent to categorical regression with optimal scaling.

Optimal scaling canonical correlation analysis has various other applications. If you have two sets of variables and one of the sets contains a nominal variable declared as single nominal, optimal scaling canonical correlation analysis results can be interpreted in a fashion similar to regression analysis. If you consider the variable to be multiple nominal, the optimal scaling analysis is an alternative to discriminant analysis. Grouping the variables in more than two sets provides a variety of ways to analyze your data.

Correspondence Analysis

The Correspondence Analysis procedure is a very general program to make biplots for correspondence tables, using either chi-squared distances, as in standard correspondence analysis, or Euclidean distances, for more general biplots. This procedure also offers the ability to constrain categories to have equal scores, a useful option to impose ordering on the categories. In addidion, it offers the ability to fit supplementary points into the space defined by the active points.

In a correspondence table, the row and column variables are assumed to represent unordered categories; therefore, we use the nominal optimal scaling level. Both variables are inspected for their nominal information only. That is, the only consideration is the fact that some objects are in the same category, while others are not. Nothing is assumed about the distance or order between categories of the same variable. One specific use of correspondence analysis is the analysis of a two-way contingency table. The SPSS Crosstabs procedure can also be used to analyze contingency tables, but correspondence analysis provides a graphic summary in the form of plots that show the relationships between categories of the two variables.

If a table has r active rows and c active columns, the number of dimensions in the correspondence analysis solution is the minimum of r minus 1 or c minus 1, whichever is less. In other words, you could perfectly represent the row categories or the column categories of a contingency table in a space of $min(r, c) - 1$ dimensions. Practically speaking, however, you would like to represent the row and column categories of a two-way table in a low-dimensional space, say two dimensions, for the obvious reason that two-dimensional plots are comprehensible and multidimensional spatial representations are usually not.

When fewer than the maximum number of possible dimensions is used, the statistics produced in the analysis describe how well the row and column categories are represented in the low-dimensional representation. Provided that the quality of representation of the two-dimensional solution is good, you can examine plots of the row points and the column points to learn which categories of the row variable are similar, which categories of the column variable are similar, and which row and column categories are similar to each other.

Independence is a common focus in contingency table analyses. However, even in small tables, detecting the cause of departures from independence may be difficult. The utility of correspondence analysis lies in displaying such patterns for two-way tables of any size. If there is an association between the row and column variables—that is, if the chi-square value is significant—correspondence analysis may help reveal the nature of the relationship.

Simple correspondence analysis is limited to two-way tables. If there are more than two variables of interest, you can combine variables to create **interaction variables**. For example, for the variables in Table 1.1, you can combine *race* and *class* to create a new variable *raclass* with the twelve categories in Table 1.4. This new variable forms a two-way table with age (twelve rows, four columns), which can be analyzed in correspondence analysis.

Table 1.4   Combinations of race and class

Category Code	Category Definition	Category Code	Category Definition
1	white, lower	7	black, middle
2	white, working	8	black, upper
3	white, middle	9	other, lower
4	white, upper	10	other, working
5	black, lower	11	other, middle
6	black, working	12	other, upper

One shortcoming of this approach is that any pair of variables can be combined. We can combine race and age, yielding another twelve category variable. Or we can combine class and age, which results in a new sixteen category variable. Each of these interaction variables forms a two-way table with the remaining variable. Correspondence analyses of these three tables will not yield identical results, yet each is a valid approach. Furthermore, if there are four or more variables, two-way tables comparing an interaction variable with another interaction variable can be constructed. The number of possible tables to analyze can get quite large for even a few variables. You can select one of these tables to analyze, or you can analyze all of them. Alternatively, the Homogeneity Analysis procedure can be used to examine all of the variables simultaneously without the need to construct interaction variables.

Homogeneity Analysis

HOMALS is an acronym for *hom*ogeneity analysis via *a*lternating *l*east *s*quares. The input for homogeneity analysis, also known as multiple correspondence analysis, is the usual rectangular data matrix, where the rows represent subjects or, more generically, **objects**, and the columns represent **variables**. There may be two or more variables in the analysis. As in correspondence analysis, all variables in a homogeneity analysis are inspected for their nominal information only. The analysis considers only the fact that some objects are in the same category, while others are not. Nothing is assumed about the distance or order between categories of the same variable.

While correspondence analysis is limited to two variables, homogeneity analysis can be thought of as the analysis of a multiway contingency table (with more than two variables). Multiway contingency tables can also be analyzed with the SPSS Crosstabs procedure, but Crosstabs gives separate summary statistics for each category of each control variable. With homogeneity analysis, it is often possible to summarize the relationship between all the variables with a single two-dimensional plot.

For a one-dimensional solution, homogeneity analysis assigns optimal scale values (category quantifications) to each category of each variable in such a way that overall, on average, the categories have maximum spread. For a two-dimensional solution, homogeneity analysis finds a second set of quantifications of the categories of each variable unrelated to the first set, again attempting to maximize spread, and so on. Because categories of a variable receive as many scorings as there are dimensions, the variables in the analysis are said to be **multiple nominal** in optimal scaling level.

Homogeneity analysis also assigns **scores** to the objects in the analysis in such a way that the category quantifications are the averages, or **centroids**, of the object scores of objects in that category.

The output for homogeneity analysis includes plots of the category quantifications and the object scores. By design, homogeneity analysis tries to produce a solution in which objects within the same category are plotted close together and objects in different categories are plotted far apart. This is done for all variables in the analysis. The plots have the property that each object is as close as possible to the category points of categories that apply to the object. In this way, the categories divide the objects into homogeneous subgroups (thus, one reason for the name "homogeneity analysis"). Variables are considered homogeneous when they classify objects in the same categories into the same subgroups.

If homogeneity analysis is used for two variables, the results are not completely identical to those produced by correspondence analysis, although both are appropriate when suitably interpreted. In the two-variable situation, correspondence analysis produces unique output summarizing the fit and the quality of representation of the solution, including stability information. Thus, correspondence analysis is probably preferable to homogeneity analysis in the two-variable case in most circumstances. Another difference between the two procedures is that the input to homogeneity analysis is a data matrix, where the rows are objects and the columns are variables, while the input to correspondence analysis can be the same data matrix, a general proximity matrix, or a joint contingency table, which is an aggregated matrix where both the rows and columns represent categories of variables.

Homogeneity analysis can be thought of as principal components analysis of nominal data with multiple optimal scaling levels. If the variables in the analysis are assumed to be numerical level (linear associations between the variables are assumed), then standard principal components analysis is appropriate.

An advanced use of homogeneity analysis is to replace the original category values with the optimal scale values from the first dimension and perform a secondary multivariate analysis. The Factor Analysis procedure produces a first principal component that is equivalent to the first dimension of homogeneity analysis. The component scores in the first dimension are equal to the object scores, and the squared component loadings are equal to the discrimination measures. The second homogeneity analysis dimension, however, is not equal to the second dimension of factor analysis. Since homogeneity analysis replaces category labels with numerical scale values, many different procedures that require interval-level (numerical) data can be applied after the homogeneity analysis. The same is true for nonlinear principal components analysis, nonlinear canonical correlation analysis, and categorical regression.

Displays with More Than Two Dimensions

All of the optimal scaling procedures involving dimension reduction allow you to select the number of dimensions included in the analysis. For analyses with three or more dimensions, HOMALS, PRINCALS, and OVERALS produce three-dimensional scatterplots. In contrast, correspondence analysis uses a matrix of scatterplots for all analyses, regardless of the dimensionality.

Three-dimensional Scatterplots

If a PRINCALS, HOMALS, or OVERALS analysis involves more than two dimensions, SPSS produces a three-dimensional plot of the first three dimensions. Figure 1.3 shows a three-dimensional plot of object scores produced by a homogeneity analysis with four dimensions.

Figure 1.3   Three-dimensional plot of object scores

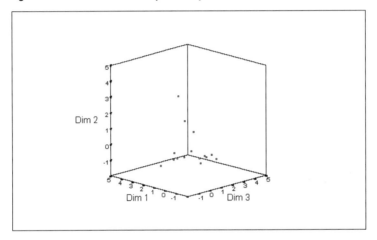

Although only the first three dimensions are displayed on the scatterplot, information about all dimensions is included when the chart is created. Each dimension constitutes a series in the Chart Editor. You can choose to display different combinations of dimensions on the scatterplot by selecting *Displayed* from the Series menu in the Chart Editor. Figure 1.4 shows the 3-D Scatterplot Displayed Data dialog box, with dimension 4 selected to be displayed in place of dimension 3. The plot displaying these selections is shown in Figure 1.5.

Figure 1.4   3-D Scatterplot Displayed Data dialog box

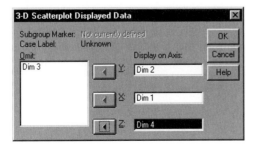

Figure 1.6   Scatterplot matrix displaying object scores for four dimensions

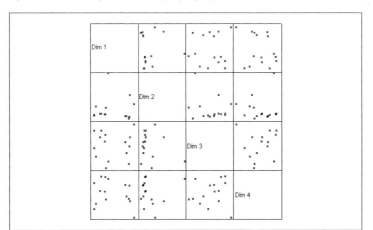

Figure 1.5   Three-dimensional plot of object scores, displaying dimensions 1, 2, and 4

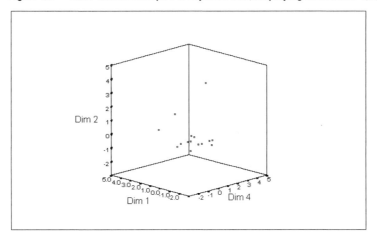

Scatterplot Matrices

To view all dimensions on a single plot, it is useful to graphically display two-dimensional scatterplots for all dimensions in a matrix scatterplot. To convert a chart into a scatterplot matrix, use the scatterplot gallery in the Chart Editor. This option offers great flexibility in converting one chart type to another. A scatterplot matrix displaying four dimensions is shown in Figure 1.6.

In contrast to the other dimension reduction techniques, correspondence analysis produces a matrix of scatterplots similar to Figure 1.6 for all analyses. If you desire individual two or three-dimensional scatterplots, use the SCATTER option on the GALLERY menu in the Chart Editor. Alternatively, to omit or add dimensions to an existing scatterplot matrix, use the DISPLAYED command on the SERIES menu. See the *SPSS Base User's Guide* for information on editing charts and using the chart gallery.

Identifying Point Labels on Charts

All of the optimal scaling procedures produce presentation-quality, high-resolution charts. Occasionally, when points on a chart fall close together, the point labels may overwrite each other, making them somewhat difficult to read. The point identification feature in the Chart Editor provides a way to identify obscured point labels and to selectively turn labels on and off for individual points. For example, Figure 1.7 shows an object scores chart in which the points in the upper portion of the chart are very close together.

Figure 1.7   Object scores chart with overwritten labels

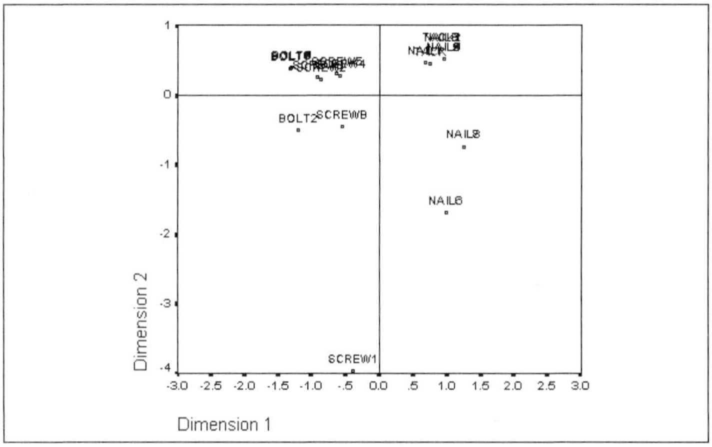

To identify the labels in the upper left cluster of points, click on the Point Selection tool on the toolbar ( ). You are now in point identification mode. Click on one of the points in the cluster. If several labels fall on that point, a list of these labels is displayed, as shown in Figure 1.8. This allows you to identify the points in this area.

Figure 1.8   Point identification

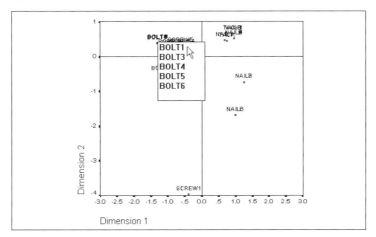

By selecting labels from this list, you can selectively toggle individual point labels on and off.

Another way to identify the points on a chart is to generate low-resolution charts. This produces a low-resolution chart with a complete listing of point values. To generate low-resolution plots, enter and run the following command in a syntax window:

```
SET HIGHRES=OFF.
```

All charts will now be generated in low-resolution until you reset HIGHRES to ON or exit the SPSS session. See the *SPSS Base Syntax Reference Guide* for more information on command syntax.

Aspect Ratio in Optimal Scaling Charts

Aspect ratio in optimal scaling plots is **isotropic**. In a two-dimensional plot, the distance representing one unit in dimension 1 is equal to the distance representing one unit in dimension 2. If you change the range of a dimension in a two-dimensional plot, the system changes the size of the other dimension to keep the physical distances equal. Isotropic aspect ratio cannot be overridden for the optimal scaling procedures.

2 Regression with Optimal Scaling (CATREG)

Regression with optimal scaling quantifies categorical data by assigning numerical values to the categories, resulting in an optimal linear regression equation for the transformed variables. Regression with optimal scaling is also known by the acronym CATREG, for *cat*egorical *reg*ression with optimal scaling.

Standard linear regression analysis involves minimizing the sum of squared differences between a response (dependent) variable and a weighted combination of predictor (independent) variables. Variables are typically quantitative, with (nominal) categorical data recoded to binary or contrast variables. As a result, categorical variables serve to separate groups of cases, and the technique estimates separate sets of parameters for each group. The estimated coefficients reflect how changes in the predictors affect the response. Prediction of the response is possible for any combination of predictor values.

An alternative approach involves regressing the response on the categorical predictor values themselves. Consequently, one coefficient is estimated for each variable. However, for categorical variables, the category values are arbitrary. Coding the categories in different ways yields different coefficients, making comparisons across analyses of the same variables difficult.

CATREG extends the standard approach by simultaneously scaling nominal, ordinal, and numerical variables. The procedure quantifies categorical variables such that the quantifications reflect characteristics of the original categories. The procedure treats quantified categorical variables in the same way as numerical variables. Using nonlinear transformations allows variables to be analyzed at a variety of levels to find the best fitting model.

Example. Regression with optimal scaling could be used to describe how job satisfaction depends on job category, geographic region, and amount of travel. You might find that high levels of satisfaction correspond to managers and low travel. The resulting regression equation could be used to predict job satisfaction for any combination of the three independent variables.

Statistics and plots. Frequencies, regression coefficients, ANOVA table, iteration history, category quantifications, correlations between untransformed predictors, correlations between transformed predictors, and transformation plots.

Data. Use integers to code categorical variables (nominal or ordinal scaling level). To minimize output, use consecutive integers beginning with 1 to code each variable. Variables scaled at the numerical level should not be recoded to consecutive integers. To minimize output, for each variable scaled at the numerical level, subtract the smallest observed value from every value and add 1. Fractional values are truncated after the decimal.

Assumptions. Only one response variable is allowed, but the maximum number of predictor variables is 200. The data must contain at least three valid cases and the number of valid cases must exceed the number of predictor variables plus one. If no variables are analyzed at a nominal level, a numerical initial configuration should be used.

Related procedures. CATREG is equivalent to categorical canonical correlation analysis with optimal scaling (OVERALS) with two sets, one of which contains only one variable. Scaling all variables at the numerical level corresponds to standard multiple regression analysis. Residual analysis and alternate plotting features are available by using the transformed variables in a standard linear regression.

To Obtain a Regression with Optimal Scaling

▶ From the menus, choose:

Statistics
  Regression
    Optimal Scaling

Figure 2.1   Regression with Optimal Scaling dialog box

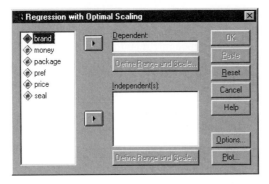

▶ Select the dependent variable and independent variable(s).

▶ Define the range and optimal scaling level for each variable.

▶ Click OK.

Define Range and Scale in CATREG

You must define a range for each variable. The maximum value specified must be an integer. Fractional data values are truncated in the analysis. A category value that is outside of the specified range is ignored in the analysis. To minimize output, use the **Automatic Recode** facility on the Transform menu to create consecutive categories beginning with 1 for variables treated as nominal or ordinal. Recoding to consecutive integers is not recommended for numerical variables. To minimize output for numerical variables, for each variable, subtract the minimum value from every value and add 1.

You must also select the scaling to be used to quantify each variable.

- **Ordinal.** The order of the categories of the observed variable is preserved in the quantified variable.
- **Nominal.** Objects in the same category receive the same score.
- **Numerical.** Categories are treated as ordered and equally spaced. The differences between category numbers and the order of the categories of the observed variable are preserved in the quantified variable. When all variables are at the numerical level, the analysis is analogous to standard multiple regression analysis.

To Define the Range and Scale in CATREG

▶   Select one or more variables in the Variables list in the Regression with Optimal Scaling dialog box.

▶   Click Define Range and Scale.

Figure 2.2   Regression with Optimal Scaling: Define Range and Scale dialog box

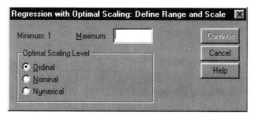

▶   Enter the maximum value for the variable. A minimum value of 1 is displayed. This minimum value cannot be changed.

▶   Select the optimal scaling level to be used in the analysis.

▶   Click Continue.

Regression with Optimal Scaling Options

The Options dialog box allows you to select the initial configuration style, select the method of handling missing values, specify iteration and convergence criteria, select optional statistics, and save quantifications as new variables in the working data file or in an external data file.

Figure 2.3   Regression with Optimal Scaling: Options dialog box

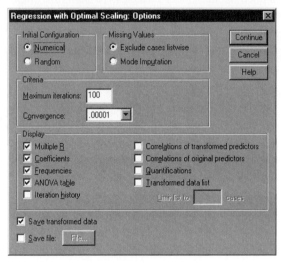

- **Initial Configuration.** If no variables are treated as nominal, select the **Numerical** configuration. If at least one variable is treated as nominal, select the **Random** configuration.

- **Missing Values.** Values outside of the defined range are treated as missing by default. Select **Exclude cases listwise** to omit all cases with missing values from the analysis. Select **Mode Imputation** to replace missing values with the most frequent category for that variable. Mode imputation results in all cases being used in the analysis.

- **Criteria.** You can specify the maximum number of iterations the regression can go through in its computations. You can also select a convergence criterion value. The regression stops iterating if the difference in total fit between the last two iterations is less than the convergence value or if the maximum number of iterations is reached.

- **Display.** Multiple R includes R, R-squared, and adjusted R-squared. Coefficients includes standardized regression coefficients, standard errors, correlations (zero-order, part, and partial), Pratt's relative importance measure, tolerances, and F tests. Frequencies includes marginal frequencies (counts), transformation types (optimal scaling levels), numbers of missing values, and modes. ANOVA table includes regression and residual sums of squares, mean squares, and an F test. Iteration history includes R^2, the square root of $(1 - R^2)$, and the increase in R^2 for each iteration. Correlations of transformed predictors displays the correlation matrix for the quantified predictors. Correlations of original predictors displays the correlation matrix of the non-transformed predictors. Quantifications lists the quantification for every category of each variable. Transformed data list yields the quantifications associated with each case.

- **Save transformed data.** Adds the transformed data to the working data file.
- **Save file.** Writes the transformed data to an external data file.

Regression with Optimal Scaling Transformation Plots

The Plot dialog box allows you to specify the variables for which transformation plots will be produced. For each of these variables, the category quantifications are plotted against the original category values. Empty categories appear on the horizontal axis but do not affect the computations. These categories are identified by breaks in the line connecting the quantifications.

To Obtain Transformation Plots in CATREG

▶ Select the dependent and independent variables in the Regression with Optimal Scaling dialog box.

▶ Click Plot.

Figure 2.4   Regression with Optimal Scaling: Plot dialog box

▶ Select the variables for which transformation plots will be produced.

▶ Click Continue.

CATREG Command Additional Features

You can customize your regression with optimal scaling if you paste your selections into a syntax window and edit the resulting CATREG command syntax. SPSS command language also allows you to:

- Specify rootnames for the transformed variables when saving them to the working data file (with the SAVE subcommand).
- Specify the number of value label characters used to label the categories along the horizontal axis (with the PLOT subcommand).
- Produce low-resolution plots that may be easier to read than the usual high-resolution plots (using the SET command).

3 Nonlinear Principal Components Analysis (PRINCALS)

Nonlinear principal components analysis is also known as categorical principal components with optimal scaling. This procedure simultaneously quantifies categorical variables while reducing the dimensionality of the data. Nonlinear principal components analysis is also known by the acronym PRINCALS, for *prin*cipal *c*omponents analysis by means of *a*lternating *l*east *s*quares.

The goal of principal components analysis is to reduce an original set of categorical variables into a smaller set of uncorrelated components that represents most of the information found in the original variables. The technique is most useful when an extreme number of variables prohibits effective interpretation of the relationships between objects. By reducing the dimensionality, you interpret a few components rather than a large number of variables.

Standard principal components analysis assumes linear relationships between numerical variables. The optimal scaling approach, on the other hand, allows variables to be scaled at different levels. Categorical variables are optimally quantified in the specified dimensionality. As a result, nonlinear relationships between variables can be modeled.

Example. Nonlinear principal components analysis could be used to graphically display the relationship between job category, job division, region, amount of travel (high, medium, low), and job satisfaction. You might find that two dimensions account for a large amount of variance. The first dimension might separate job category from region, whereas the second dimension might separate job division from amount of travel. You also might find that high job satisfaction is related to a medium amount of travel.

Statistics and plots. Frequencies, eigenvalues, iteration history, object scores, category quantifications, component loadings, transformed variables correlation matrix, object scores plots, category quantifications plots, component loadings plots.

Data. Use integers to code categorical variables (nominal or ordinal scaling level). To minimize output, use consecutive integers beginning with 1 to code each variable. Variables scaled at the numerical level should not be recoded to consecutive integers. To minimize output, for each variable scaled at the numerical level, subtract the smallest observed value from every value and add 1. Fractional values are truncated after the decimal.

Assumptions. Variables in the analysis have category quantifications that do not differ for each dimension (single quantification), unless a variable is specified as multiple nominal. Only one set of variables will be used in the analysis. The maximum number of dimensions used in the procedure depends on the scaling level of the variables. If all variables are scaled as single nominal, ordinal, or numerical, the maximum number of dimensions is the minimum of the number of observations minus 1 and the number of variables. If some variables are scaled as multiple nominal, the maximum number of dimensions is the minimum of the number of observations minus 1 and the total number of valid multiple nominal categories plus the number of non-multiple nominal variables, minus the number of multiple nominal variables without missing values. If you specify a number greater than the maximum, the maximum value is used.

Related procedures. If all variables are multiple nominal, nonlinear principal components analysis is identical to homogeneity analysis. If sets of variables are of interest, nonlinear canonical correlation analysis should be used.

To Obtain a Nonlinear Principal Components Analysis

▶ From the menus, choose:

Statistics
  Data Reduction
    Optimal Scaling

Figure 3.1   Optimal Scaling by Alternating Least Squares dialog box

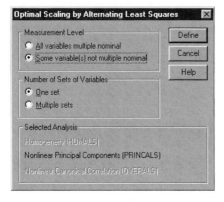

▶ Select **Some variable(s) not multiple nominal.**

▶ Select **One set.**

▶ Click **Define.**

Figure 3.2   Nonlinear Principal Components Analysis (PRINCALS) dialog box

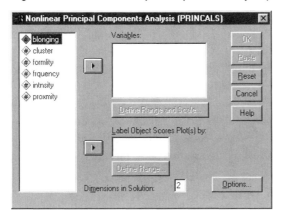

▶ Select two or more variables.

▶ Define the value ranges and measurement scale (optimal scaling level) for the variables.

▶ Click **OK**.

Optionally, you can:

• Select one or more variables to provide point labels for object scores plots. Each variable produces a separate plot, with the points labeled by the values of that variable. You must define a range for each of these plot label variables. Using the dialog box, a single variable cannot be used both in the analysis and as a labeling variable. If labeling the object scores plot with a variable used in the analysis is desired, use the **Compute** facility on the Transform menu to create a copy of that variable. Use the new variable to label the plot. Alternatively, command syntax can be used.

• Specify the number of dimensions you want in the solution. In general, choose as few dimensions as needed to explain most of the variation. If the analysis involves more than two dimensions, SPSS produces three-dimensional plots of the first three dimensions. Other dimensions can be displayed by editing the chart.

Define Range and Scale in PRINCALS

You must define a range for each variable. The maximum value specified must be an integer. Fractional data values are truncated in the analysis. A category value that is outside of the specified range is ignored in the analysis. To minimize output, use the **Automatic Recode** facility on the Transform menu to create consecutive categories beginning with 1 for variables treated as nominal or ordinal. Recoding to consecutive integers is not recommended for variables scaled at the numerical level. To minimize output for variables treated as numerical, for each variable, subtract the minimum value from every value and add 1.

You must also select the scaling to be used to quantify each variable.

- **Ordinal.** The order of the categories of the observed variable is preserved in the quantified variable.

- **Single nominal.** In the quantified variable, objects in the same category receive the same score. When all variables are single nominal, the first dimension of this solution is the same as that of the first homogeneity analysis dimension.

- **Multiple nominal.** The quantifications can be different for each dimension. When all variables are multiple nominal, principal components analysis with optimal scaling produces the same results as homogeneity analysis.

- **Discrete numeric.** Categories are treated as ordered and equally spaced. The differences between category numbers and the order of the categories of the observed variable are preserved in the quantified variable. When all variables are at the numerical level, principal components analysis with optimal scaling is analogous to classical principal components analysis.

To Define an Optimal Scaling Range and Scale in PRINCALS

▶ In the PRINCALS dialog box, select one or more variables in the variables list.

▶ Click Define Range and Scale.

Figure 3.3   PRINCALS Define Range and Scale dialog box

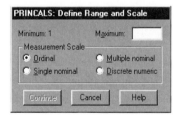

▶ Enter the maximum value for the variable. A minimum value of 1 is displayed. This minimum value cannot be changed.

▶ Select the Measurement (Optimal Scaling) Scale to be used in the analysis.

▶ Click Continue.

Define Range in PRINCALS

You must define a range for each variable used to label the object scores plots. The maximum value specified must be an integer. Fractional data values are truncated in the analysis. Labels for categories outside of the specified range for a labeling variable do appear in the plots.

To Define an Optimal Scaling Range in PRINCALS

▶ Select a variable to Label Object Scores Plot(s) by in the Nonlinear Principal Components Analysis (PRINCALS) dialog box.

▶ Click Define Range.

Figure 3.4   PRINCALS Define Range dialog box

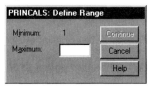

▶ Enter the maximum value for the variable. A minimum value of 1 is displayed. This minimum value cannot be changed.

▶ Click Continue.

Nonlinear Principal Components Analysis Options

The Options dialog box allows you to select optional statistics and plots, save object scores as new variables in the working data file, and specify iteration and convergence criteria.

Figure 3.5   PRINCALS Options dialog box

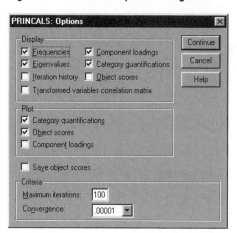

- **Display.** Available statistics include marginal frequencies (counts), eigenvalues, iteration history, transformed variables correlation matrix, component loadings, category quantifications, and object scores.
- **Plot.** You can produce plots of category quantifications, object scores, and component loadings.
- **Save object scores.** You can save the object scores as new variables in the working data file. Object scores are saved for the number of dimensions specified in the main dialog box.
- **Criteria.** You can specify the maximum number of iterations the nonlinear principal components analysis can go through in its computations. You can also select a convergence criterion value. The analysis stops iterating if the difference in total fit between the last two iterations is less than the convergence value or if the maximum number of iterations is reached.

PRINCALS Command Additional Features

You can customize your nonlinear principal components analysis if you paste your selections into a syntax window and edit the resulting PRINCALS command syntax. SPSS command language also allows you to:

- Specify the dimension pairs to be plotted, rather than plotting all extracted dimensions (using the NDIM keyword on the PLOT subcommand).
- Specify the number of value label characters used to label points on the plots (with the PLOT subcommand).

- Designate more than five variables as labeling variables for object scores plots (with the PLOT subcommand).
- Select variables used in the analysis as labeling variables for the object scores plots (with the PLOT subcommand).
- Select variables to provide point labels for the quantification score plot (with the PLOT subcommand).
- Specify the number of cases to be included in the analysis, if you do not want to use all cases in the working data file (with the NOBSERVATIONS subcommand).
- Specify rootnames for variables created by saving object scores (with the SAVE subcommand).
- Specify the number of dimensions to be saved, rather than saving all extracted dimensions (with the SAVE subcommand).
- Write category quantifications to a matrix file (using the MATRIX subcommand).
- Produce low-resolution plots that may be easier to read than the usual high-resolution plots (using the SET command).

4 Nonlinear Canonical Correlation Analysis (OVERALS)

Nonlinear canonical correlation analysis corresponds to categorical canonical correlation analysis with optimal scaling. The purpose of this procedure is to determine how similar sets of categorical variables are to one another. Nonlinear canonical correlation analysis is also known by the acronym OVERALS.

Standard canonical correlation analysis is an extension of multiple regression, where the second set does not contain a single response variable, but multiple ones. The goal is to explain as much as possible of the variance in the relationships among two sets of numerical variables in a low dimensional space. Initially, the variables in each set are linearly combined such that the linear combinations have a maximal correlation. Given these combinations, subsequent linear combinations are determined which are uncorrelated with the previous combinations and which have the largest correlation possible.

The optimal scaling approach expands the standard analysis in three crucial ways. First, OVERALS allows more than two sets of variables. Second, variables can be scaled as either nominal, ordinal, or numerical. As a result, nonlinear relationships between variables can be analyzed. Finally, instead of maximizing correlations between the variable sets, the sets are compared to an unknown compromise set defined by the object scores.

Example. Categorical canonical correlation analysis with optimal scaling could be used to graphically display the relationship between one set of variables containing job category and years of education and another set of variables containing minority classification and gender. You might find that years of education and minority classification discriminate better than the remaining variables. You might also find that years of education discriminates best on the first dimension.

Statistics and plots. Frequencies, centroids, iteration history, object scores, category quantifications, weights, component loadings, single and multiple fit, object scores plots, category coordinates plots, component loadings plots, category centroids plots, transformation plots.

Data. Use integers to code categorical variables (nominal or ordinal scaling level). To minimize output, use consecutive integers beginning with 1 to code each variable. Variables scaled at the numerical level should not be recoded to consecutive integers. To minimize output, for each variable scaled at the numerical level, subtract the smallest observed value from every value and add 1. Fractional values are truncated after the decimal.

Assumptions. Variables can be classified into two or more sets. Variables in the analysis are scaled as multiple nominal, single nominal, ordinal, or numerical. The maximum number of dimensions used in the procedure depends on the optimal scaling level of the variables. If all variables are specified as ordinal, single nominal, or numerical, the maximum number of dimensions is the minimum of the number of observations minus 1 and the total number of variables. However, if only two sets of variables are defined, the maximum number of dimensions is the number of variables in the smaller set. If some variables are multiple nominal, the maximum number of dimensions is the total number of multiple nominal categories plus the number of non-multiple nominal variables minus the number of multiple nominal variables. For example, if the analysis involves five variables, one of which is multiple nominal with four categories, the maximum number of dimensions is $(4 + 4 - 1)$, or 7. If you specify a number greater than the maximum, the maximum value is used.

Related procedures. If each set contains one variable, nonlinear canonical correlation analysis is equivalent to nonlinear principal components analysis. If each of these variables is multiple nominal, the analysis corresponds to homogeneity analysis. If two sets of variables are involved and one of the sets contains only one variable, the analysis is identical to categorical regression with optimal scaling.

To Obtain a Nonlinear Canonical Correlation Analysis

▶ From the menus, choose:

Statistics
  Data Reduction
    Optimal Scaling

Figure 4.1   Optimal Scaling by Alternating Least Squares dialog box

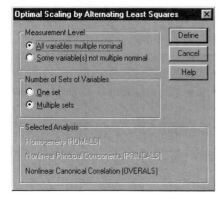

▶ Select **Multiple sets**.

▶ Select either **Some variable(s) not multiple nominal** or **All variables multiple nominal**.

▶ Click **Define**.

Figure 4.2   **Nonlinear Canonical Correlation Analysis (OVERALS) dialog box**

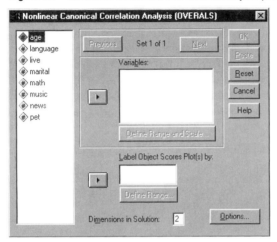

▶ Define at least two sets of variables. Select the variable(s) that you want to include in the first set. To move to the next set, click **Next**, and select the variables that you want to include in the second set. You can add additional sets as desired. Click **Previous** to return to the previously defined variable set.

▶ Define the value range and measurement scale (optimal scaling level) for each selected variable.

▶ Click **OK**.

Optionally, you can:

• Select one or more variables to provide point labels for object scores plots. Each variable produces a separate plot, with the points labeled by the values of that variable. You must define a range for each of these plot label variables. Using the dialog box, a single variable cannot be used both in the analysis and as a labeling variable. If labeling the object scores plot with a variable used in the analysis is desired, use the **Compute** facility on the Transform menu to create a copy of that variable. Use the new variable to label the plot. Alternatively, command syntax can be used.

• Specify the number of dimensions you want in the solution. In general, choose as few dimensions as needed to explain most of the variation. If the analysis involves more than two dimensions, SPSS produces three-dimensional plots of the first three dimensions. Other dimensions can be displayed by editing the chart.

Define Range and Scale in OVERALS

You must define a range for each variable. The maximum value specified must be an integer. Fractional data values are truncated in the analysis. A category value that is outside of the specified range is ignored in the analysis. To minimize output, use the **Automatic Recode** facility on the Transform menu to create consecutive categories beginning with 1 for variables treated as nominal or ordinal. Recoding to consecutive integers is not recommended for variables scaled at the numerical level. To minimize output for variables treated as numerical, for each variable, subtract the minimum value from every value and add 1.

You must also select the scaling to be used to quantify each variable.

• **Ordinal.** The order of the categories of the observed variable is preserved in the quantified variable.

• **Single nominal.** Objects in the same category receive the same score. When all variables are single nominal, the first dimension of this solution is the same as that of the first homogeneity analysis dimension.

• **Multiple nominal.** The quantifications can be different for each dimension. When all variables are multiple nominal and there is only one variable in each set, categorical canonical correlation analysis with optimal scaling produces the same results as homogeneity analysis.

• **Discrete numeric.** Categories are treated as ordered and equally spaced. The differences between category numbers and the order of the categories of the observed variable are preserved in the quantified variable. When all variables are at the numerical level and there are two sets, the analysis is analogous to classical canonical correlation analysis.

To Define an Optimal Scaling Range and Scale in OVERALS

▶ In the OVERALS dialog box, select one or more variables in the variables list.

▶ Click Define Range and Scale.

Figure 4.3   OVERALS Define Range and Scale dialog box

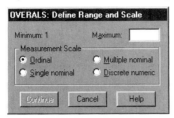

▶ Enter the maximum value for the variable. A minimum value of 1 is displayed. This minimum value cannot be changed.

▶ Select the Measurement (Optimal Scaling) Scale to be used in the analysis.

▶ Click Continue.

Define Range in OVERALS

You must define a range for each variable used to label the object scores plots. The maximum value specified must be an integer. Fractional data values are truncated in the analysis. Labels for category values outside of the specified range for a labeling variable do not appear in the plots. All cases with such category values are labeled with a single label corresponding to a data value outside of the defined range.

To Define an Optimal Scaling Range in OVERALS

▶ Select a variable to Label Object Scores Plot(s) by in the Nonlinear Canonical Correlation Analysis (OVERALS) dialog box.

▶ Click Define Range.

Figure 4.4   OVERALS Define Range dialog box.

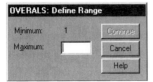

▶ Enter the maximum value for the variable. A minimum value of 1 is displayed. This minimum value cannot be changed.

▶ Click Continue.

Nonlinear Canonical Correlation Analysis Options

The Options dialog box allows you to select optional statistics and plots, save object scores as new variables in the working data file, specify iteration and convergence criteria, and specify an initial configuration for the analysis.

Figure 4.5   OVERALS Options dialog box

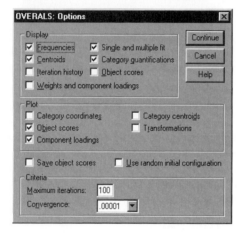

- **Display.** Available statistics include marginal frequencies (counts), centroids, iteration history, weights and component loadings, category quantifications, object scores, and single and multiple fit statistics.
- **Plot.** You can produce plots of category coordinates, object scores, component loadings, category centroids, and transformations.
- **Save object scores.** You can save the object scores as new variables in the working data file. Object scores are saved for the number of dimensions specified in the main dialog box.
- **Use random initial configuration.** A random initial configuration should be used if all or some of the variables are single nominal. If this option is not selected, a nested initial configuration is used.
- **Criteria.** You can specify the maximum number of iterations the nonlinear canonical correlation analysis can go through in its computations. You can also select a convergence criterion value. The analysis stops iterating if the difference in total fit between

the last two iterations is less than the convergence value or if the maximum number of iterations is reached.

OVERALS Command Additional Features

You can customize your nonlinear canonical correlation analysis if you paste your selections into a syntax window and edit the resulting OVERALS command syntax. SPSS command language also allows you to:

- Specify the dimension pairs to be plotted, rather than plotting all extracted dimensions (using the NDIM keyword on the PLOT subcommand).
- Specify the number of value label characters used to label points on the plots (with the PLOT subcommand).
- Designate more than five variables as labeling variables for object scores plots (with the PLOT subcommand).
- Select variables used in the analysis as labeling variables for the object scores plots (with the PLOT subcommand).
- Select variables to provide point labels for the quantification score plot (with the PLOT subcommand).
- Specify the number of cases to be included in the analysis, if you do not want to use all cases in the working data file (with the NOBSERVATIONS subcommand).
- Specify rootnames for variables created by saving object scores (with the SAVE subcommand).
- Specify the number of dimensions to be saved, rather than saving all extracted dimensions (with the SAVE subcommand).
- Write category quantifications to a matrix file (using the MATRIX subcommand).
- Produce low-resolution plots that may be easier to read than the usual high-resolution plots (using the SET command).
- Produce centroid and transformation plots for specified variables only (with the PLOT subcommand).

5 Correspondence Analysis

One of the goals of correspondence analysis is to describe the relationships between two nominal variables in a correspondence table in a low-dimensional space, while simultaneously describing the relationships between the categories for each variable. For each variable, the distances between category points in a plot reflect the relationships between the categories with similar categories plotted close to each other. Projecting points for one variable on the vector from the origin to a category point for the other variable describes the relationship between the variables.

An analysis of contingency tables often includes examining row and column profiles and testing for independence via the chi-square statistic. However, the number of profiles can be quite large, and the chi-square test does not reveal the dependence structure. The Crosstabs procedure offers several measures of association and tests of association, but cannot graphically represent any relationships between the variables.

Factor analysis is a standard technique for describing relationships between variables in a low-dimensional space. However, factor analysis requires interval data, and the number of observations should be five times the number of variables. Correspondence analysis, on the other hand, assumes nominal variables and can describe the relationships between categories of each variable, as well as the relationship between the variables. In addition, correspondence analysis can be used to analyze any table of positive correspondence measures.

Example. Correspondence Analysis could be used to graphically display the relationship between staff category and smoking habits. You might find that with regards to smoking, junior managers differ from secretaries, but secretaries do not differ from senior managers. You might also find that heavy smoking is associated with junior managers, whereas light smoking is associated with secretaries.

Statistics and plots. Correspondence measures, row and column profiles, singular values, row and column scores, inertia, mass, row and column score confidence statistics, singular value confidence statistics, transformation plots, row point plots, column point plots, and biplots.

Data. Categorical variables to be analyzed are scaled nominally. For aggregated data or for a correspondence measure other than frequencies, use a weighting variable with positive similarity values. Alternatively, for table data, use syntax to read the table.

Assumptions. The maximum number of dimensions used in the procedure depends on the number of active rows and column categories and the number of equality constraints. If no equality constraints are used and all categories are active, the maximum dimensionality is one fewer than the number of categories for the variable with the fewest categories. For example, if one variable has five categories and the other has four, the maximum number of dimensions is three. Supplementary categories are not active. For example, if one variable has five categories, two of which are supplementary, and the other variable has four categories, the maximum number of dimensions is two. Treat all sets of categories that are constrained to be equal as one category. For example, if a variable has five categories, three of which are constrained to be equal, that variable should be treated as having three categories when determining the maximum dimensionality. Two of the categories are unconstrained, and the third category corresponds to the three constrained categories. If you specify a number of dimensions greater than the maximum, the maximum value is used.

Related procedures. If more than two variables are involved, use homogeneity analysis. If the variables should be scaled ordinally, use nonlinear principal components analysis.

To Obtain a Correspondence Analysis

▶ From the menus, choose:

Statistics
  Data Reduction
    Correspondence Analysis

Figure 5.1   Correspondence Analysis dialog box

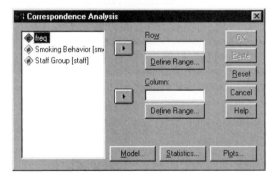

▶ Select a Row variable.

▶ Select a Column variable.

▶ Define the ranges for the variables.

▶ Click OK.

Define Row Range in Correspondence Analysis

You must define a range for the row variable. The minimum and maximum values specified must be integers. Fractional data values are truncated in the analysis. A category value that is outside of the specified range is ignored in the analysis.

All categories are initially unconstrained and active. You can constrain row categories to equal other row categories, or you can define a row category as supplementary.

- **Category is supplemental.** Supplementary categories do not influence the analysis, but are represented in the space defined by the active categories. Supplementary categories play no role in defining the dimensions. The maximum number of supplementary row categories is the total number of row categories minus 2.

- **Categories must be equal.** Categories must have equal scores. Use equality constraints if the obtained order for the categories is undesirable or counterintuitive. The maximum number of row categories that can be constrained to be equal is the total number of active row categories minus 1. To impose different equality constraints on sets of categories, use syntax. For example, use syntax to constrain categories 1 and 2 to be equal and categories 3 and 4 to be equal.

To Define a Row Range in Correspondence Analysis

▶ Select the row variable in the Correspondence Analysis dialog box.

▶ Click **Define Range**.

Figure 5.2   Correspondence Analysis: Define Row Range dialog box

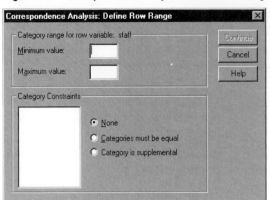

▶ Enter the minimum and maximum values for the row variable.

▶ Click **Continue**.

• Optionally, you can specify equality constraints on the row variable categories and define categories to be supplementary. For each category to be constrained or supplementary, select the category from the list of categories and choose **Category is supplemental** or **Categories must be equal**. For equality constraints, at least two categories must be designated as equal.

Define Column Range in Correspondence Analysis

You must define a range for the column variable. The minimum and maximum values specified must be integers. Fractional data values are truncated in the analysis. A category value that is outside of the specified range is ignored in the analysis.

All categories are initially unconstrained and active. You can constrain column categories to equal other column categories or you can define a column category as supplementary.

• **Category is supplemental.** Supplementary categories do not influence the analysis, but are represented in the space defined by the active categories. Supplementary categories play no role in defining the dimensions. The maximum number of supplementary column categories is the total number of column categories minus 2.

- **Categories must be equal.** Categories must have equal scores. Use equality constraints if the obtained order for the categories is undesirable or counterintuitive. The maximum number of column categories that can be constrained to be equal is the total number of active column categories minus 1. To impose different equality constraints on sets of categories, use syntax. For example, use syntax to constrain categories 1 and 2 to be equal and categories 3 and 4 to be equal.

To Define a Column Range in Correspondence Analysis

▶ Select the column variable in the Correspondence Analysis dialog box.

▶ Click Define Range.

Figure 5.3   Correspondence Analysis: Define Column Range dialog box

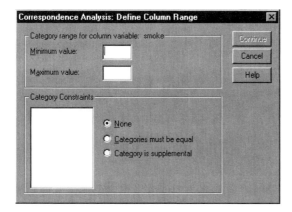

▶ Enter the minimum and maximum values for the column variable.

▶ Click Continue.

- Optionally, you can specify equality constraints on the column variable categories and define categories to be supplementary. For each category to be constrained or supplementary, select the category from the list of categories and choose Category is supplemental or Categories must be equal. For equality constraints, at least two categories must be designated as equal.

Correspondence Analysis Model

The Model dialog box allows you to specify the number of dimensions, the distance measure, the standardization method, and the normalization method.

Figure 5.4   Correspondence Analysis: Model dialog box

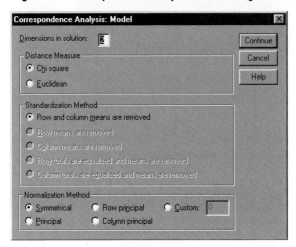

Dimensions in solution. Specify the number of dimensions. In general, choose as few dimensions as needed to explain most of the variation. The maximum number of dimensions depends on the number of active categories used in the analysis and on the equality constraints. The maximum number of dimensions is the smaller of:

• the number of active row categories minus the number of row categories constrained to be equal, plus the number of constrained row category sets.

and

• the number of active column categories minus the number of column categories constrained to be equal, plus the number of constrained column category sets.

Distance measure. You can select the measure of distance among the rows and among the columns of the correspondence table. Choose one of the following alternatives:

• **Chi-square.** Use a weighted profile distance, where the weight is the mass of the rows or columns. This measure is required for standard correspondence analysis.

• **Euclidean.** Use the square root of the sum of squared differences between pairs of rows and between pairs of columns.

Standardization Method. Choose one of the following alternatives:

• **Row and column means are removed.** Both the rows and columns are centered. This method is required for standard correspondence analysis.

• **Row means are removed.** Only the rows are centered.

- **Column means are removed.** Only the columns are centered.
- **Row totals are equalized and means are removed.** Before centering the rows, the row margins are equalized.
- **Column totals are equalized and means are removed.** Before centering the columns, the column margins are equalized.

Normalization Method. Choose one of the following alternatives:

- **Symmetrical.** For each dimension, the row scores are the weighted average of the column scores divided by the matching singular value, and the column scores are the weighted average of row scores divided by the matching singular value. Use this method if you want to examine the differences or similarities between the categories of the two variables.
- **Principal.** The distances between row points and between column points are approximations of the distances in the correspondence table according to the selected distance measure. Use this method if you want to examine differences between categories of either or both variables instead of differences between the two variables.
- **Row principal.** The distances between row points are approximations of the distances in the correspondence table according to the selected distance measure. The row scores are the weighted average of the column scores. Use this method if you want to examine differences or similarities between categories of the row variable.
- **Column principal.** The distances between column points are approximations of the distances in the correspondence table according to the selected distance measure. The column scores are the weighted average of the row scores. Use this method if you want to examine differences or similarities between categories of the column variable.
- **Custom.** You must specify a value between –1 and 1. A value of –1 corresponds to column principal. A value of 1 corresponds to row principal. A value of 0 corresponds to symmetrical. All other values spreads the inertia over both the row and column scores to varying degrees. This method is useful for making tailor-made biplots.

Correspondence Analysis Statistics

The Statistics dialog box allows you to specify the numerical output produced.

Figure 5.5   Correspondence Analysis: Statistics dialog box

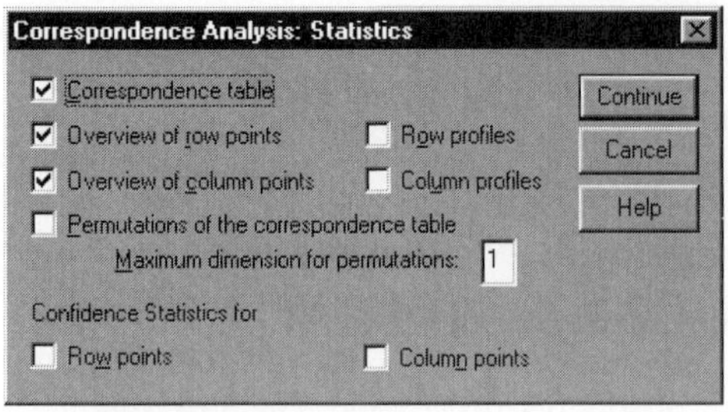

- **Correspondence table.** A crosstabulation of the input variables with row and column marginal totals.
- **Overview of row points.** For each row category, the scores, mass, inertia, contribution to the inertia of the dimension, and the contribution of the dimension to the inertia of the point.
- **Overview of column points.** For each column category, the scores, mass, inertia, contribution to the inertia of the dimension, and the contribution of the dimension to the inertia of the point.
- **Row profiles.** For each row category, the distribution across the categories of the column variable.
- **Column profiles.** For each column category, the distribution across the categories of the row variable.
- **Permutations of the correspondence table.** The correspondence table reorganized such that the rows and columns are in increasing order according to the scores on the first dimension. Optionally, you can specify the maximum dimension number for which permuted tables will be produced. A permuted table for each dimension from 1 to the number specified is produced.
- **Confidence Statistics for Row points.** Includes standard deviation and correlations for all nonsupplementary row points.
- **Confidence Statistics for Column points.** Includes standard deviation and correlations for all nonsupplementary column points.

Correspondence Analysis Plots

The Plots dialog box allows you to specify which plots are produced.

Figure 5.6   Correspondence Analysis: Plots dialog box

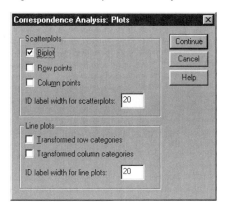

Scatterplots. Produces a matrix of all pairwise plots of the dimensions. Available scatterplots include:

- **Biplot.** Produces a matrix of joint plots of the row and column points. If principal normalization is selected, the biplot is not available.
- **Row points.** Produces a matrix of plots of the row points.
- **Column points.** Produces a matrix of plots of the column points.

Optionally, you can specify how many value label characters to use when labeling the points. This value must be a non-negative integer less than or equal to 20.

Line plots. Produces a plot for every dimension of the selected variable. Available line plots include:

- **Transformed row categories.** Produces a plot of the original row category values against their corresponding row scores.
- **Transformed column categories.** Produces a plot of the original column category values against their corresponding column scores.

Optionally, you can specify how many value label characters to use when labeling the category axis. This value must be a non-negative integer less than or equal to 20.

CORRESPONDENCE Command Additional Features

You can customize your correspondence analysis if you paste your selections into a syntax window and edit the resulting CORRESPONDENCE command syntax. SPSS command language also allows you to:

- Specify table data as input instead of using casewise data (using the TABLE = ALL subcommand).

- Specify the number of value-label characters used to label points for each type of scatterplot matrix or biplot matrix (with the PLOT subcommand).

- Specify the number of value-label characters used to label points for each type of line plot (with the PLOT subcommand).

- Write a matrix of row and column scores to an SPSS matrix data file (with the OUTFILE subcommand).

- Write a matrix of confidence statistics (variances and covariances) for the singular values and the scores to an SPSS matrix data file (with the OUTFILE subcommand).

- Specify multiple sets of categories to be equal (with the EQUAL subcommand).

6 Homogeneity Analysis (HOMALS)

Homogeneity analysis quantifies nominal (categorical) data by assigning numerical values to the cases (objects) and categories. Homogeneity analysis is also known by the acronym HOMALS, for *hom*ogeneity analysis by means of *a*lternating *l*east *s*quares.

The goal of HOMALS is to describe the relationships between two or more nominal variables in a low-dimensional space containing the variable categories as well as the objects in those categories. Objects within the same category are plotted close to each other, whereas objects in different categories are plotted far apart. Each object is as close as possible to the category points for categories that contain that object.

Homogeneity analysis is similar to correspondence analysis but is not limited to two variables. As a result, homogeneity analysis is also known in the literature as multiple correspondence analysis. Homogeneity analysis can also be viewed as a principal components analysis of nominal data.

Homogeneity analysis is preferred over standard principal components analysis when linear relationships between the variables may not hold or when variables are measured at a nominal level. Moreover, output interpretation is more straightforward in HOMALS than in other categorical techniques, such as crosstabulation tables and loglinear modeling. Because variable categories are quantified, techniques which require numerical data can be applied to the quantifications in subsequent analyses.

Example. Homogeneity analysis could be used to graphically display the relationship between job category, minority classification, and gender. You might find that minority classification and gender discriminate between people, but that job category does not. You might also find that the Latino and African-American categories are similar to each other.

Statistics and plots. Frequencies, eigenvalues, iteration history, object scores, category quantifications, discrimination measures, object scores plots, category quantifications plots, discrimination measures plots.

Data. All variables are categorical (nominal optimal scaling level). Use integers to code the categories. To minimize output, use consecutive integers beginning with 1 to code each variable.

Assumptions. All variables in the analysis have category quantifications that can be different for each dimension (multiple nominal). Only one set of variables will be used in the analysis. The maximum number of dimensions used in the procedure is either the total number of categories minus the number of variables with no missing data, or the number of cases minus 1, whichever is smaller. For example, if one variable has five categories and the other has four (with no missing data), the maximum number of dimensions is seven ((5 + 4) − 2). If you specify a number greater than the maximum, the maximum value is used.

Related procedures. For two variables, homogeneity analysis is analogous to correspondence analysis. If you believe that variables possess ordinal or numerical properties, nonlinear principal components should be used. If you are interested in sets of variables, nonlinear canonical correlation analysis should be used.

To Obtain a Homogeneity Analysis

▶ From the menus, choose:

Statistics
 Data Reduction
  Optimal Scaling

Figure 6.1   Optimal Scaling by Alternating Least Squares dialog box

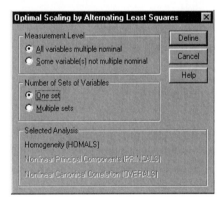

▶ In the Optimal Scaling dialog box, select **All variables multiple nominal**.

▶ Select **One set**.

▶ Click **Define**.

Figure 6.2   Homogeneity Analysis (HOMALS) dialog box

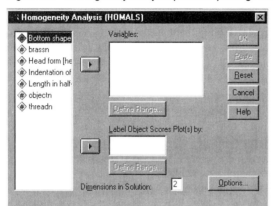

▶   Select two or more variables.

▶   Define the ranges for the variables.

▶   Click **OK**.

Optionally, you can:

• Select one or more variables to provide point labels for object scores plots. Each variable produces a separate plot, with the points labeled by the values of that variable. You must define a range for each of these plot label variables. Using the dialog box, a single variable cannot be used both in the analysis and as a labeling variable. If labeling the object scores plot with a variable used in the analysis is desired, use the Compute facility on the Transform menu to create a copy of that variable. Use the new variable to label the plot. Alternatively, command syntax can be used.

• Specify the number of dimensions you want in the solution. In general, choose as few dimensions as needed to explain most of the variation. If the analysis involves more than two dimensions, SPSS produces three-dimensional plots of the first three dimensions. Other dimensions can be displayed by editing the chart.

Define Range in Homogeneity Analysis

You must define a range for each variable. The maximum value specified must be an integer. Fractional data values are truncated in the analysis. A category value that is outside of the specified range is ignored in the analysis. To minimize output, use the Automatic Recode facility on the Transform menu to create consecutive categories beginning with 1.

You must also define a range for each variable used to label the object scores plots. However, labels for categories with data values outside of the defined range for the variable do appear on the plots.

To Define an Optimal Scaling Range in Homogeneity Analysis

▶ Select one or more variables in the Variables list in the Homogeneity Analysis (HOMALS) dialog box.

▶ Click Define Range.

Figure 6.3   HOMALS Define Range dialog box

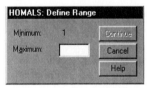

▶ Enter the maximum value for the variable. A minimum value of 1 is displayed. This minimum value cannot be changed.

▶ Click Continue.

Homogeneity Analysis Options

The Options dialog box allows you to select optional statistics and plots, save object scores as new variables in the working data file, and specify iteration and convergence criteria.

Figure 6.4   HOMALS Options dialog box

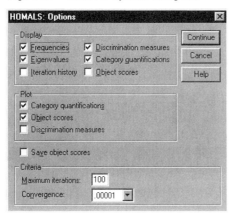

- **Display.** These options control what statistics are included in the output. Available statistics include marginal frequencies, eigenvalues, iteration history, discrimination measures, category quantifications, and object scores.

- **Plot.** These options produce plots of category quantifications, object scores, and discrimination measures.

- **Save object scores.** You can save the object scores as new variables in the working data file. Object scores are saved for the number of dimensions specified in the main dialog box.

- **Criteria.** You can specify the maximum number of iterations the homogeneity analysis can go through in its computations. You can also select a convergence criterion value. The homogeneity analysis stops iterating if the difference in total fit between the last two iterations is less than the convergence value, or if the maximum number of iterations is reached.

HOMALS Command Additional Features

You can customize your homogeneity analysis if you paste your selections into a syntax window and edit the resulting HOMALS command syntax. SPSS command language also allows you to:

- Specify the dimension pairs to be plotted, rather than plotting all extracted dimensions (using the NDIM keyword on the PLOT subcommand).

- Specify the number of value label characters used to label points on the plots (with the PLOT subcommand).

- Designate more than five variables as labeling variables for object scores plots (with the PLOT subcommand).

- Select variables used in the analysis as labeling variables for the object scores plots (with the PLOT subcommand).
- Select variables to provide point labels for the quantification score plot (with the PLOT subcommand).
- Specify the number of cases to be included in the analysis if you do not want to use all cases in the working data file (with the NOBSERVATIONS subcommand).
- Specify rootnames for variables created by saving object scores (with the SAVE subcommand).
- Specify the number of dimensions to be saved, rather than saving all extracted dimensions (with the SAVE subcommand).
- Write category quantifications to a matrix file (using the MATRIX subcommand).
- Produce low-resolution plots that may be easier to read than the usual high-resolution plots (using the SET command.)

7
Regression with Optimal Scaling Examples

The goal of categorical regression with optimal scaling is to describe the relationship between a response and a set of predictors. By quantifying this relationship, values of the response can be predicted for any combination of predictors.

Standard linear regression maximizes the squared correlation between the response and a linear combination of interval level predictors. Categorical variables can either be recoded as indicator variables or can be treated in the same fashion as interval level variables. In the first approach, the model contains a separate intercept and slope for each combination of the levels of the categorical variables. This results in a large number of parameters to interpret. In the second approach, only one parameter is estimated for each variable. However, the arbitrary nature of the category codings makes generalizations impossible.

An alternative approach is to quantify the categories to maximize the squared correlation between the quantified response and a linear combination of the quantified predictors. In other words, the categories are scaled optimally to account for as much variation in the transformed response as possible. All interpretations are relative to the transformed variables, but can be related to the original variables through the relationship between the quantifications and the original categories.

Whereas standard linear regression requires numerical predictors, regression with optimal scaling offers three scaling levels for each variable. Combinations of these levels can account for a wide range of nonlinear relationships for which standard linear regression is ill-suited. Consequently, optimal scaling offers greater flexibility than the standard approach with minimal added complexity.

In this chapter, two examples serve to illustrate the analyses involved in optimal scaling regression. The first example uses a small data set to illustrate the basic concepts. The second example uses a much larger set of variables and observations in a practical example.

An Example: Carpet Cleaner Data

We'll be using a popular example by Green and Wind (1973). In their example, a company interested in marketing a new carpet cleaner wants to examine the influence of five factors on consumer preference—package design, brand name, price, a *Good Housekeeping* seal, and a money-back guarantee. There are three factor levels for package design, each one differing in the location of the applicator brush; three brand names (*K2R*, *Glory*, and *Bissell*); three price levels; and two levels (either no or yes) for each of the last two factors. Table 7.1 displays the variables used in the carpet-cleaner study, with their variable labels and values.

Table 7.1   Variables in the carpet-cleaner study

Variable name	Variable label	Value labels
package	Package design	*A*, B*, C**
brand	Brand name	*K2R, Glory, Bissell*
price	Price	$1.19, $1.39, $1.59
seal	*Good Housekeeping* seal	*No, yes*
money	Money-back guarantee	*No, yes*

Ten consumers rank twenty-two profiles defined by these factors. The variable *pref* contains the rank of the average rankings for each profile. Low rankings correspond to high preference. This variable reflects an overall measure of preference for each profile. Using CATREG, we will explore how the five factors in Table 7.1 are related to preference.

Standard Linear Regression

The standard approach for describing the relationships in this problem is linear regression. The most common measure of how well a regression model fits the data is R^2. This statistic represents how much of the variance in the response is explained by the weighted combination of predictors. The closer R^2 is to 1, the better the model fits. Regressing *pref* on the five predictors results in an R^2 of 0.707, indicating that 71% of the variance in the preference rankings is explained by the predictor variables in the linear regression.

The standardized coefficients are shown in Figure 7.1. The sign of the coefficient indicates whether the predicted response increases or decreases when the predictor increases, all other predictors being constant. For categorical data, the category coding determines the meaning of an increase in a predictor. For instance, an increase in money, package, or seal will result in a decrease in predicted preference ranking. Money is coded 1 for no money-back guarantee and 2 for money-back guarantee. An increase in money corresponds to the addition of a money-back guarantee. Thus, adding a money-back guarantee reduces the predicted preference ranking, which corresponds to an increased predicted preference.

Figure 7.1   Regression coefficients

Variables	Standardized Coefficients Beta	t	Sig.
BRAND	.056	.407	.689
MONEY	-.197	-1.447	.167
PACKAGE	-.560	-4.015	.001
PRICE	.366	2.681	.016
SEAL	-.330	-2.423	.028

The value of the coefficient reflects the amount of change in the predicted preference ranking. Using standardized coefficients, interpretations are based on the standard deviations of the variables. Each coefficient indicates the number of standard deviations that the predicted response changes for a one standard deviation change in a predictor, all other predictors remaining constant. For example, a one standard deviation change in *brand* yields an increase in predicted preference of 0.056 standard deviations. The standard deviation of *pref* is 6.44, so *pref* increases by 0.361 (0.056 * 6.44). Changes in *package* yield the greatest changes in predicted preference.

A regression analysis should always include an examination of the residuals. The standardized residuals are plotted against the standardized predicted values in Figure 7.2. No patterns should be present if the model fits well. Here we see a U-shape in which both low and high standardized predicted values have positive residuals. Standardized predicted values near 0 tend to have negative residuals.

Figure 7.2   Residuals versus predicted values

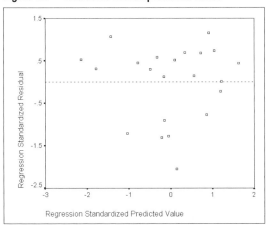

This shape is more pronounced in the plot of the standardized residuals against *package* in Figure 7.3. Every residual for Design B* is negative, whereas all but one of the residuals is positive for the other two designs. Because the regression model fits one parameter for each variable, the relationship cannot be captured by the standard approach.

Figure 7.3   Residuals versus package

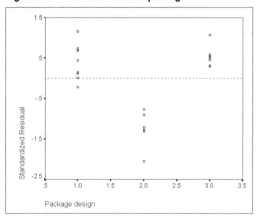

Optimal Scaling

The categorical nature of the variables and the nonlinear relationship between *pref* and *package* suggest that regression on optimal scores may perform better than standard regression. The U-shape of Figure 7.3 indicates that a nominal treatment of *package* should be used. All other predictors will be treated at the numerical scaling level.

The response variable warrants special consideration. We want to predict the values of *pref*. Thus, recovering as many properties of its categories as possible in the quantifications is desirable. Using an ordinal or nominal scaling level ignores the differences between the response categories. However, linearly transforming the response categories preserves category differences. Consequently, scaling the response numerically is generally preferred and will be employed here.

Intercorrelations

The intercorrelations among the predictors are useful for identifying multicollinearity in the regression. Variables that are highly correlated will lead to unstable regression estimates. However, due to their high correlation, omitting one of them from the model only minimally affects prediction. The variance in the response that can be explained by the omitted variable is still explained by the remaining correlated variable. However, zero-order correlations are sensitive to outliers and also cannot identify multicollinearity due to a high correlation between a predictor and a combination of other predictors.

Figure 7.4 and Figure 7.5 show the intercorrelations of the predictors for both the untransformed and transformed predictors. All values are near 0, indicating that multicollinearity between individual variables is not a concern.

Notice that the only correlations that change involve package. Because all other predictors are treated numerically, the differences between the categories and the order of the categories are preserved for these variables. Consequently, the correlations cannot change.

Figure 7.4   Original predictor correlations

	Package design	Brand name	Price	Good Housekeeping seal	Money-back guarantee
Package design	1.000	-.189	-.126	.081	.066
Brand name	-.189	1.000	.065	-.042	-.034
Price	-.126	.065	1.000	.000	.000
Good Housekeeping seal	.081	-.042	.000	1.000	-.039
Money-back guarantee	.066	-.034	.000	-.039	1.000

Figure 7.5   Transformed predictor correlations

	Package design	Brand name	Price	Good Housekeeping seal	Money-back guarantee
Package design	1.000	-.156	-.089	.032	.102
Brand name	-.156	1.000	.065	-.042	-.034
Price	-.089	.065	1.000	.000	.000
Good Housekeeping seal	.032	-.042	.000	1.000	-.039
Money-back guarantee	.102	-.034	.000	-.039	1.000

Model Fit and Coefficients

Regression with optimal scaling yields an R^2 of 0.948, indicating that almost 95% of the variance in the transformed preference rankings is explained by the regression on the optimally transformed predictors. Transforming the predictors improves the fit over the standard approach. The F statistic of 58.46 with corresponding p value less than 0.001 also indicates that the model is performing well.

Figure 7.1 shows the standardized regression coefficients. CATREG standardizes the variables, so only standardized coefficients are reported. These values are divided by their corresponding standard errors, yielding an F test for each variable. However, the test for each variable is contingent upon the other predictors being in the model. In other words, the test determines if omission of a predictor variable from the model with all other predictors present significantly worsens the predictive capabilities of the model. These values should not be used to omit several variables at one time for a subsequent model. Moreover, alternating least squares optimizes the quantifications, implying that these tests must be interpreted conservatively.

Figure 7.6   Standardized coefficients for transformed predictors

	Standardized Coefficients		
	Beta	Std. Error	F
Package design	-.748	.058	165.614
Brand name	4.575E-02	.058	.627
Price	.370	.057	41.860
Good Housekeeping seal	-.350	.057	37.660
Money-back guarantee	-.159	.057	7.666

The largest coefficient occurs for *package*. A one standard deviation increase in *package* yields a 0.748 standard deviation decrease in predicted preference ranking. However, *package* is treated nominally, so an increase in the quantifications need not correspond to an increase in the original category codes.

Standardized coefficients are often interpreted as reflecting the importance of each predictor. However, regression coefficients cannot fully describe the impact of a predictor or the relationships between the predictors. Alternative statistics must be used in conjunction with the standardized coefficients to fully explore predictor effects.

Correlational Analyses

To interpret the contributions of the predictors to the regression, it is not sufficient to only inspect the regression coefficients. In addition, the correlations, partial correlations, and part correlations should be inspected. Figure 7.7 contains these correlational measures for each variable.

The zero-order correlation is the correlation between the transformed predictor and the transformed response. For this data, the largest correlation occurs for *package*. However, if we can explain some of the variation in either the predictor or the response, we will get a better representation of how well the predictor is doing.

Figure 7.7   Zero-order, part, and partial correlations (transformed variables)

	Correlations		
	Zero-order	Partial	Part
Package design	-.816	-.955	-.733
Brand name	.207	.194	.045
Price	.440	.851	.368
Good Housekeeping seal	-.370	-.838	-.350
Money-back guarantee	-.223	-.569	-.158

Other variables in the model can confound the performance of a given predictor in predicting the response. The partial correlation coefficient removes the linear effects of other predictors from both the predictor and the response. This measure equals the correlation between the residuals from regressing the predictor on the other predictors and the residuals from regressing the response on the other predictors. The squared partial correlation corresponds to the proportion of the variance explained relative to the residual variance of the response remaining after removing the effects of the other variables. For example, in Figure 7.7, *package* has a partial correlation of –0.955. Removing the effects of the other variables, package explains 91% (-0.955^2) of the variation in the preference rankings. Both *price* and *seal* also explain a large portion of variance if the effects of the other variables are removed.

Figure 7.8 displays the partial correlations for the untransformed variables. All of the partial correlations increase when optimal scores are used. In the standard approach, *package* explained 50% of the variation in *pref* when other variable effects were removed from both. In contrast, *package* explains 91% of the variation if optimal scaling is used. Similar results occur for *price* and *seal*

Figure 7.8   Zero-order, part, and partial correlations (untransformed variables)

	Correlations		
	Zero-order	Partial	Part
Brand name	.206	.101	.055
Money-back guarantee	-.223	-.340	-.196
Package design	-.657	-.708	-.544
Price	.440	.557	.363
Good Housekeeping seal	-.370	-.518	-.328

As an alternative to removing the effects of variables from both the response and a predictor, we can remove the effects from just the predictor. The correlation between the response and the residuals from regressing a predictor on the other predictors is the part correlation. Squaring this value yields a measure of the proportion of variance explained relative to the total variance of response. From Figure 7.7, if we remove the effects of *brand, seal, money,* and *price* from *package*, the remaining part of *package* explains $(-0.733)^2$, or 54% of the variation in preference rankings.

Importance

In addition to the regression coefficients and the correlations, Pratt's measure of relative importance (Pratt, 1987) aids in interpreting predictor contributions to the regression. Large individual importances relative to the other importances correspond to predictors that are crucial to the regression. Also, the presence of suppressor variables is signaled by a low importance for a variable that has a coefficient of similar size to the important predictors.

Figure 7.9 displays the importances for the carpet cleaner predictors. In contrast to the regression coefficients, this measure defines the importance of the predictors additively—that is, the importance of a set of predictors is the sum of the individual importances of the predictors. Pratt's measure equals the product of the regression coefficient and the zero-order correlation for a predictor. These products add to R^2, so they are divided by R^2, yielding a sum of one. The set of predictors *package* and *brand*, for example, have an importance of 0.654. The largest importance corresponds to *package*, with *package, price,* and *seal* accounting for 95% of the importance for this combination of predictors.

Multicollinearity

Large correlations between predictors will dramatically reduce a regression model's stability. Correlated predictors result in unstable parameter estimates. Tolerance reflects how much the independent variables are linearly related to one another. This measure is the proportion of a variable's variance *not* accounted for by other independent variables in the equation. If the other predictors can explain a large amount of a predictor's variance, that predictor is not needed in the model. A tolerance value near 1 indicates that the variable cannot be predicted very well from the other predictors. In contrast, a variable with a very low tolerance contributes little information to a model, and can cause computational problems. Moreover, large negative values of Pratt's importance measure indicate multicollinearity.

Figure 7.9 shows the tolerance for each predictor. All of these measures are very high. None of the predictors are predicted very well by the other predictors and multicollinearity is not present.

Figure 7.9   Predictor tolerances and importances

	Importance	Tolerance	
		After Transformation	Before Transformation
Package design	.644	.959	.942
Brand name	.010	.971	.961
Price	.172	.989	.982
Good Housekeeping seal	.137	.996	.991
Money-back guarantee	.037	.987	.993

Transformation Plots

Plotting the original category values against their corresponding quantifications can reveal trends which might not be noticed in a list of the quantifications. Such plots are commonly referred to as transformation plots. Attention should be given to categories that receive similar quantifications. These categories affect the predicted response in the same manner. However, the transformation type dictates the basic appearance of the plot.

Variables treated as numerical result in a linear relationship between the quantifications and the original categories, corresponding to a straight line in the transformation plot. The order and the difference between the original categories is preserved in the quantifications.

The order of the quantifications for variables treated as ordinal correspond to the order of the original categories. However, the differences between the categories are not preserved. As a result, the transformation plot is nondecreasing but need not be a straight line. If consecutive categories correspond to similar quantifications, the category distinction may be unnecessary and the categories could be combined. Such categories result in a plateau on the transformation plot. However, this pattern can also result from imposing an ordinal structure on a variable that should be treated as nominal. If a subsequent nominal treatment of the variable reveals the same pattern, combining categories is warranted. Moreover, if the quantifications for a variable treated as ordinal fall along a straight line, a numerical transformation may be more appropriate.

For variables treated as nominal, the order of the categories along the horizontal axis corresponds to the order of the codes used to represent the categories. Interpretations of category order or of the distance between the categories is unfounded. The plot can assume any nonlinear or linear form. If an increasing trend is present, an ordinal treatment should be attempted. If the nominal transformation plot displays a linear trend, a numerical transformation may be more appropriate.

Figure 7.10 displays the transformation plot for *price*, which was treated as numerical. Notice that the order of the categories along the straight line correspond to the order of the original categories. Also, the difference between the quantifications for *$1.19* and *$1.39* (–1.173 and 0) is the same as the difference between the quantifications for *$1.39* and *$1.59* (0 and 1.173). The fact that categories 1 and 3 are the same distance from category 2 is preserved in the quantifications.

Figure 7.10   Transformation plot for price (numerical)

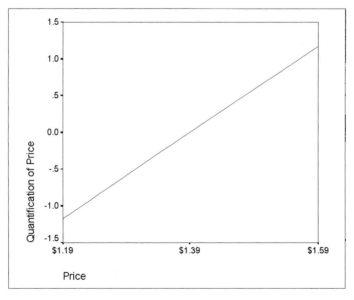

The nominal transformation of *package* yields the transformation plot in Figure 7.11. Notice the distinct nonlinear shape in which the second category has the largest quantification. In terms of the regression, the second category decreases predicted preference ranking, whereas the first and third categories have the opposite effect.

Figure 7.11   Transformation plot for package (nominal)

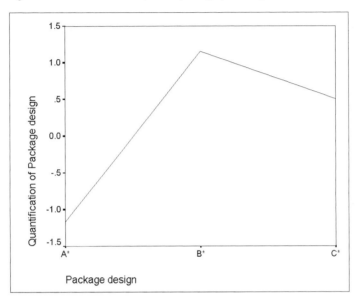

Residual Analysis

Any regression should be accompanied by a residual analysis. However, CATREG does not produce residuals. To perform a residual analysis, save the transformed data to an external file. Using the transformed data in a standard linear regression allows you to save and analyze the residuals. The resulting coefficients correspond to the coefficients from CATREG.

Figure 7.12 shows the standardized residuals plotted against the optimal scores for *package*. All of the residuals are within two standard deviations of 0. A random scatter of points replaces the U-shape present in Figure 7.3. Predictive abilities are improved by optimally quantifying the categories.

Figure 7.12   Residuals for regression with optimal scaling

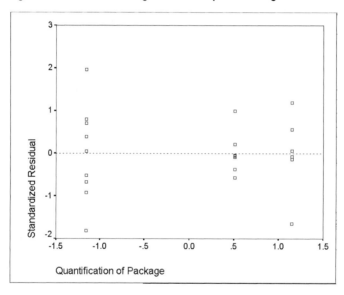

In addition to the standard residual plots, you can create partial residual plots using the transformed data. The residuals from regressing a predictor on the other predictors can be plotted against the residuals from regressing the response on the other predictors. The more linear the resulting scatter, the higher the part correlation between the predictor and the response.

Regressing *package* on *brand*, *price*, *money*, and *seal* yields one set of residuals. Regressing *pref* on *brand*, *price*, *money*, and *seal* yields another. Both residual sets reflect information left in the variables after removing the effects of the other variables. These two sets are plotted against each other in Figure 7.13. The rather compact cluster of points illustrates the large amount of variation in *pref* explained by *package* when the effects of the other predictors are removed from both. The decreasing linear trend indicates that as transformed *package* increases, predicted preference increases.

Figure 7.13   Partial residual plot

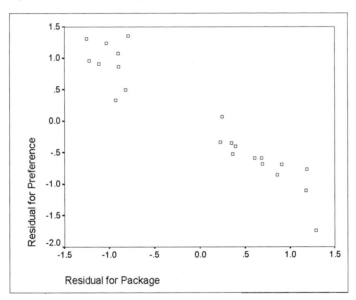

Regressing *brand* on *price*, *package*, *money*, and *seal* yields the residuals plotted against the residuals from regressing *pref* on *price*, *package*, *money*, and *seal* in Figure 7.14. No discernible trend is apparent, and the points are widely scattered. The correlation between these residuals of 0.194, indicates that only 4% of the variance in preference is explained by *brand*.

Figure 7.14   Partial residual plot

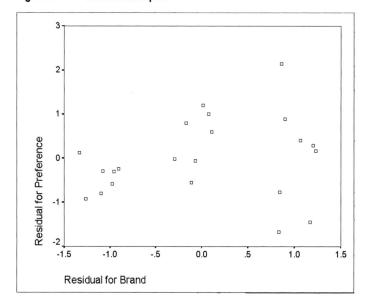

Another Example: Ozone Data

In this example, we will use a larger set of data to illustrate the selection and effects of optimal scaling transformations. The data include 330 observations on six meteorological variables analyzed by Breiman and Friedman (1985), and Hastie and Tibshirani (1990), among others. Table 7.2 describes the original variables. Our regression with optimal scaling attempts to predict the ozone concentration from the remaining variables.

Previous researchers found nonlinearities among these variables, which hinder standard regression approaches.

Table 7.2

Variable	Description
ozon	daily ozone level; categorized into one of 38 categories
ibh	inversion base height
dpg	pressure gradient (mm Hg)
vis	visibility (miles)
temp	temperature (degrees F)
doy	day of the year

Categorizing Variables

In many analyses, variables need to be categorized or recoded before a regression with optimal scaling can be performed. For example, CATREG truncates any decimals and treats negative values as missing. If either of these applications is undesirable, the data must be recoded before performing the optimal scaling regression. Moreover, if a variable has more categories than is practically interpretable, a modification before the analysis can reduce the category range to a more manageable number.

The variable *doy* has a minimum value of 3 and a maximum value of 365. Using this variable in CATREG corresponds to using a variable with 365 categories. Similarly, *vis* ranges from 0 to 350. To simplify analyses, divide each variable by 10, add 1, and round the result to the nearest integer. The resulting variables, denoted *ddoy* and *dvis*, have only 38 and 36 categories respectively, and are consequently much easier to interpret.

The variable *ibh* ranges from 111 to 5000. A variable with this many categories results in very complex relationships. However, dividing by 100 and rounding the result to the nearest integer yields categories ranging from 1 to 50 for the variable *dibh*. Using a 50 category variable rather than a 5000 category variable simplifies interpretations significantly.

Categorizing *dpg* differs slightly from categorizing the previous three variables. This variable ranges from –69 to 107. CATREG omits any categories coded with negative numbers from the analysis. To adjust for the negative values, add 70 to all observations to yield a range from 1 to 177. Dividing this range by 10 and adding 1 results in *ddpg*, a variable with categories ranging from 1 to 19.

The temperatures for *temp* range from 25 to 93 on the Fahrenheit scale. Converting to Celsius and rounding yields a range from –4 to 34. Adding 5 eliminates all negative numbers and results in *tempc*, a variable with 39 categories.

As described above, different modifications for variables may be required before conducting a regression with optimal scaling. The divisors used here are purely subjective. If you desire fewer categories, divide by a larger number. For example, *doy* could have been divided into months of the year or seasons.

Selection of Transformation Type

Each variable can be analyzed at one of three different levels. However, because prediction of the response is the goal, we recommend scaling the response "as is" by employing the numerical optimal scaling level. Consequently, the order and the differences between categories will be preserved in the transformed variable.

Treating all predictors as nominal yields an R^2 of 0.883. This large amount of variance accounted for is not surprising because nominal treatment imposes no restrictions on the quantifications. However, interpreting the results can be quite difficult.

Figure 7.15 shows the standardized regression coefficients of the predictors. A common mistake made when interpreting these values involves focusing on the coefficients while neglecting the quantifications. You cannot assert that the large positive value of the *tempc* coefficient implies that as *tempc* increases, predicted *ozon* increases. Similarly, the negative coefficient for *dibh* does not suggest that as *dibh* increases, predicted *ozon* decreases. All interpretations must be relative to the *transformed* variables. As the quantifications for *tempc* increase, or as the quantifications for *dibh* decrease, predicted *ozon* increases. To examine the effects of the original variables, you must relate the categories to the quantifications.

Figure 7.15   Regression coefficients (all predictors nominal)

	Standardized Coefficients		
	Beta	Std. Error	F
DDPG	-.264	.021	165.512
DDOY	.358	.021	290.275
DVIS	.200	.020	104.459
TEMPC	.631	.021	924.505
DIBH	-.267	.020	178.259

Figure 7.16 displays the transformation plot for *ddpg*. The initial categories (1 through 7) receive small quantifications and thus have minimal contributions to the predicted response. Categories 8 through 10 receive somewhat higher, negative values, resulting in a moderate increase in predicted *ozon*. The quantifications increase up to category 17, where *ddpg* has its greatest decreasing effect on predicted *ozon*. Although the line decreases after this category, using an ordinal scaling level for *ddpg* may not significantly reduce the fit, while simplifying the interpretations of the effects. However, the importance measure of 0.04 and the regression coefficient for *ddpg* indicates that this variable is not very useful in the regression.

Figure 7.16   Transformation plot for ddpg (nominal)

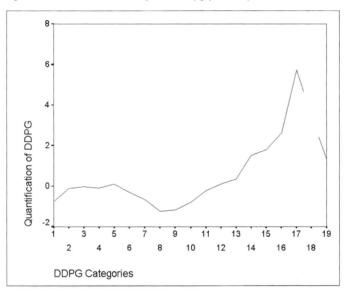

The transformation plots for *dvis* and *dibh* (Figure 7.17 and Figure 7.18) show no apparent pattern. As evidenced by the jagged nature of the plots, moving from low categories to high categories yields fluctuations in the quantifications in both directions. Thus, describing the effects of these variables requires focusing on the individual categories. Imposing ordinal or linear restrictions on the quantifications for either of these variables might significantly reduce the fit.

Figure 7.17   Transformation plot for dvis (nominal)

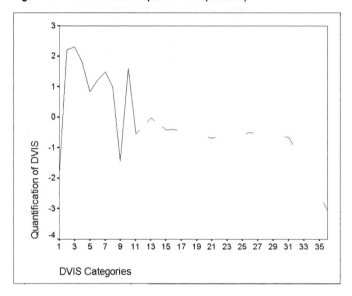

Figure 7.18   Transformation plot for dibh (nominal)

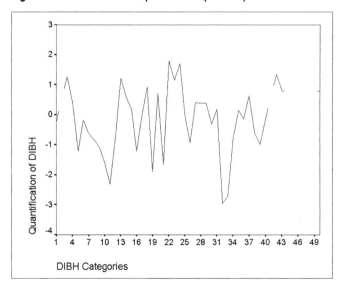

Figure 7.19 shows the transformation plot for *ddoy*. In contrast to Figure 7.18, this plot displays a pattern. The quantifications tend to increase up to category 21, at which point they tend to decrease, yielding an inverted U-shape. Considering the sign of the regression coefficient for *ddoy*, the initial categories (1 through 5) receive quantifications that have a decreasing effect on predicted *ozon*. From category 6 onward, the effect of the quantifications on predicted *ozon* gets more increasing, reaching a maximum around category 21. Beyond category 21, the quantifications tend to decrease the predicted *ozon*. Although the line is quite jagged, the general shape is still identifiable.

Figure 7.19   Transformation plot for ddoy (nominal)

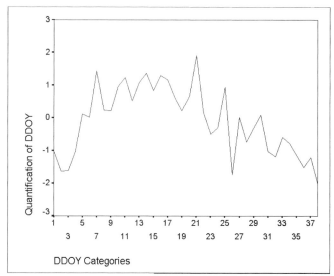

The transformation plot for *tempc* (Figure 7.20) displays an alternative pattern. As the categories increase, the quantifications tend to increase. As a result, as *tempc* increases, predicted *ozon* tends to increase. This pattern suggests scaling *tempc* at the ordinal level.

Figure 7.20   Transformation plot for tempc (nominal)

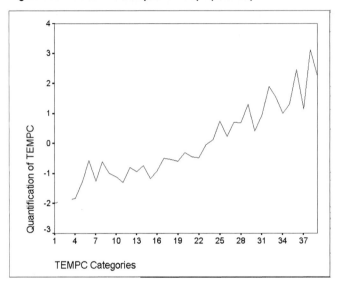

Thus, the transformation plots suggest scaling *tempc* at the ordinal level while keeping all other predictors nominally scaled. This model results in an R^2 of .873, so the variance accounted for decreases negligibly when the quantifications for *tempc* are restricted to be ordered.

Figure 7.21 displays the coefficients, correlations, and importances. Comparing the coefficients to those in Figure 7.15, no large changes occur. The importance measures suggest that *tempc* is much more important to the regression than the other variables. When the effects of the other variables are removed, 73% of the variance in transformed *ozon* is accounted for by transformed *tempc*. However, as a result of the ordinal scaling level of *tempc* and the positive regression coefficient, we can assert that as *tempc* increases, predicted *ozon* increases.

Figure 7.21   Coefficients, correlations, and importances

	Standardized Coefficients		Correlations			
	Beta	Std. Error	Zero-order	Partial	Part	Importance
DDPG	-.252	.021	-.110	-.547	-.233	.032
DDOY	.349	.022	.335	.667	.319	.134
DVIS	.198	.020	.329	.477	.193	.075
TEMPC	.646	.022	.816	.857	.593	.604
DIBH	-.273	.021	-.499	-.585	-.257	.156

The transformation plot in Figure 7.22 illustrates the ordinal restriction on the quantifications for *tempc*. The jagged line in Figure 7.20 is here replaced by a smooth increasing line. Moreover, no long plateaus are present, indicating that collapsing categories is not needed.

Figure 7.22   Transformation plot for tempc (ordinal)

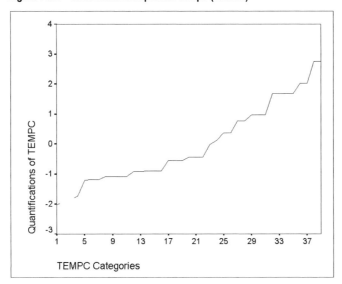

Optimality of the Quantifications

As stated previously, the transformed variables from regression with optimal scaling can be used in a standard linear regression, yielding identical results. However, the quantifications are only optimal for the model that produced them. Using a subset of the predictors in linear regression does not correspond to an optimal scaling regression on the same subset.

For example, a linear regression of *ozon* on the five predictors has an R^2 of 0.677. At the 0.001 level, only *tempc*, *dvis*, and *dibh* are significant. A linear model including only these three predictors results in a decrease in R^2 to 0.661.

Employing regression with optimal scaling yields a fit of 0.873 if the response is scaled numerically, *tempc* is scaled ordinally, and all other predictors are scaled nominally. Using the quantifications for the response, *tempc*, *dvis*, and *dibh* in a standard linear regression results in a fit of 0.758. However, a CATREG analysis using only these three predictors has a fit of 0.791.

Effects of Transformations

Transforming the variables makes a nonlinear relationship between the original response and the original set of predictors linear for the transformed variables. However, when there are multiple predictors, pairwise relationships are confounded by the other variables in the model.

Figure 7.23 illustrates the relationship between *ozon* and *ddoy*. As *ddoy* increases to approximately 25, *ozon* increases. However, for *ddoy* values greater than 25, *ozon* decreases. This inverted U pattern suggests a quadratic relationship between the two variables. A linear regression cannot capture this relationship.

Figure 7.23   Scatterplot of ozon and ddoy

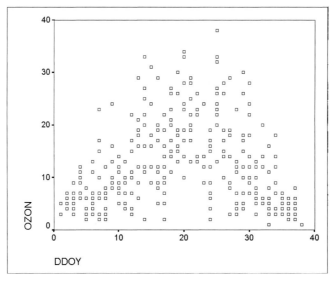

By excluding the other variables from the model, we can focus on the relationship between *ozon* and *ddoy*. However, all interpretations based on the reduced model apply only to the reduced model. Do not generalize the results to the regression involving all predictors.

The regression of *ozon* on *ddoy* yields an R^2 of 0.004. This fit suggests that *ddoy* has no predictive value for *ozon*. This is not surprising, given the pattern in Figure 7.23. By using optimal scaling, however, we can linearize the quadratic relationship and use the transformed *ddoy* to predict the response.

The optimal scaling regression treats *ozon* as numerical and *ddoy* as nominal. This results in an R^2 of 0.562. Although only 56% of the variation in *ozon* is accounted for by the linear regression, this is a substantial improvement over the original regression. Transforming *ddoy* allows for the prediction of *ozon*.

Figure 7.24 displays the transformation plot for *ddoy*. The extremes of *ddoy* both receive negative quantifications, whereas the central values have positive quantifications. By applying this transformation, the low and high *ddoy* values have similar effects on predicted *ozon*.

Figure 7.24   Transformation plot for ddoy (nominal)

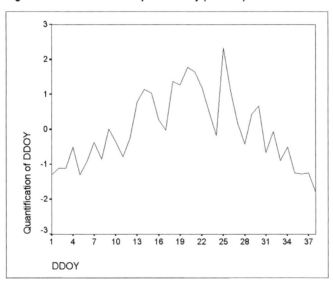

Figure 7.25 depicts the relationship between the transformed variables. An increasing trend replaces the inverted U in Figure 7.23. The regression line has a slope of 0.750, indicating that as transformed *ddoy* increases, predicted *ozon* increases. Using optimal scaling linearizes the relationship and allows interpretations which would otherwise go unnoticed.

Figure 7.25   Scatterplot of the transformed variables

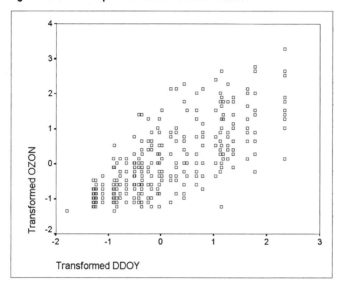

Nonlinear Principal Components Analysis Examples

Nonlinear principal components analysis corresponds to categorical principal components analysis with optimal scaling and is also known by the acronym PRINCALS, for *prin*cipal *c*omponents analysis by means of *a*lternating *l*east *s*quares. As with homogeneity analysis, nonlinear canonical correlation analysis, and categorical regression with optimal scoring, nonlinear principal components analysis uses alternating least squares as the computational algorithm to estimate parameters.

Like classical principal components analysis, nonlinear principal components analysis can be thought of as a method of dimension reduction. A set of variables is analyzed to reveal major dimensions of variation. The original data set can then be replaced by a new, smaller data set with minimal loss of information. The method reveals relationships among variables, among cases, and among variables and cases.

The most important differences between nonlinear principal components analysis and classical principal components analysis are that the former can perform nonlinear analysis and the variables can have different scaling levels—nominal, ordinal, interval, or ratio.

Two examples of nonlinear principal components analysis will be presented. The first employs a rather small data set useful for illustrating the basic concepts and interpretations associated with the procedure. The second example examines the effects of different optimal scaling levels in a practical application.

Basic Terminology

Although the optimal scaling literature has much in common with other traditional areas of data analysis, it has some unique terms for describing phrases such as "unit of analysis" and "factor levels." The following are descriptions of terms unique to categorical principal components analysis with optimal scaling:

Objects. What we usually refer to in other areas of data analysis as cases are called objects in nonlinear principal components analysis. These objects are the basic units of analysis.

Categories. The values or levels of the objects on some variables separate the objects into categories. Objects with the same value on a variable are in the same category.

An important process in nonlinear principal components analysis is the quantification of the data:

Object scores. Categorical principal components analysis with optimal scaling quantifies objects by assigning each one an object score. Object scores have a mean of 0 and unit variance.

Category quantifications. Categorical principal components analysis with optimal scaling also assigns numerical values to the different categories of each variable. These are the category quantifications.

The criterion used by nonlinear principal components analysis for quantifying the observed data is that the object scores should have large correlations with each of the variables in the quantified data matrix. A solution is good to the extent that this criterion is satisfied.

Optimal Scaling Level

In addition to accepting observed variables measured at different levels of measurement, nonlinear principal components analysis allows you to specify the optimal scaling level at which the variables are quantified.

This can be a very confusing concept when you first use nonlinear principal components analysis. When specifying the level, you specify not the level at which variables are *measured,* but the level at which they are *scaled.* The idea is that the variables to be scaled may have nonlinear relations regardless of the scale (nominal, ordinal, interval, or ratio) on which they are measured. The purpose of the analysis is not to determine the scale on which variables are measured, but to investigate possible nonlinear relationships. This highlights an important feature of nonlinear principal components analysis and most of the other SPSS Categories procedures—they are mainly exploratory rather than confirmatory techniques. There is much more emphasis in these techniques on visually discovering possible relationships among variables and objects in a multidimensional space than in hypothesis testing.

The four ways that variables can be quantified in nonlinear principal components analysis are:

Ordinal. Categories of the quantified variable have the same original order as that of the observed variable.

Single nominal. Objects in the same category (cases with the same value on a variable) obtain the same score. When all of the variables are scaled as single nominal and the number of dimensions is 1, the nonlinear principal components analysis solution is equal to the first-dimension homogeneity analysis solution.

Multiple nominal. With variables scaled at the multiple-nominal level, the quantifications can be different for each dimension. (With the other three levels, the category quantifications are the same across all dimensions.) This leads to different computations, output, and interpretation of output.

Numeric. This option assumes that the variable already has numerical values for its categories. During optimal scaling quantification, only interval-level transformation is performed. When all of the variables are scaled as numerical, nonlinear principal components analysis is analogous to classical principal analysis applied to categorical data.

It is important to understand that there are no intrinsic properties of a variable that automatically predefine what optimal scaling level you should specify for it. You can explore your data in any way that makes sense and makes interpretation easier. By analyzing an interval-level variable at the ordinal level, for example, the use of a nonlinear transformation may allow a solution in fewer dimensions.

Selecting the Optimal Scaling Level

The following two examples illustrate how the "obvious" level of measurement might not be the best optimal scaling level. Suppose that a variable sorts objects into age groups. Although age can be scaled as a numerical variable, you may decide to scale age as ordinal if, for example, the study is on driver safety. It may be that safety is related linearly to age only for people younger than 25. Ordinal treatment of age might then be more realistic than numerical treatment. On the other hand, it may be true that for people younger than 25 safety has a positive relation with age, whereas for people older than 60 safety has a negative relation with age. In this case, it might be better to treat age as a nominal variable.

As another example, a variable that sorts persons by political preference appears to be essentially nominal. If you order the parties from political left to political right, you might want the quantification of parties to respect this order by using an ordinal level of analysis. If you had some a priori reasons to assume interval properties in this political preference scale, you might require it to be quantified as a numerical variable.

A brief geometric explanation of the differences might provide some additional insight. Suppose you have a three-dimensional nonlinear principal components analysis problem. The categories of multiple-nominal variables can be placed anywhere in these three dimensions. The categories of single-nominal variables are restricted to be placed anywhere on a line through the origin of these dimensions. The categories of an ordinal variable are also restricted to be on such a line, and the order of the categories is important. Numerical variables have these restrictions, and in addition, the distance between all categories on the line must be equal.

Even though there are no predefined properties of a variable that make it exclusively one level or another, there are some general guidelines to help the novice user. With single-nominal quantification, you usually don't know the order of the categories but you want the nonlinear principal components analysis to impose one. If the order of the categories is known, you should probably try ordinal quantification. If the categories are unorderable, you might try multiple-nominal quantification.

How you decide to quantify the variables will affect, for example, the number of dimensions needed, computation of statistics, plot display, and interpretation of the output. Ultimately, it is up to you, and you will probably want to compare the results of several nonlinear principal components analyses using different optimal scaling levels. For a more detailed discussion of the different levels, see Gifi (1991).

Example 1

This example examines Guttman's (1968) adaptation of a table by Bell (1961). The data are also discussed by Lingoes (1968). Guttman and Lingoes used this data set to illustrate their multidimensional scalogram analysis (MSA) programs, and we will do the same to demonstrate categorical principal components analysis with optimal scaling.

Bell presented a table to illustrate possible clusters of social systems. Guttman used a portion of this table, in which five variables describing such things as social interaction, feelings of belonging to a group, physical proximity of members, and formality of the relationship were crossed with seven theoretical clusters of people including *crowds* (for example, people at a football game), *audiences* (for example, people at a theater or classroom lecture), *public* (for example, newspaper or television audiences), *mobs* (like a crowd but with much more intense interaction), *primary groups* (intimate), *secondary groups* (voluntary), and the *modern community* (loose confederation resulting from close physical proximity and a need for specialized services).

Table 8.1 shows the variables in the data set resulting from the classification of the seven clusters used in the Guttman-Bell data, with their variable labels and the value labels (categories) associated with the levels of each variable. In addition to selecting variables to be included in the computation of the nonlinear principal components analysis, you can select variables that are used to label plots. In this example, all variables in the data are included in the analysis. When you specify a nonlinear principal components analysis, you must specify the optimal scaling level for each variable. In this example, an ordinal level is specified for all variables.

Table 8.1   Variables in the Guttman-Bell data set

Variable name	Variable label	Value labels
intnsity	Intensity of interaction	Slight, low, moderate, high
frquency	Frequency of interaction	Slight, nonrecurring, infrequent, frequent
blonging	Feeling of belonging	None, slight, variable, high
proxmity	Physical proximity	Distant, close
formlity	Formality of relationship	No relationship, formal, informal

Number of Dimensions

Figure 8.1 shows some of the initial output for the nonlinear principal components analysis. After a list of the variables and a table showing marginal frequencies, the eigenvalues of each dimension are displayed. These eigenvalues are similar to those of classical principal components analysis. They are measures of how much variance is accounted for by each dimension.

Figure 8.1   Frequency and eigenvalue output from nonlinear principal components analysis

```
Marginal Frequencies
====================
Variable  Missing  Categories
                     1     2     3     4
BLONGING      0      1     2     2     2
FRQUENCY      0      2     2     2     1
INTNSITY      0      2     2     1     2
FORMLITY      0      1     4     2
PROXMITY      0      2     5


The iterative process stops because the convergence test value is reached.
Dimension  Eigenvalue
---------  ----------
    1         .6784
    2         .2668
```

The eigenvalues can be used as an indication of how many dimensions are needed. In this example, the default number of dimensions, 2, was used. Is this the right number? In general, when all variables are either single nominal, ordinal, or numerical, the eigenvalue for a dimension should be larger than $1/$ number of variables . In this example, you can see that both dimensions have eigenvalues larger than 0.2 ($1/5$ variables). Since the second dimension is just barely greater than 0.2, a third dimension probably would not add much more information.

For multiple-nominal variables, there is no easy rule of thumb to determine the correct number of dimensions. If the number of variables is replaced by the total number of categories minus the number of variables, the above rule still holds, as do the rules for the maximum number of dimensions (see the Syntax Reference section of this manual). But these rules alone would probably allow more dimensions than are needed. When choosing the number of dimensions, perhaps one of the most useful guidelines is to keep the number small enough so that meaningful interpretations are possible.

If an analysis involves more than two dimensions, SPSS produces three-dimensional plots of the first three dimensions. Other dimensions can be displayed by editing the chart. See the *SPSS Base User's Guide* for information on editing charts and using the chart gallery.

Quantifications

The Categories output presents, for each variable, the quantifications, the single-category coordinates, and the multiple-category coordinates for each dimension. The quantifications are the values assigned to each category. The single category coordinates are the coordinates of the categories on a line representing the variable in the object space, and are found by multiplying the quantifications by the component loadings. The multiple category coordinates are the category coordinates in the object space before ordinal or linear constraints are imposed. These values equal the average of the object scores for objects in the same category.

For variables scaled as ordinal, single nominal, or numerical, the single-category coordinates are plotted in a quantification plot. For multiple-nominal variables, multiple coordinates are found under the heading *Category Quantifications* and are the coordinates plotted in quantification plots.

Figure 8.2 shows the quantification plot for the present example. Glancing at the quantifications, you can see that some of the categories of some variables were not separated by the nonlinear principal components analysis as cleanly as would have been expected if the level had been truly ordinal. (Use the point identification feature described in Chapter 1 to read obscured point labels.) Variables *intnsity* and *frquency*, for example, have equal or almost equal quantifications for their two middle categories. This kind of result might suggest trying alternative nonlinear principal components analyses, perhaps with some categories collapsed, or perhaps with a different level of analysis, such as multiple nominal.

Figure 8.2   Category coordinates labeled with the category values

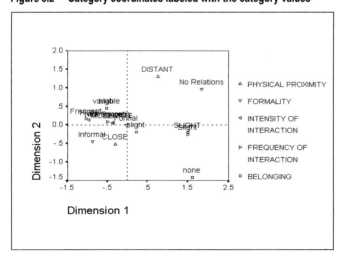

The two variables measuring interaction, *intnsity* and *frquency*, appear very close together and, along with *formlity*, account for much of the variance in dimension 1. *formlity* appears close to *proxmity* (labeled *PHYSICAL PROXIMITY*).

By focusing on the category values, you can see the relationships even more clearly. Not only are *intnsity* and *frquency* close, but the directions of their scales are similar; that is, slight intensity is close to slight frequency, and frequent interaction is near high intensity of interaction. You also see that close physical proximity seems to go hand-in-hand with an informal type of relationship, and physical distance is related to no relationship.

Object Scores

The nonlinear principal components analysis can also request a listing and plot of object scores. The plot of the object scores can be useful for detecting outliers, detecting typical groups of objects, or revealing some special patterns.

Figure 8.3 shows the listing of object scores for the Guttman-Bell data. By examining the object scores, which are the two-dimensional coordinate values for the points, you can identify specific objects on the plot for information.

Figure 8.3   Object scores

```
The Object Scores are:
 ======================
           *
Object  *       Dimension
           *
                  1          2
       1 *      1.27      -1.81
       2 *      -.28       -.45
       3 *      1.72       1.20
       4 *      -.93       -.23
       5 *     -1.09       -.16
       6 *      -.19       1.41
       7 *      -.50        .04
```

The first dimension appears to separate objects 1 (*crowds*) and 3 (*public*), which have relatively large positive scores, from objects 4 (*mobs*) and 5 (*primary groups*), which have relatively large negative scores. The second dimension appears to separate objects 3 (*public*) and 6 (*secondary groups*) from object 1 (*crowds*).

Figure 8.4   Object scores plot

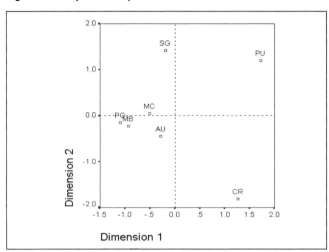

Figure 8.4 shows the plot of the object scores labeled by Guttman's theoretical clusters. The plot indicates the points for each of the seven clusters. You can see that *secondary group* (labeled *SG*) at the top of the plot is quite different from *crowd* (labeled *CR*) at the bottom of the plot. Examining patterns among individual objects depends on the unit of analysis and might not always be very meaningful. In this case, however, the *secondary group* is characterized by distant physical proximity and a high feeling of belonging, while the *crowd* has close physical proximity and no feeling of belonging. You can also see that the nonlinear principal components analysis does not separate the *mob* (labeled *MB*) from the *primary group* (labeled *PG*). Although we usually don't think of our families as mobs, on the variables measured, these two groups received the same score on four of the five variables! Obviously, you might want to explore possible shortcomings of the variables and categories used. For example, *high* intensity of interaction and *informal* relationships probably mean different things to these two groups. Alternatively, you might consider a higher dimensional solution.

Component Loadings

Figure 8.5 shows the plot of component loadings. If you draw lines by hand or by using a third-party application from the origin to each variable, you see that the lines are relatively long, indicating again that the first two dimensions account for most of the variance of all the quantified variables. On the first dimension, all variables have high (negative) component loadings. The plot also shows that the second dimension is correlated mainly with quantified variables *blonging* and *proxmity*, in opposite directions. This means that objects with a high score in dimension 2 will have a high score in feeling of belonging and a low score in physical proximity. The second dimension, therefore, reveals a contrast between these two variables while having little relation with the quantified variables *frquency* and *intnsity*.

Figure 8.5   Component loadings

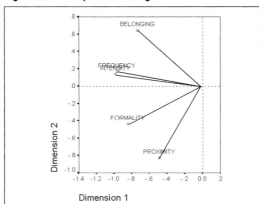

Additional Dimensions

As in standard principal components analysis, there is no general rule defining how many dimensions to use in categorical principal components analysis with optimal scaling. General rules of thumb are merely suggestions. Increasing the number of dimensions will increase the amount of variation accounted for, and may reveal differences concealed in lower dimensional solutions.

As noted previously, in two dimensions, *mob* and *primary group* cannot be separated. However, increasing the dimensionality may allow the two groups to be differentiated. A three dimensional solution has eigenvalues of 0.7206, 0.1578, and 0.1216. Although the last two eigenvalues are relatively small, interpretation may be improved by the addition of the third dimension.

The object scores for a three-dimensional solution were saved and plotted in the scatterplot matrix in Figure 8.6. In a scatterplot matrix, every dimension is plotted against every other dimension in a series of two-dimensional scatterplots.

Figure 8.6   Three-dimensional object scores scatterplot matrix

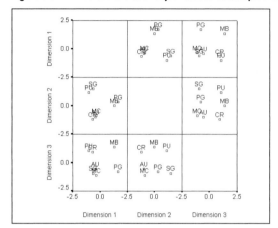

The first column of plots reveals that the first dimension separates *primary group* and *mob* from the other groups. Notice that the order of the objects along the horizontal axis does not change in any of the plots in the first column; each of these plots employs dimension 1 as the *x*-axis.

The second column of plots allows for interpretation of dimension 2. The second dimension has changed slightly from the two-dimensional solution. *Audience* (labeled *AU*) and *modern community* (labeled *MC*) are much closer to *crowd*.

The third dimension separates *mob*, *crowd*, and *public* (labeled *PU*), which all have high positive scores, from the other objects, which have high negative scores. The addition of a third dimension separates *mob* from *primary group*, which did not occur in the two-dimensional solution. However, *audience* and *modern community*, which differ on two variables, cannot be separated in the three-dimensional space.

The matrix plot reveals a unique structure underlying these objects. Plotting dimension 1 against dimension 2 yields three distinct clusters of objects. These clusters are {*primary group, mob*}, {*secondary group, public*}, and {*modern community, audience, crowd*}. The third dimension separates each of these clusters. *Public* is plotted above *secondary group*. *Mob* is plotted above *primary group*. *Crowd* is plotted above *audience/modern community*. As a result, the objects lie at the vertices of the triangular prism in Figure 8.7. To aid in viewing the three dimensionality of the figure, the space has been rotated and lines connecting the points have been added. One triangular face is defined by *public*, *mob*, and *crowd*. The opposite face has vertices corresponding to *secondary group*, *primary group*, and *audience/modern community*. *Public* is positioned opposite *secondary group*, *mob* is opposite *primary group*, and *crowd* is opposite the final two objects.

Figure 8.7   Three-dimensional object scores space

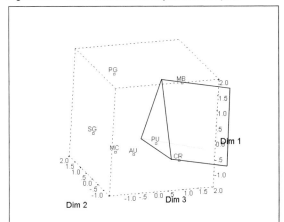

Knowing how the objects are separated does not reveal what variables correspond to which dimensions. This is accomplished using the component loadings, which are presented in Figure 8.8. The first dimension corresponds primarily to *blonging*, *intnsity*, and *formlity*, the second dimension corresponds to *proxmity*, and the third dimension corresponds to *frquency*. Notice that the third dimension, which allows for a separation of mobs from primary groups not present in the two-dimensional solution, is associated with *frquency*, the one variable on which these two groups differ.

Figure 8.8   Three-dimensional component loadings

```
Component Loadings
------------------

Variable            Dimension
--------            1       2       3

BLONGING            .977    .119    .177
FRQUENCY            .682    .144   -.717
INTNSITY            .976    .129    .176
FORMLITY            .979    .106    .173
PROXMITY            .521   -.852   -.048
```

Example 2

The following example uses data on the professional journal preferences of 39 psychologists. They were asked to rank 10 journals from 1 (most preferred) to 10 (least preferred). These data were originally reported by Roskam (1968) and used by Gifi

(1990) to illustrate PRINCALS analysis. The journal titles, journal labels, and psychology department labels are shown in Table 8.2. For this example, the 39 psychologists are treated as the variables, and the 10 journals are considered the objects (cases).

Table 8.2   Journal and department codes

Code	Journal	Code	Department
JEXP	Journal of Experimental Psychology	S	Social psychology
JAPP	Journal of Applied Psychology	D	Educational & developmental psychology
JPSP	Journal of Personality & Social Psychology	C	Clinical psychology
MUBR	Multivariate Behavioral Research	M	Mathematical psych. & psych. statistics
JCLP	Journal of Consulting Psychology	E	Experimental psychology
JEDP	Journal of Educational Psychology	R	Cultural psych. & psych. of religion
PMEK	Psychometrika	T	Industrial psychology
HURE	Human Relations	A	Physiological & animal psychology
BULL	Psychological Bulletin		
HUDE	Human Development		

Numerical Variables

The variables are initially analyzed at the numerical scaling level. The maximum number of dimensions that can be extracted is 9, the number of objects (journals) minus 1. A two dimensional solution in which all psychologists are treated as numerical variables has eigenvalues of 0.4052 and 0.1639, yielding a total fit of 0.5691. Only 57% of the variance in psychologist rankings is accounted for by two principal components.

The object scores are plotted in Figure 8.9. Three groups of objects are evident. *JEXP*, *PMEK*, *MUBR*, *JAPP*, and possibly *BULL* cluster on the left of the plot. These journals are commonly referred to as "hard" journals due to their technical nature. A developmental group consisting of *HUDE* and *JEDP* emerges at the top right. The third group consists of *HURE, JCLP*, and possibly *JPSP*, which are "soft" journals lacking technical descriptions.

Figure 8.9   Object scores labeled with journal name

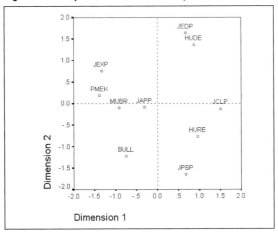

Figure 8.10 contains the component loadings for the psychologists. By looking at how the points cluster, you can see the similarities or differences between psychologists in the various departments. Unfortunately, the academic departments are not separated very well and the loadings vary considerably. The developmental psychologists are separated from the other psychologists but the loadings are not very large on either dimension. The first dimension does separate the experimental, mathematical, and animal psychologists from most of the other psychologists.

Figure 8.10   Component loadings labeled with department code

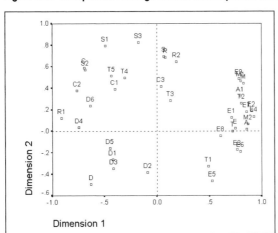

If vectors are drawn from the origin to each variable in Figure 8.10, all but one of the developmental vectors point toward the lower left of the figure. However, the developmental journals are positioned at the top right of the object scores plot. The cause of this apparent anomaly is that low ranks correspond to most preferred journals. Consequently, the component loadings point in the least preferred direction; the developmental journals are most preferred by the developmental psychologists.

Ordinal Variables

Although identifiable clusters of journals are present when the psychologists are scaled at the numerical level, the components do not have a clear interpretation. A better fit may possibly be obtained by changing the optimal scaling level of the variables.

If all of the psychologists are treated as ordinal variables, the two-dimensional solution has eigenvalues of 0.4616 and 0.3554. The total fit of 0.8171 (0.4616 + 0.3554) indicates that 82% of the variation in the original data is accounted for by two principal components. These two components represent quite a substantial reduction in the data (from thirty-nine variables to two principal components) while still accounting for a large proportion of the variance. Moreover, employing an ordinal level improves the fit over the numerical level while retaining the same dimensionality.

The object scores are plotted in Figure 8.11. This plot is similar to the object scores plot for the numerical case with minor differences. *BULL* is closer to the first dimension. The hard and soft groups are each more compactly clustered. However, the developmental journals have moved further apart. *JEDP* is now part of the hard group.

Figure 8.11   Object scores labeled with journal name (ordinal)

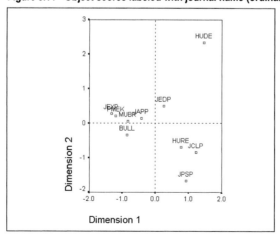

Figure 8.12 shows the component loadings for each of the 39 psychologists, with the points labeled with the first letter of the variable name. Vectors from the origin to the variables are approximately the same length and form a roughly circular pattern. Groups of psychologists are much more defined than in the numerical case.

Figure 8.12   Component loadings labeled with department code (ordinal)

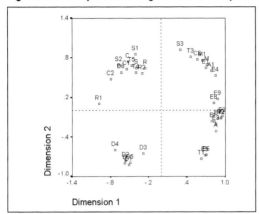

For example, you can see that all but one member of the educational and developmental psychology department (labeled *D* on the plot) cluster together in a distinct group in the lower left corner of the plot. These psychologists have negative loadings on both components. Furthermore, the first component separates the experimental, mathematical, and animal psychologists from the developmental and cultural psychologists. The second component separates the developmental from the social, cultural, and clinical psychologists.

A comparison of the object scores and components indicates that psychologists tend to favor journals closely associated with their own departments. For example, developmental psychologists prefer *HUDE* the most. Experimental psychologists favor *JEXP*. In contrast, *JEDP* is situated near the origin and is not preferred by any one particular department.

Transformation Plots

The relationship between the categories and their quantifications can be illustrated in a transformation plot. Although PRINCALS does not offer these plots, you can construct them by plotting the quantifications against the original categories. For ordinal or nominal scaling levels, a line chart is recommended. For variables treated as numerical, the presence of empty categories can complicate making interpretations. A scatterplot is preferred to a line chart for variables treated numerically.

Figure 8.13 displays the transformation plot for one of the developmental psychologists scaled at a numerical level. Because no empty categories are present, the line chart and the scatterplot perform equally well, and a line chart is illustrated here. The quantifications lie on a straight line because the numerical optimal scaling level results in quantifications that are equally spaced. Although such a pattern is desirable for a ranking scale, equally spaced categories are a rarity in practice.

Figure 8.13   Transformation plot for D1(numerical)

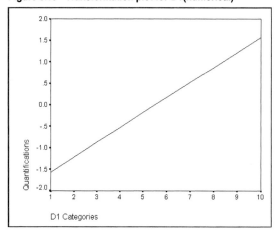

An ordinal treatment of the developmental psychologist yields the transformation plot in Figure 8.14. The linear trend is replaced by a nondecreasing trend. The first two categories are very far apart, whereas categories three through seven receive similar quantifications. The final three categories have quantifications of approximate equal value. Moving from a numerical scaling level to an ordinal scaling level dramatically alters the relationship between the quantifications and the categories, yielding a significantly improved fit for the latter optimal scaling level.

Figure 8.14   Transformation plot for D1(ordinal)

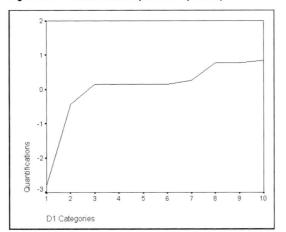

Thus the ordinal solution not only accounts for more variance than the numerical solution, but also has more compact groups and interpretable components. Consideration of the scaling level for each variable is crucial to obtaining the best fit. In this case, standard principal components analysis requires a higher dimensional solution (and more complex interpretations) to account for as much variance as the nonlinear approach.

9

Nonlinear Canonical Correlation Analysis Examples

Nonlinear canonical correlation analysis corresponds to categorical canonical correlation analysis with optimal scaling. This procedure, also known as OVERALS, analyzes two or more sets of variables using the iterative alternating least-squares method also used in homogeneity analysis, nonlinear principal components analysis, and categorical regression with optimal scaling.

The purpose of nonlinear canonical correlation analysis is to determine how similar the sets of variables are to one another. As in linear canonical correlation analysis, the aim is to account for as much of the variance in the relationships among the sets as possible in a low dimensional space. Unlike linear canonical analysis, however, nonlinear canonical correlation analysis does not assume an interval level of measurement or that the relationships are linear. Another important difference is that nonlinear canonical correlation analysis establishes the similarity between the sets by simultaneously comparing linear combinations of the variables in each set to an unknown set—the object scores.

Basic Terminology

Most of the terms used in nonlinear canonical correlation analysis have already been introduced in regression with optimal scaling and nonlinear principal components analysis. In addition, this chapter assumes some familiarity with canonical correlation. The following are some terms that are fairly specific to nonlinear canonical correlation analysis:

Set. A set is a group of variables formed by some theoretical reason. Nonlinear canonical correlation analysis concentrates on relationships among these sets rather than the individual variables themselves. An individual variable is important only when it provides information that is independent of the other variables in the same set.

Centroids. The centroids are the averages of all objects belonging to the same category. These are similar to the multiple category coordinates but differ in that they do not depend on the contribution of other variables in the set. When there is only one variable per set (as is the case in homogeneity analysis and nonlinear principal components analysis), centroids are the same as multiple category coordinates for single variables and category quantifications for multiple variables.

Projected centroids. Projected centroids are projections (not necessarily orthogonal) of the category quantifications onto a straight line through the origin. They are the product of the quantifications and the component loadings. They can be produced for single nominal, ordinal, and numerical variables. When there is only one variable per set, projected centroids are the same as single category coordinates, which are the product of the quantifications and the weights.

Weights. Weights are the regression coefficients in each dimension for every quantified variable in a set, where the object scores are regressed on the quantified variables. Weights provide an indication of the unique contribution each variable makes to the dimension within each set.

Optimal Scaling Level

The same four optimal scaling levels defined for categorical principal components analysis with optimal scaling—numerical, ordinal, single nominal, and multiple nominal—are available in nonlinear canonical correlation analysis as well.

In addition, the discussion in Chapter 8 on the specified optimal scaling level applies to nonlinear canonical correlation analysis as well. The variable's level at the time of observation might not be the level you want to specify for the analysis. See Chapter 8 for more information on how to choose the best level of analysis.

An Example

The example in this chapter is from a survey by Verdegaal (1985). The responses of 15 subjects to eight variables were recorded. The variables, variable labels, and value labels (categories) in the data set are shown in Table 9.1.

Table 9.1   The survey data

Variable name	Variable label	Value labels
age	Age in years	20–25, 26–30, 31–35, 36–40, 41–45, 46–50, 51–55, 56–60, 61–65, 66–70
marital	Marital status	Single, Married, Other
pet	Pets owned	No, Cat(s), Dog(s), Other than cat or dog, Various domestic animals
news	Newspaper read most often	None, Telegraaf, Volkskrant, NRC, Other

Table 9.1   The survey data (Continued)

Variable name	Variable label	Value labels
music	Music preferred	Classical, New wave, Popular, Variety, Don't like music
live	Neighborhood preference	Town, Village, Countryside
math	Math test score	0–5, 6–10, 11–15
language	Language test score	0–5, 6–10, 11–15, 16–20

The variables of interest are the first six, and they are divided into three sets. Set 1 includes *age* and *marital*, set 2 includes *pet* and *news*, and set 3 includes *music* and *live*. *pet* is scaled as multiple nominal and *age* is scaled as ordinal; all of the other variables are scaled as single nominal. This analysis requests a random initial configuration. By default, the initial configuration is numerical. However, when some of the variables are treated as single nominal with no possibility of ordering, it is best to choose a random initial configuration. This is the case with most of the variables in this study.

Examining the Data

After a list of the variables with their levels of optimal scaling, categorical canonical correlation analysis with optimal scaling produces a table showing the frequencies of objects in categories. This table is especially important if there are missing data, since almost-empty categories are more likely to dominate the solution. In this example, there are no missing data.

A second preliminary check is to examine the plot of object scores. You want to see if there are any outliers that might tend to dominate the solution. Outliers have such different quantifications from the other objects that they will be at the boundaries of the plot, thus dominating one or more dimensions.

If you find outliers, you can handle them in one of two ways. First, you can simply eliminate them from the data and run the nonlinear canonical correlation analysis again. Second, you can try recoding the extreme responses of the outlying object(s) by collapsing (merging) some categories.

As shown in the plot of object scores in Figure 9.1, there were no outliers for the survey data.

Figure 9.1   Object scores

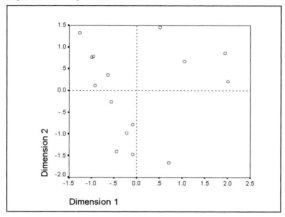

Accounting for Similarity between Sets

The fit and loss values tell you how well the nonlinear canonical correlation analysis solution fits the optimally quantified data with respect to the association between the sets. Figure 9.2 shows the fit value, loss values, and eigenvalues for the survey example.

Figure 9.2   Fit, loss, and eigenvalues

```
Loss per Set
------------                    Dimension
                      Sum        1        2
Set 1                .423     .240     .183
Set 2                .593     .184     .409
Set 3                .376     .172     .204
                    -------  -------  -------
Mean                 .464     .199     .265
Fit                 1.536
Eigenvalue                    .801     .735
```

Loss is partitioned across dimensions and sets. For each dimension and set, loss represents the proportion of variation in the object scores that cannot be accounted for by the weighted combination of variables in the set. The average loss is labeled *Mean*. In this example, the average loss over sets is 0.464. Notice that more loss occurs for the second dimension than for the first.

The eigenvalue for each dimension equals 1 minus the average loss for the dimension, and indicates how much of the relationship is shown by each dimension. The eigenvalues add up to the total fit. For Verdegaal's data, $0.801 / 1.536 = 52\%$ of the actual fit is accounted for by the first dimension.

The maximum fit value equals the number of dimensions, and if obtained, indicates that the relationship is perfect. The average loss value over sets and dimensions tells you the difference between the maximum fit and the actual fit. *Fit* plus *average loss* equals the number of dimensions. Perfect similarity rarely happens and usually capitalizes on trivial aspects in the data.

Another measure of association is the multiple correlation between linear combinations from each set and the object scores. If no variables in a set are multiple nominal, you can compute this by multiplying the weight and component loading of each variable within the set, adding these products, and taking the square root of the sum.

Figure 9.3 gives the weights and component loadings for the variables in this example. The multiple correlation (R) for the first weighted sum of optimally scaled variables (*age* and *marital*) with the first dimension of object scores is

$$R = \sqrt{(0.683 \times 0.835 + 0.294 \times 0.649)}$$
$$= \sqrt{(0.5703 + 0.1908)}$$
$$= 0.872$$

For each dimension, $1 - \text{loss} = R^2$. For example, from Figure 9.2, $1 - 0.240 = 0.760$, which is 0.872 squared. Consequently, small loss values indicate large multiple correlations between weighted sums of optimally scaled variables and dimensions. Weights are not unique for multiple nominal variables. For multiple nominal variables, use $1 - \text{loss}$ per set.

Figure 9.3   Weights and component loadings

```
Weights
-------                          Dimension
                                    1      2
AGE                                .683   .785
MARITAL                            .294  -1.014
----------------------------- ----------------
PET                                 -      -
NEWS                               .846   .359
----------------------------- ----------------
MUSIC                             -.627   .752
LIVE                              -.489  -.777


Component Loadings for Single Variables
------------------
Projections of the Single Quantified Variables in the Object Space
                                 Dimension
                                    1      2
AGE                                .835   .257
MARITAL                            .649  -.607
----------------------------- ----------------
PET                                 -      -
NEWS                               .669   .389
----------------------------- ----------------
MUSIC                             -.783   .503
LIVE                              -.690  -.536


Component Loadings for Multiple Variables
------------------
Projections of the Multiple Quantified Variables in the Object Space
                                 Dimension
                      Dimension     1      2
----------------------------------------------
PET                       1        .395  -.432
                          2       -.276   .680
```

Another popular statistic with two sets of variables is the canonical correlation. Since the canonical correlation is related to the eigenvalue and thus provides no additional information, it is not included in the nonlinear canonical correlation analysis output. For two sets of variables, the canonical correlation per dimension is obtained by the formula:

$$\rho_d = 2 \times E_d - 1$$

where d is the dimension number and E is the eigenvalue. You can generalize the canonical correlation for more than two sets with the formula:

$$\rho_d = ((K \times E_d) - 1)/(K - 1)$$

where d is the dimension number, K is the number of sets, and E is the eigenvalue. For our example,

$$\rho_1 = ((3 \times 0.801) - 1)/2 = 0.701$$

and

$$\rho_2 = ((3 \times 0.735) - 1)/2 = 0.603$$

The loss of each set is partitioned by the nonlinear canonical correlation analysis in several ways. Figure 9.4 presents the multiple fit, single fit, and single loss tables produced by the nonlinear canonical correlation analysis for the survey example. Note that *multiple fit* minus *single fit* equals *single loss*.

Figure 9.4   Partitioning fit and loss

```
Multiple Fit
------------                    Dimension
                    Sum        1        2
AGE               1.167      .498     .670
MARITAL           1.116      .087    1.029
-------------------------------- ----------------
PET                .840      .400     .440
NEWS               .912      .726     .186
-------------------------------- ----------------
MUSIC              .998      .416     .582
LIVE               .843      .239     .605


Single Fit
----------                      Dimension
                    Sum        1        2
AGE               1.082      .466     .616
MARITAL           1.115      .086    1.029
-------------------------------- ----------------
PET                 -          -        -
NEWS               .845      .716     .129
-------------------------------- ----------------
MUSIC              .959      .394     .566
LIVE               .843      .239     .604


Single Loss
-----------                     Dimension
                    Sum        1        2
AGE                .085      .031     .054
MARITAL            .001      .001     .000
-------------------------------- ----------------
PET                 -          -        -
NEWS               .067      .010     .057
-------------------------------- ----------------
MUSIC              .039      .023     .016
LIVE               .000      .000     .000
```

Single loss indicates the loss resulting from restricting variables to one set of quantifications (that is, single nominal, ordinal, or nominal). If *single loss* is large, it is better to treat the variables as multiple nominal. In this example, however, *single fit* and *multiple fit* are almost equal, which means that the multiple coordinates are almost on a straight line in the direction given by the weights.

Multiple fit equals the variance of the multiple category coordinates for each variable. These measures are analogous to the discrimination measures found in homogeneity analysis. You can examine the multiple fit table to see which variables discriminate best. For example, look at the multiple fit table for *marital* and *news*. The fit values, summed across the two dimensions, are 1.116 for *marital* and 0.912 for *news*. This tells us that variable *news* discriminates less than *marital*.

Single fit corresponds to the squared weight for each variable and equals the variance of the single category coordinates. As a result, the weights equal the standard deviations of the single category coordinates. Examining how the single fit is broken down across dimensions, we see that variable *news* discriminates mainly on the first dimension, and that variable *marital* discriminates almost totally on the second. In other words, the categories of news are further apart in the first dimension than in the second, whereas the pattern is reversed for marital. In contrast, *age* discriminates in both the first and second dimensions; thus the spread of the categories is equal along both dimensions.

Component Loadings

Figure 9.5 shows the plot of component loadings for the survey data. When there are no missing data, the component loadings are equivalent to the Pearson correlations between the quantified variables and the object scores.

If you draw lines on the plot either by hand or with a third-party product, the length of the line drawn from the origin to each variable point approximates the importance of that variable. The canonical variables are not plotted but can be represented by horizontal and vertical lines drawn through the origin.

Figure 9.5   Component loadings

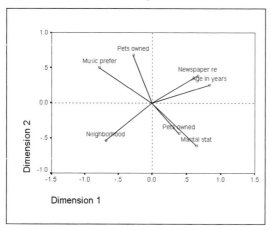

The relationships between variables are apparent. There are two directions which do not coincide with the horizontal and vertical axes. One direction is determined by *age* (labeled *Age in years*), *news* (labeled *Newspaper re*), and *live* (labeled *Neighborhood*). The other direction is defined by the variables *marital* (labeled *Marital stat*), *music* (labeled *Music prefer*), and *pet* (labeled *Pets owned*). The *pet* variable is a multiple nominal variable, so there are two points plotted for it. Each quantification is interpreted as a single variable.

Transformation Plots

The different levels at which each variable can be scaled impose restrictions on the quantifications. Transformation plots illustrate the relationship between the quantifications and the original categories resulting from the selected optimal scaling level. Figure 9.6, Figure 9.7, and Figure 9.8 show the transformation plots for *age*, *news*, and *live*.

Figure 9.6   Transformation plot for variable age (ordinal)

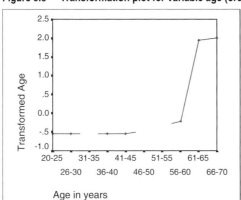

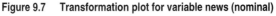

Figure 9.7   Transformation plot for variable news (nominal)

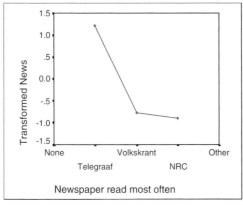

Figure 9.8   Transformation plot for variable live (nominal)

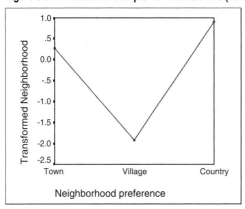

The transformation plot for *live* (Figure 9.8), which was treated as nominal, displays a U-shaped pattern, in which the middle category receives the lowest quantification and the extreme categories receive values similar to each other. This pattern indicates a quadratic relationship between the original variable and the transformed variable. Using an alternative optimal scaling level is not suggested for *live*.

The quantifications for *news*, in contrast, correspond to a decreasing trend across the three categories that have observed cases (Figure 9.7). The first category receives the highest quantification, the second category receives a smaller value, and the third category receives the smallest value. Although the variable is scaled as nominal, the category order is retrieved in the quantifications.

In contrast, the transformation plot for *age* displays an S-shaped curve (Figure 9.6). The four youngest observed categories all receive the same negative quantification, whereas the two oldest categories receive similar positive values. Consequently, collapsing all of the younger ages into one common category (that is, below 50), and collapsing the two oldest categories into one may be attempted. However, the exact equality of the quantifications for the younger groups indicates that restricting the order of the quantifications to the order of the original categories may not be desirable. Because the quantifications for the 26–30, 36–40, and 41–45 groups cannot be lower than the quantification for the 20–25 group, these values are set equal to the boundary value. Allowing these values to be smaller than the quantification for the youngest group (that is, treating age as nominal) may improve the fit. So although *age* may be considered an ordinal variable, treating it as such does not appear appropriate in this case. Moreover, treating *age* as numerical, and thus maintaining the distances between the categories, would substantially reduce the fit.

Single versus Multiple Category Coordinates

For every variable treated as single nominal, ordinal, or numerical, quantifications, single category coordinates, and multiple category coordinates are determined. These statistics for *age* are presented in Figure 9.9.

Figure 9.9   Coordinates for variable Age

```
Variable:  AGE       Age in years                              Set: 1
---------
Type:      ORDINAL              Missing: 0
Category                        Marginal Frequency          Quantification
--------                        ------------------          --------------
     1     20-25                        3                         -.55
     2     26-30                        5                         -.55
     3     31-35                        0                          .00
     4     36-40                        1                         -.55
     5     41-45                        1                         -.55
     6     46-50                        0                          .00
     7     51-55                        0                          .00
     8     56-60                        2                         -.22
     9     61-65                        1                         1.95
    10     66-70                        2                         2.01

Single Category Coordinates
---------------------------
Category      Dimension
                 1        2
     1         -.38     -.43
     2         -.38     -.43
     4         -.38     -.43
     5         -.38     -.43
     8         -.15     -.17
     9         1.33     1.53
    10         1.37     1.57

Multiple Category Coordinates
----------------------------
Category      Dimension
                 1        2
     1         -.19     -.14
     2         -.41     -.62
     4         -.32     -.73
     5         -.36     -.54
     8         -.44      .08
     9         1.72     1.20
    10         1.22     1.70
```

Every category for which no cases were recorded receives a quantification of 0. For *age*, this includes the 31–35, 46–50, and 51–55 categories. These categories are not restricted to be ordered with the other categories and do not affect any computations.

For multiple nominal variables, each category receives a different quantification on each dimension. For all other transformation types, a category has only one quantification, regardless of the dimensionality of the solution. The single category coordinates represent the locations of the categories on a line in the object space, and equal the quantifications multiplied by the weights. For example, in Figure 9.9, the single category coordinates of (–0.15, –0.17) for category 8 are the quantification multiplied by the weights (see Figure 9.3).

The multiple category coordinates for variables treated as single nominal, ordinal, or numerical represent the coordinates of the categories in the object space before ordinal or linear constraints are applied. These values are unconstrained minimizers of the loss. For multiple nominal variables, these coordinates represent the quantifications of the categories.

The effects of imposing constraints on the relationship between the categories and their quantifications are revealed by comparing the single with the multiple category coordinates. On the first dimension, the multiple category coordinates for *age* decrease to category 2 and remain relatively at the same level until category 9, at which point a dramatic increase occurs. A similar pattern is evidenced for the second dimension. These relationships are removed in the single category coordinates, in which the ordinal constraint is applied. On both dimensions, the coordinates are now nondecreasing. The differing structure of the two sets of coordinates suggests that a nominal treatment may be more appropriate.

Centroids and Projected Centroids

Figure 9.10 shows the plot of centroids labeled by variables. This plot should be interpreted in the same way as the category quantifications plot in homogeneity analysis, or the multiple category coordinates in nonlinear principal components analysis. By itself, such a plot shows how well variables separate groups of objects (the centroids are in the center of gravity of the objects).

Notice that the categories for *age* are not separated very clearly. The younger age categories are grouped together at the left of the plot. As suggested previously, ordinal may be too strict a scaling level to impose on *age*.

Figure 9.10 Centroids labeled by variables

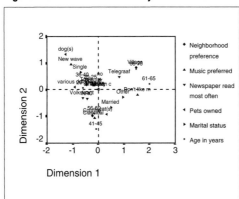

When you request centroid plots, individual centroid and projected centroid plots for each variable labeled by value labels are also produced. The projected centroids are on a line in the object space. These plots should be interpreted in the same way as single category coordinates in nonlinear principal components analysis. Figure 9.11, Figure 9.12, and Figure 9.13 are the plots of centroids and projected centroids for *age*, *news*, and *live*, the variables of the first direction in the loadings plot.

Figure 9.11   Centroids and projected centroids for variable age

Figure 9.12   Centroids and projected centroids for variable news

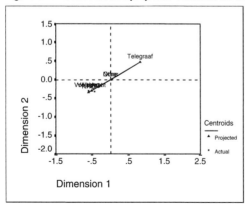

Figure 9.13   Centroids and projected centroids for variable live

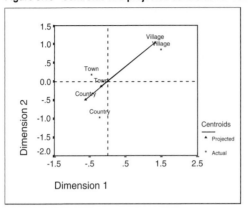

The actual centroids are projected onto the vectors defined by the component loadings. These vectors have been added to the centroid plots to aid in distinguishing the projected from the actual centroids. The projected centroids fall in one of four quadrants formed by extending two perpendicular reference lines through the origin. The interpretation of the direction of single nominal, ordinal, or numerical variables is obtained from the position of the projected centroids. For example, the variable *news* is specified as single nominal. The projected centroids show that *Volkskrant* and *NRC* are contrasted with *Telegraaf.*

The problem with *age* is evident from the projected centroids. Treating *age* as ordinal implies that the order of the age groups must be preserved. To satisfy this restriction, all age groups below age 45 are projected into the same point. Along the direction defined by *age*, *news*, and *live*, there is no separation of the younger age groups. Such a finding suggests treating the variable as nominal.

To understand the relationships among variables, find out what the specific categories (values) are for clusters of categories in the centroid plots. The relationships among *age*, *news*, and *live* can be described by looking at the upper right and lower left of the plots. In the upper right, the *age* groups are the older respondents (61–65 and 66–70) (Figure 9.11); they read the newspaper *Telegraaf* (Figure 9.12), and prefer living in a *Village* (Figure 9.13). Looking at the lower left corner of each plot, we see that the younger to middle-aged respondents read the *Volkskrant* or *NRC,* and want to live in the *Country* or in a *Town.* However, separating the younger groups is very difficult.

The same types of interpretations can be made about the other direction (*music*, *marital*, and *pet*) by focusing on the upper left and the lower right of the centroid plots. In the upper left corner, we find that single people tend to have dogs and like new wave music. The *married* and *other* categories for *marital* have cats; the former group prefers classical music and the latter group does not like music.

An Alternative Analysis

The results of the analysis suggest that treating *age* as ordinal does not appear appropriate. Although *age* is measured at an ordinal level, its relationships with other variables are not monotonic. To investigate the effects of changing the optimal scaling level to single nominal, you may rerun the analysis.

The eigenvalues for a two-dimensional solution are 0.806 and 0.757 respectively, for a total fit of 1.564. The multiple fit and single fit tables are presented in Figure 9.14. *Age* is still a highly discriminating variable, as evidenced by the sum of the multiple fit values. In contrast to the earlier results, however, examination of the single fit values reveals the discrimination to be almost entirely along the second dimension.

Figure 9.14   Partitioning fit and loss

```
Multiple Fit
------------                        Dimension
                        Sum         1         2
AGE                     1.440       .247      1.193
MARITAL                 1.401       .273      1.128
-------------------------------     ----------------
PET                      .921       .529       .392
NEWS                     .826       .642       .184
-------------------------------     ----------------
LIVE                     .898       .075       .823
MUSIC                   1.044       .602       .442


Single Fit
----------                          Dimension
                        Sum         1         2
AGE                     1.381       .196      1.185
MARITAL                 1.399       .271      1.128
-------------------------------     ----------------
PET                       -          -          -
NEWS                     .782       .633       .148
-------------------------------     ----------------
LIVE                     .898       .075       .823
MUSIC                   1.043       .601       .442

Single Loss
-----------                         Dimension
                        Sum         1         2
AGE                      .059       .051       .008
MARITAL                  .002       .001       .000
-------------------------------     ----------------
PET                       -          -          -
NEWS                     .044       .008       .036
-------------------------------     ----------------
LIVE                     .000       .000       .000
MUSIC                    .001       .000       .001
```

Figure 9.15 displays the transformation plot for *age*. The quantifications for a nominal variable are unrestricted, so the nondecreasing trend displayed when *age* was treated ordinally is no longer present (see Figure 9.6). We find a decreasing trend until the age of 40 and an increasing trend thereafter, corresponding to a U-shaped (quadratic) relationship. The two older categories still receive similar scores, and subsequent analyses may involve combining these categories.

Figure 9.15   Transformation plot for variable age (nominal)

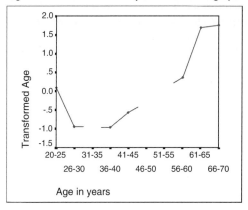

The transformation plot for *live* is given in Figure 9.16. Treating *age* as nominal does not affect the quantifications for *live* to any significant degree. The middle category receives the smallest quantification, with the extremes receiving large positive values.

Figure 9.16   Transformation plot for variable live (age nominal)

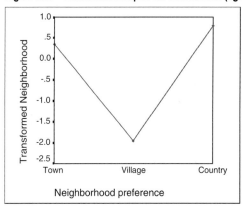

A change is found in the transformation plot for *news* in Figure 9.17. Previously (Figure 9.7), a decreasing trend was present in the quantifications, possibly suggesting an ordinal treatment for this variable. However, treating *age* as nominal removes this trend from the *news* quantifications.

Figure 9.17   Transformation plot for variable news (age nominal)

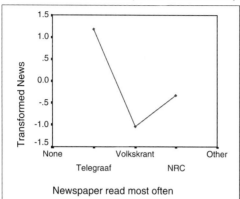

Figure 9.18 displays the centroid plot for *age*. Notice that the categories do not fall in chronological order along the line joining the projected centroids. The 20–25 group is situated in the middle rather than at the end. The spread of the categories is much improved over the ordinal counterpart presented previously.

Figure 9.18   Centroids and projected centroids for variable age (nominal)

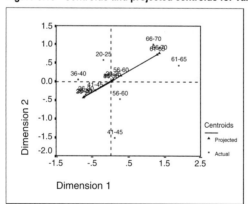

Interpretation of the younger age groups is now possible from the centroid plot given in Figure 9.19. The *Volkskrant* and the *NRC* categories are also further apart than in the previous analysis, allowing for separate interpretations of each. The groups between the ages of 26 and 45 read the *Volkskrant* and prefer *Country* living. The 20–25 and 56–60 age groups read the *NRC*; the former group prefers to live in a *Town*, and the latter group prefers *Country* living. The oldest groups read the *Telegraaf* and prefer *Village* living.

Interpretation of the other direction (*music*, *marital*, and *pet*) is basically unchanged from the previous analysis. The only obvious difference is that people with a marital status of *other* have either cats or no pets.

Figure 9.19 Centroids labeled by variables (age nominal)

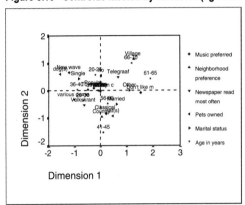

General Suggestions

Once you have examined the initial results, you will probably want to refine your analysis by changing some of the specifications on the nonlinear canonical correlation analysis. Here are some tips for structuring your analysis:

- Create as many sets as possible. Put an important variable that you want to predict in a separate set by itself.
- Put variables that you consider predictors together in a single set. If there are many predictors, try to partition them into several sets.
- Put each multiple nominal variable in a separate set by itself.
- If variables are highly correlated to each other and you don't want this relationship to dominate the solution, put those variables together in the same set.

10 Correspondence Analysis Examples

Correspondence analysis analyzes correspondence tables. A **correspondence table** is any two-way table whose cells contain some measurement of correspondence between the rows and the columns. The measure of correspondence can be any indication of the similarity, affinity, confusion, association, or interaction between the row and column variables. A very common type of correspondence table is a crosstabulation, where the cells contain frequency counts.

Such tables can be obtained easily with the Crosstabs procedure. However, a crosstabulation does not always provide a clear picture of the nature of the relationship between the two variables. This is particularly true if the variables of interest are nominal (with no inherent order or rank) and contain numerous categories. Crosstabulation may tell you that the observed cell frequencies differ significantly from the expected values in a 10×9 crosstabulation of *occupation* and *breakfast cereal*, but it may be difficult to discern which occupational groups have similar tastes or what those tastes are.

Correspondence analysis allows you to examine the relationship between two nominal variables graphically in a multidimensional space. It computes row and column scores and produces plots based on the scores. Categories that are similar to each other appear close to each other in the plots. In this way, it is easy to see which categories of a variable are similar to each other or which categories of the two variables are related. The Correspondence Analysis procedure also allows you to fit supplementary points into the space defined by the active points.

If the ordering of the categories according to their scores is undesirable or counter-intuitive, order restrictions can be imposed by constraining the scores for some categories to be equal. For example, suppose you expect the variable *smoking behavior* with categories *none*, *light*, *medium* and *heavy* to have scores which correspond to this ordering. However, if the analysis orders the categories *none*, *light*, *heavy* and *medium*, constraining the scores for *heavy* and *medium* to be equal preserves the ordering of the categories in their scores.

The interpretation of correspondence analysis in terms of distances depends on the normalization method used. The Correspondence Analysis procedure can be used to analyze either the differences between categories of a variable or differences between variables. With the default normalization, it analyzes the differences between the row and column variables.

The correspondence analysis algorithm is capable of many kinds of analyses. Centering the rows and columns and using chi-square distances corresponds to standard correspondence analysis. However, using alternative centering options combined with Euclidean distances allows for an alternative representation of a matrix in a low-dimensional space.

Three examples will be presented. The first employs a relatively small correspondence table and illustrates the concepts inherent in correspondence analysis. The second example demonstrates a practical marketing application. The final example uses a table of distances in a multidimensional scaling approach.

Example 1

The aim of correspondence analysis is to show the relationships between the rows and columns of a correspondence table. We will use a hypothetical table introduced by Greenacre (1984) to illustrate the basic concepts. Table 10.1 shows the distribution of smoking behavior for five levels of job category. The rows of the correspondence table represent the job categories. The columns of the correspondence table represent the smoking behavior.

Table 10.1 Correspondence table

	None	Light	Medium	Heavy	No Alcohol	Alcohol	Active Margin
Senior Managers	4	2	3	2	0	11	11
Junior Managers	4	3	7	4	1	17	18
Senior Employees	25	10	12	4	5	46	51
Junior Employees	18	24	33	13	10	78	88
Secretaries	10	6	7	2	7	18	25
National Average	42	29	20	9			
Active Margin	61	45	62	25			193

In addition, the table contains one supplementary row and two supplementary columns. The supplementary row identifies the percentage of people in each of the smoking categories nationwide. The two supplementary columns contain the number of people in each staff category who do not drink alcohol and the number of people who do. Supplementary rows and columns do not influence the analysis and are not part of the marginal sums.

The marginal row totals show that the company has far more employees, both junior and senior, than managers and secretaries. However, the distribution of senior and junior positions for the managers is approximately the same as the distribution of senior and junior positions for the employees. Looking at the column totals, we see that there are similar numbers of nonsmokers and medium smokers. Furthermore, heavy smokers are outnumbered by each of the other three categories. But what, if anything, do any of these job categories have in common regarding smoking behavior? And what is the relationship between job category and smoking?

Using correspondence analysis, we can take these data and generate a variety of plots that graphically illustrate the underlying relationships between categories and between variables. Figure 10.1 shows the scatterplot matrix of row scores for a three-dimensional solution.

Figure 10.1   Scatterplot matrix of row scores (row principal normalization)

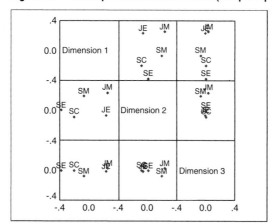

Scatterplot matrices can easily be converted to two or three dimensional scatterplots using the chart gallery available through the Chart Editor. Figure 10.2 displays the two-dimensional plot of the row scores for the first two dimensions. The remainder of this chapter uses two-dimensional plots derived from scatterplot matrices.

Figure 10.2   Two-dimensional plot of row column (row principal normalization)

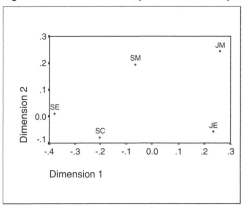

An important choice in correspondence analysis is the normalization method. Although solutions under different choices of normalization are completely equivalent in terms of fit (the singular values), the plots, among other things, can be quite different. Figure 10.3 shows the correspondence analysis plot of row and column scores for the first two dimensions. We use row principal normalization to focus on the differences or similarities between job categories. Row principal normalization results in the Euclidean distance between a row point and the origin, approximating the chi-square distance between the row category and the average row category. Moreover, the Euclidean distance between any two points in the plot approximate the chi-square distance between the corresponding rows of the correspondence table. The chi-square distance is a weighted Euclidean distance, where the weights equal the masses.

Figure 10.3   Plot of row and column scores (row principal normalization)

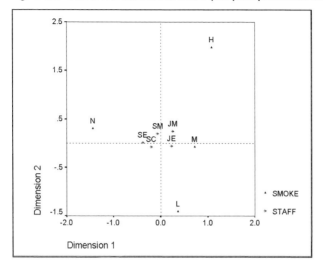

The interpretation of the plot is fairly simple—row points that are close together are more alike than row points that are far apart. In Figure 10.3, we see that *secretaries* and *senior employees* are plotted near each other. This indicates that *secretaries* and *senior employees* are similar in their smoking behavior. *Junior managers* are relatively far from *senior employees* and are therefore very unlike them.

Although the distances between column points are artificially exaggerated by the row principal normalization, you can still get a general idea about the relationship between the row and column variables from this joint plot. If you draw a line from the origin to each column point (*smoke*) and then make an orthogonal projection (perpendicular line) from the row points (*staff categories*) to these lines, the distance from the intersection of the two lines to the column point gives you an indication of how categories of the two variables are related to each other. For example, in Figure 10.4, vectors for *none* and *heavy* smoking help describe the relationship between each of these categories and staff. You can see that senior employees (*SE*) are closest to none (*N*), followed by secretaries (*SC*) and senior managers (*SM*). Junior employees (*JE*) are farthest from none. In contrast, junior managers (*JM*) are closest to heavy (H), followed by senior managers and junior employees. Similar interpretations are possible for the other two smoking categories. This order is identical for all normalization methods but principal normalization.

Figure 10.4 Orthogonal projections (row principal normalization)

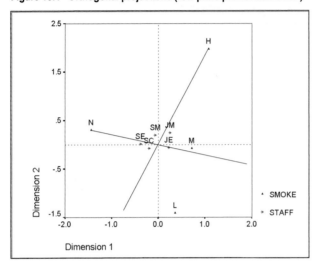

Profiles and Distances

To determine the distance between categories, correspondence analysis considers the marginal distributions as well as the individual cell frequencies. It computes **row** and **column profiles**, which give the row and column proportions for each cell, based on the marginal totals. Figure 10.5 shows the row profiles for this example.

Figure 10.5 Row profiles

		Smoking Behavior						
		None	Light	Medium	Heavy	No Alcohol[1]	Alcohol[1]	Active Margin
Staff Group	Senior Managers	.364	.182	.273	.182	.000	1.000	1.000
	Junior Managers	.222	.167	.389	.222	.056	.944	1.000
	Senior Employees	.490	.196	.235	.078	.098	.902	1.000
	Junior Employees	.205	.273	.375	.148	.114	.886	1.000
	Secretaries	.400	.240	.280	.080	.280	.720	1.000
	National Average[2]	.420	.290	.200	.090	.000	.000	1.000
	Mass	.316	.233	.321	.130	.119	.881	

1. Supplementary column
2. Supplementary row

The row profiles indicate the proportion of the row category in each column category. For example, among the senior employees, most are nonsmokers and very few are heavy smokers. In contrast, among the junior managers, most are medium smokers and very few are light smokers.

Figure 10.6 contains the column profiles. These values indicate the proportion of the column in each row category. For example, most of the light smokers are junior employees. Similarly, most of the medium and heavy smokers are junior employees. Recall that the sample contains predominantly junior employees. It is not surprising that this staff category dominates the smoking categories.

Figure 10.6   Column profiles

		Smoking Behavior						
		None	Light	Medium	Heavy	No Alcohol[1]	Alcohol[1]	Mass
Staff Group	Senior Managers	.066	.044	.048	.080	.000	.065	.057
	Junior Managers	.066	.067	.113	.160	.043	.100	.093
	Senior Employees	.410	.222	.194	.160	.217	.271	.264
	Junior Employees	.295	.533	.532	.520	.435	.459	.456
	Secretaries	.164	.133	.113	.080	.304	.106	.130
	National Average[2]	.689	.644	.323	.360	.000	.000	.518
	Active Margin	1.000	1.000	1.000	1.000	1.000	1.000	

[1.] Supplementary column

[2.] Supplementary row

If we think of difference in terms of distance, then the greater the difference between row profiles, the greater the distance between points in a plot. The goal of correspondence analysis with row principal normalization is to find a configuration in which Euclidean distances between row points in the full dimensional space equal the chi-square distances between rows of the correspondence table. In a reduced space, the Euclidean distances approximate the chi-square distances.

Chi-square distances are weighted profile distances. These weighted distances are based on the concept of mass. **Mass** is a measure that indicates the influence of an object based on its marginal frequency. Mass affects the **centroid**, which is the weighted mean row or column profile. The **row centroid** is the mean row profile. Points with a large mass, like *junior employees*, pull the centroid strongly to their location. A point with a small mass, like *senior managers*, pulls the row centroid only slightly to its location.

Inertia

If the entries in the correspondence table are frequencies and row principal normalization is used, then the weighted sum over all squared distances between the row profiles and the mean row profile equals the chi-square statistic. Euclidean distances between row points in the plot approximate chi-square distances between rows of the table.

The **total inertia** is defined as the weighted sum of all squared distances to the origin divided by the total over all cells, where the weights are the masses. Rows with a small mass influence the inertia only when they are far from the centroid. Rows with a large mass influence the total inertia, even when they are located close to the centroid. The same applies to columns.

Row and Column Scores

The row and column scores are the coordinates of the row and column points in Figure 10.3. Figure 10.7 and Figure 10.8 show the row and column scores, respectively.

Figure 10.7   Row scores

		Mass	Score in Dimension			Inertia
			1	2	3	
Staff Group	Senior Managers	.057	-.066	.194	-.071	.003
	Junior Managers	.093	.259	.243	.034	.012
	Senior Employees	.264	-.381	.011	.005	.038
	Junior Employees	.456	.233	-.058	-.003	.026
	Secretaries	.130	-.201	-.079	.008	.006
	National Average[1]	.518	-.258	-.118	-.159	.055
	Active Total	1.000				.085

[1.] Supplementary point

Figure 10.8   Column scores

		Mass	Score in Dimension			Inertia
			1	2	3	
Smoking Behavior	None	.316	-1.438	.305	.044	.049
	Light	.233	.364	-1.409	-1.082	.007
	Medium	.321	.718	-.074	1.262	.013
	Heavy	.130	1.074	1.976	-1.289	.016
	No Alcohol[1]	.119	-.420	-3.616	8.725	.039
	Alcohol[1]	.881	.057	.489	-1.180	.005
	Active Total	1.000				.085

[1.] Supplementary point

For row principal normalization, geometrically, the column scores are proportional to the weighted centroid of the active row points. The row points are in the weighted centroid of the active column points, where the weights correspond to the entries in the row profiles table. For example, the score of –0.066 for *senior managers* on the first dimension equals (see Figure 10.5 for the row profile):

$$(-1.438 \times 0.364) + (0.364 \times 0.182) + (0.718 \times 0.273) + (1.074 \times 0.182)$$

When the row points are the weighted average of the column points and the maximum dimensionality is used, the Euclidean distance between a row point and the origin equals the chi-square distance between the row and the average row. For example, the chi-square distance between the row profile for *secretaries* and the row centroid is:

$$\sqrt{\frac{(0.400 - 0.316)^2}{0.316} + \frac{(0.240 - 0.233)^2}{0.233} + \frac{(0.280 - 0.321)^2}{0.321} + \frac{(0.080 - 0.130)^2}{0.130}} = 0.217$$

The Euclidean distance from the *secretaries* point to the origin is:

$$\sqrt{(-0.201)^2 + (-0.079)^2 + 0.008^2} = 0.216$$

Inertia of a row equals the weighted chi-squared distance to the average row. With row principal normalization, inertia of a row point equals the weighted squared Euclidean distance to the origin in the full dimensional space, where the weight is the mass. Figure 10.7 and Figure 10.8 display the inertias for all points. These inertias sum to the total inertia across rows and columns. Because the chi-square statistic is equivalent to the total inertia times the sum of all cells of the correspondence table, we can think of the orientation of the row points as a pictorial representation of the chi-square statistic. For other normalization methods, interpretations differ and are discussed later.

Supplementary Profiles

In correspondence analysis, additional categories can be represented in the space describing the relationships between the active categories. A supplementary profile defines a profile across categories of either the row or column variable and does not influence the analysis in any way. Table 10.1 contains one supplementary row and two supplementary columns.

The national average of people in each smoking category defines a supplementary row profile. The two supplementary columns define two column profiles across the categories of staff. The supplementary profiles define a point in either the row space or the column space. Because we will focus on both the rows and the columns separately, we will use principal normalization.

Figure 10.9 shows the first two dimensions for the row points with the supplementary point for *national average*. *National average* lies far from the origin, indicating that the sample is not representative of the nation in terms of smoking behavior. *Secretaries* and *senior employees* are close to the national average, whereas *junior managers* are not. Thus, secretaries and senior employees have smoking behaviors similar to the national average, but junior managers do not.

Figure 10.9   Row points (principal normalization)

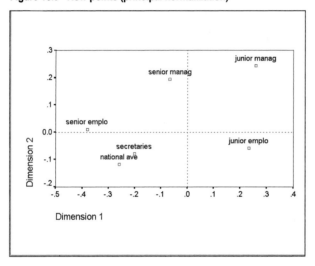

Figure 10.10 displays the column space with the two supplementary points for alcohol consumption. Alcohol lies near the origin, indicating a close correspondence between the alcohol profile and the average column profile (see Figure 10.6). However, no alcohol differs from the average column profile, illustrated by the large distance from the origin. The closest point to no alcohol is light smokers. The light profile is most similar to the nondrinkers. Among the smokers, medium is next closest and heavy is farthest. Thus, there is a progression in similarity to non-drinking from light to heavy smoking.

However, the relatively high proportion of secretaries in the no alcohol group prevents any close correspondence to any of the smoking categories.

Figure 10.10   Column points (principal normalization)

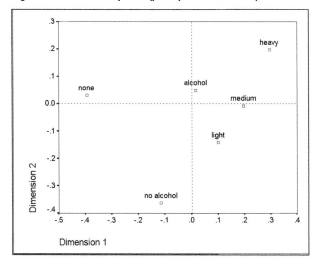

Dimensionality

Ideally, you want a correspondence analysis solution that represents the relationship between the row and column variables in as few dimensions as possible. But it is frequently useful to look at the maximum number of dimensions to see the relative contribution of each dimension. The maximum number of dimensions for a correspondence analysis solution equals the number of active rows minus 1 or the number of active columns minus 1, whichever is less. An active row or column is one for which a distinct set of scores is found. Supplementary rows or columns are not active. If two row or column categories are constrained to be equal, one set of scores is determined for both. Consequently, each equality constraint is equivalent to one active row or column. In the present example, the maximum number of dimensions is $min(5, 4) - 1$, or 3.

The first dimension displays as much of the inertia as possible, the second is orthogonal to the first and displays as much of the remaining inertia as possible, and so on. It is possible to split the total inertia into components attributable to each dimension. You can then evaluate the inertia shown by a particular dimension by comparing it to the total inertia. For example, Figure 10.11 shows that the first dimension displays 87.8%

(0.075/0.085) of the total inertia, whereas the second dimension displays only 11.8% (0.010/0.085).

Figure 10.11   Inertia per dimension

		Singular Value	Inertia	Chi Square
Dimension	1	.273	.075	
	2	.100	.010	
	3	.020	.000	
	Total		.085	16.442

If you decide that the first p dimensions of a q dimensional solution, where $q>p$, show enough of the total inertia, then you do not have to look at higher dimensions. In this example, you might decide to omit the last dimension, knowing that it represents only 0.5% of the total inertia.

The singular values shown in Figure 10.11 can be interpreted as the correlation between the row and column scores. They are analogous to the Pearson correlation coefficient (r) in correlation analysis. For each dimension, the singular value squared (eigenvalue) equals the inertia and thus is another measure of the importance of that dimension.

Contributions

As discussed in the section on "Dimensionality" above, it is possible to compute the inertia displayed by a particular dimension. The scores on each dimension correspond to an orthogonal projection of the point onto that dimension. Thus, the inertia for a dimension equals the weighted sum of the squared distances from the scores on the dimension to the origin. However, whether this applies to row or column scores (or both) depends on the normalization method used. Each row and column point contributes to the inertia. Row and column points that contribute substantially to the inertia of a dimension are important to that dimension. The contribution of a point to the inertia of a dimension is the weighted squared distance from the projected point to the origin divided by the inertia for the dimension. Figure 10.12 and Figure 10.13 show these contributions for the row and column points respectively for a two-dimensional representation.

Figure 10.12   Contributions of row points

		Contribution	
		Of Point to Inertia of Dimension	
		1	2
Staff Group	Senior Managers	.003	.214
	Junior Managers	.084	.551
	Senior Employees	.512	.003
	Junior Employees	.331	.152
	Secretaries	.070	.081
	National Average[1]	.000	.000
	Active Total	1.000	1.000

[1.] Supplementary point

Figure 10.13   Contributions of column points

		Contribution	
		Of Point to Inertia of Dimension	
		1	2
Smoking Behavior	None	.654	.029
	Light	.031	.463
	Medium	.166	.002
	Heavy	.150	.506
	No Alcohol[1]	.000	.000
	Alcohol[1]	.000	.000
	Active Total	1.000	1.000

[1.] Supplementary point

The diagnostics that measure the contributions of points are an important aid in the interpretation of a correspondence analysis solution. Dominant points in the solution can easily be detected. For example, *senior employees* and *junior employees* are dominant points in the first dimension, contributing 84% of the inertia. Among the column points, *none* contributes 65% of the inertia for the first dimension alone.

The contribution of a point to the inertia of the dimensions depends on both the mass and the distance from the origin. Points that are far from the origin and have a large mass contribute most to the inertia of the dimension. Because supplementary points do not play any part in defining the solution, they do not contribute to the inertia of the dimensions.

In addition to examining the contribution of the points to the inertia per dimension, you can examine the contribution of the dimensions to the inertia per point. We can examine how the inertia of a point is spread over the dimensions by computing the percentage of the point inertia contributed by each dimension. Figure 10.14 and Figure 10.15 display these contributions.

Figure 10.14   Contributions of dimensions to the row point inertias

		Contribution		
		Of Dimension to Inertia of Point		
		1	2	Total
Staff Group	Senior Managers	.092	.800	.893
	Junior Managers	.526	.465	.991
	Senior Employees	.999	.001	1.000
	Junior Employees	.942	.058	1.000
	Secretaries	.865	.133	.999
	National Average[1]	.631	.131	.761

[1]. Supplementary point

Figure 10.15   Contributions of dimensions to the column point inertias

		Contribution		
		Of Dimension to Inertia of Point		
		1	2	Total
Smoking Behavior	None	.994	.006	1.000
	Light	.327	.657	.984
	Medium	.982	.001	.983
	Heavy	.684	.310	.995
	No Alcohol[1]	.040	.398	.439
	Alcohol[1]	.040	.398	.439

[1]. Supplementary point

Notice that the contributions of the dimensions to the point inertias do not all sum to one. In a reduced space, the inertia that is contributed by the higher dimensions is not represented. Using the maximum dimensionality would reveal the unaccounted inertia amounts.

In Figure 10.14, the first two dimensions contribute all of the inertia for *senior employees* and *junior employees*, and virtually all of the inertia for *junior managers* and *secretaries*. For senior managers, 11% of the inertia is not contributed by the first two dimensions. Two dimensions contribute a very large proportion of the inertias of the row points.

Similar results occur for the column points in Figure 10.15. For every active column point, two dimensions contribute at least 98% of the inertia. The third dimension contributes very little to these points. The low totals for the supplementary column points indicate that these points are not very well represented in the space defined by the active points. Including these points in the analysis as active might result in quite a different solution.

Normalization

Normalization is used to distribute the inertia over the row scores and column scores. Some aspects of the correspondence analysis solution, such as the singular values, the inertia per dimension, and the contributions, do not change under the various normalizations. The row and column scores and their variances are affected.

Correspondence analysis has several ways to spread the inertia. The three most common include spreading the inertia over the row scores only, spreading the inertia over the column scores only, or spreading the inertia symmetrically over both the row scores and the column scores. The normalization used in this example is called **row principal normalization**. In row principal normalization, the Euclidean distances between the row points approximate chi-square distances between the rows of the correspondence table. The row scores are the weighted average of the column scores. The column scores are standardized to have a weighted sum of squared distances to the centroid of 1. Since this method maximizes the distances between row categories, you should use row principal normalization if you are primarily interested in seeing how categories of the row variable differ from each other.

On the other hand, you might want to approximate the chi-square distances between the columns of the correspondence table. In that case, the column scores should be the weighted average of the row scores. The row scores are standardized to have a weighted sum of squared distances to the centroid of 1. This is called **column principal normalization**. This method maximizes the distances between column categories and should be used if you are primarily concerned with how categories of the column variable differ from each other.

You can also treat the rows and columns symmetrically. This normalization spreads inertia symmetrically over the rows and over the columns. The inertia is divided equally over the row scores and the column scores. Note that neither the distances between the row points nor the distances between the column points are approximations of chi-square distances in this case. This is called **symmetrical normalization**. Use this method if you are primarily interested in the differences or similarities between the two variables. Usually, this is the preferred method to make biplots.

A fourth option is called **principal normalization**, in which the inertia is spread twice in the solution, once over the row scores and once over the column scores. You should use this method if you are interested in the distances between the row points and the distances between the column points separately, but not in how the row and column points are related to each other. Biplots, such as the one in Figure 10.3, are not appropriate for this normalization option and are therefore not available if you have specified the principal normalization method.

The normalization options allow you to rescale the desired graphical representation in a flexible way. For example, Figure 10.16 shows the biplot of row and column points using symmetrical normalization. In this plot, *junior managers* are closest to *heavy* and *senior employees* are closest to *none*. However, this plot does not indicate the relationship between categories of the row variable or of the column variable.

Figure 10.16   Biplot with symmetrical normalization

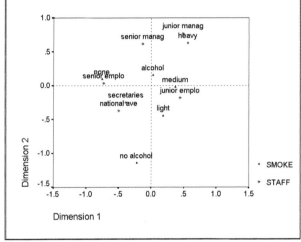

Row principal normalization results in the biplot in Figure 10.3. Notice that the column points have moved toward the edges and the row points have clustered about the origin. Row points are in the weighted centroid of the corresponding column points.

Figure 10.17 displays the biplot for column principal normalization. The column points have moved toward the origin and the row points have moved away from it. Here, column points are in the weighted centroid of the corresponding row points.

Figure 10.17   Biplot with column principal normalization

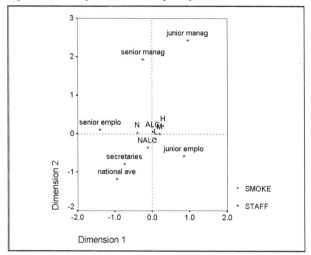

The most flexible way to spread the inertia involves dividing the inertia unevenly over the row and column scores. This option results in an expansion of one set of points and a contraction of the other set of points. The points in the resulting biplot are oriented somewhere between the corresponding points for row and column principal normalization. This option is particularly useful for constructing a tailor-made biplot.

Permutations of the Correspondence Table

Sometimes it is useful to order the categories of the rows and the columns. For example, you might have reason to believe that the categories of a variable correspond to a certain order, but you don't know the precise order. This ordination problem is found in various disciplines—the seriation problem in archaeology, the ordination problem in phytosociology, and Guttman's scalogram problem in the social sciences. Ordering can be achieved by taking the row and column scores as ordering variables. If you have row and column scores in p dimensions, p permuted tables can be made. When the first singular value is large, the first table will show a particular structure, with larger-than-expected relative frequencies close to the "diagonal."

Figure 10.18 shows the permutation of the correspondence table along the first dimension for the example. Looking at the row scores for dimension 1 in Figure 10.7, you can see that the ranking from lowest to highest is *senior employees* (–0.381), *national average* (–0.258), *secretaries* (–0.201), *senior managers* (–0.066), *junior employees* (0.233), and *junior managers* (0.259). Looking at the column scores for dimension 1 in Figure 10.8, you see that the ranking is *none, no alcohol, alcohol, light, medium,* and then *heavy*. These rankings are reflected in the ordering of the rows and columns of the table.

Figure 10.18   Permutation of the correspondence table

		Smoking Behavior						
		None	No Alcohol[1]	Alcohol[1]	Light	Medium	Heavy	Active Margin
Staff Group	Senior Employees	25	5	46	10	12	4	51
	National Average[2]	42			29	20	9	
	Secretaries	10	7	18	6	7	2	25
	Senior Managers	4	0	11	2	3	2	11
	Junior Employees	18	10	78	24	33	13	88
	Junior Managers	4	1	17	3	7	4	18
	Active Margin	61			45	62	25	193

1. Supplementary column
2. Supplementary row

Confidence Statistics

Assuming that the table to be analyzed is a frequency table and that the data are a random sample from an unknown population, the cell frequencies follow a multinomial distribution. From this, it is possible to compute the standard deviations and correlations of the singular values, row scores, and column scores.

In a one-dimensional correspondence analysis solution, you can compute a confidence interval for each score in the population. If the standard deviation is large, correspondence analysis is very uncertain of the location of the point in the population. On the other hand, if the standard deviation is small, then the correspondence analysis is fairly certain that this point is located very close to the point given by the solution.

In a multidimensional solution, if the correlation between dimensions is large, it may not be possible to locate a point in the correct dimension with much certainty. In such cases, multivariate confidence intervals must be calculated using the variance/covariance matrix that can be written to a file.

The standard deviations for the singular values are 0.07 for the first dimension and 0.076 for the second dimension. These small values indicate that the correspondence analysis would produce the same solution for a slightly different sample from the same population. The fact that the first two singular values are very different is reflected in the small correlation of 0.02 between the two dimensions.

Figure 10.19 and Figure 10.20 show the confidence statistics for the row and column scores. The standard deviations for the rows are quite small, so we can conclude that the correspondence analysis has obtained an overall stable solution. The standard deviations for the column scores are much larger due to the row principal normalization. If we look at the correlations between the dimensions for the scores, we see that the correlations are small for the row scores and the column scores with one exception. The column scores for *none* have a correlation of 0.617. However, the correlations for the column scores can be inflated by using column principal normalization.

Figure 10.19   Confidence statistics for row scores

		Standard Deviation in Dimension		Correlation
		1	2	1-2
Staff Group	Senior Managers	.321	.316	.101
	Junior Managers	.248	.225	.067
	Senior Employees	.102	.050	.046
	Junior Employees	.081	.056	.350
	Secretaries	.094	.070	-.184

Figure 10.20   Confidence statistics for column scores

		Standard Deviation in Dimension		Correlation
		1	2	1-2
Smoking Behavior	None	.138	.442	.617
	Light	.534	.861	.054
	Medium	.328	1.044	.016
	Heavy	.682	1.061	-.250

Example 2

The previous example involved a small table of hypothetical data. Actual applications often involve much larger tables. In this example, we will use data introduced by Kennedy, Riquier, and Sharp (1996) pertaining to perceived images of six iced coffee brands.

For each of twenty-three iced coffee image attributes, people selected all brands that were described by the attribute. Table 10.2 contains the attributes and their corresponding labels. The six brands are denoted *AA*, *BB*, *CC*, *DD*, *EE*, and *FF* to preserve confidentiality.

Table 10.2   Iced coffee attributes

Image Attribute	Label	Image Attribute	Label
good hangover cure	cure	fattening brand	fattening
low fat/calorie brand	low fat	appeals to men	men
brand for children	children	South Australian brand	South Australian
working class brand	working	traditional/old fashioned brand	traditional
rich/sweet brand	sweet	premium quality brand	premium
unpopular brand	unpopular	healthy brand	healthy
brand for fat/ugly people	ugly	high caffeine brand	caffeine
very fresh	fresh	new brand	new
brand for yuppies	yuppies	brand for attractive people	attractive
nutritious brand	nutritious	tough brand	tough
brand for women	women	popular brand	popular
minor brand	minor		

Dimensionality

Figure 10.21 shows the decomposition of the total inertia along each dimension. Two dimensions account for 83% of the total inertia. Adding a third dimension adds only 8.6% to the accounted for inertia. Thus, we elect to use a two dimensional representation.

Figure 10.21   Inertia per dimension

		Singular Value	Inertia	Chi Square	Proportion of Inertia	
					Accounted for	Cumulative
Dimension	1	.711	.506		.629	.629
	2	.399	.159		.198	.827
	3	.263	.069		.086	.913
	4	.234	.055		.068	.982
	5	.121	.015		.018	1.000
	Total		.804	3746.97	1.000	1.000

Contributions

Figure 10.22 shows the contributions of the row points to the inertia of the dimensions and the contributions of the dimensions to the inertia of the row points. If all points contributed equally to the inertia, the contributions would be 0.043. *Healthy* and *low fat* both contribute a substantial portion to the inertia of the first dimension. *Men* and *tough* contribute the largest amounts to the inertia of the second dimension. Both *ugly* and *fresh* contribute very little to either dimension.

Figure 10.22   Attribute contributions

		Contribution				
		Of Point to Inertia of Dimension		Of Dimension to Inertia of Point		
		1	2	1	2	Total
IMAGE	fattening	.042	.035	.652	.173	.825
	men	.073	.219	.512	.480	.992
	South Australian	.010	.044	.114	.152	.266
	traditional	.039	.071	.454	.260	.715
	premium	.016	.090	.296	.509	.805
	healthy	.152	.010	.953	.020	.973
	caffeine	.019	.005	.702	.053	.755
	new	.086	.006	.893	.021	.914
	attractive	.035	.001	.911	.007	.918
	tough	.056	.246	.404	.560	.964
	popular	.058	.001	.771	.003	.774
	cure	.008	.011	.446	.209	.655
	low fat	.175	.013	.941	.021	.962
	children	.006	.041	.179	.380	.559
	working	.055	.064	.693	.255	.948
	sweet	.020	.112	.212	.368	.580
	unpopular	.011	.005	.585	.085	.670
	ugly	.000	.002	.000	.131	.131
	fresh	.001	.002	.196	.214	.410
	yuppies	.010	.019	.392	.246	.637
	nutritious	.041	.001	.946	.006	.951
	women	.062	.001	.965	.007	.972
	minor	.027	.001	.593	.007	.600
	Active Total	1.000	1.000			

Two dimensions contribute a large amount to the inertia for most row points. The large contributions of the first dimension to *healthy, new, attractive, low fat, nutritious,* and *women* indicate that these points are very well represented in one dimension. Consequently, the higher dimensions contribute little to the inertia of these points, which will lie very near the horizontal axis. The second dimension contributes most to *men, premi-um*, and *tough*. Both dimensions contribute very little to the inertia for *South Australian* and *ugly*, so these points are poorly represented.

Figure 10.23 displays the contributions involving the column points. Brands *CC* and *DD* contribute the most to the first dimension, whereas *EE* and *FF* explain a large amount of the inertia for the second dimension. *AA* and *BB* contribute very little to either dimension.

Figure 10.23   Brand contributions

		Contribution				
		Of Point to Inertia of Dimension		Of Dimension to Inertia of Point		
		1	2	1	2	Total
BRAND	AA	.187	.003	.744	.004	.748
	BB	.021	.134	.135	.272	.407
	CC	.362	.007	.951	.006	.957
	DD	.267	.010	.928	.011	.939
	EE	.127	.477	.420	.494	.914
	FF	.036	.369	.169	.550	.718
	Active Total	1.000	1.000			

In two dimensions, all brands but *BB* are well represented. *CC* and *DD* are represented well in one dimension. The second dimension contributes the largest amounts for *EE* and *FF*. Notice that *AA* is represented well in the first dimension, but does not have a very high contribution to that dimension.

Principal Normalization

Initially, we will focus on how the attributes are related to each other and how the brands are related to each other. Using principal normalization spreads the total inertia once over the rows and once over the columns. Although this prevents biplot interpretation, the distances between the categories for each variable can be examined.

Figure 10.24 displays the plot of the row points. *Fresh* and *ugly* are both very close to the origin, indicating that they differ little from the average row profile. Three general classifications emerge. Located in the upper left of the plot, *tough, men*, and *working* are all similar to each other. The lower left contains *sweet, fattening, children*, and *premium*. In contrast, *healthy, low fat, nutritious*, and *new* cluster on the right side of the plot.

Figure 10.24   Plot of image attributes (principal normalization)

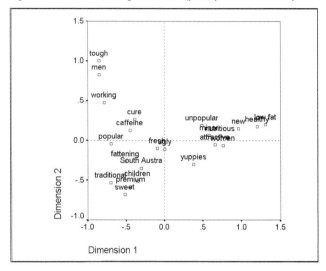

Figure 10.25 shows the plot of the brands. Notice that all brands are far from the origin, so no brand is similar to the overall centroid. Brands *CC* and *DD* group together at the right, whereas brands *BB* and *FF* cluster in the lower half of the plot. Brands *AA* and *EE* are not similar to any other brand.

Figure 10.25   Plot of brands (principal normalization)

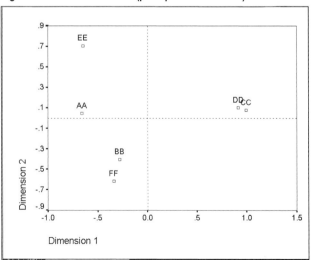

Symmetrical Normalization

How are the brands related to the image attributes? Principal normalization cannot address these relationships. To focus on how the variables are related to each other, use symmetrical normalization. Rather than spread the inertia twice (as in principal normalization), symmetrical normalization divides the inertia equally over both the rows and columns. Distances between categories for a single variable cannot be interpreted, but distances between the categories for different variables are meaningful.

Figure 10.26 displays the biplot of the row and column scores. In the upper left, brand *EE* is the only tough, working brand and appeals to men. Brand *AA* is the most popular and also viewed as the most highly caffeinated. The *sweet, fattening* brands include *BB* and *FF*. Brands *CC* and *DD*, while perceived as *new* and *healthy*, are also the most *unpopular*.

For further interpretation, you can draw a line through the origin and the two image attributes *men* and *yuppies*, and project the brands onto this line. The two attributes are opposed to each other, indicating that the association pattern of brands for *men* is reversed compared to the pattern for *yuppies*. That is, *men* are most frequently associated with brand *EE* and least frequently with brand *CC*, whereas *yuppies* are most frequently associated with brand *CC* and least frequently with brand *EE*.

Figure 10.26   Biplot of the brands and the attributes (symmetrical normalization)

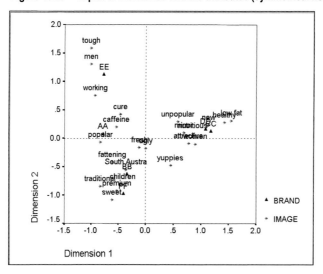

Example 3

Correspondence analysis is not restricted to frequency tables. The entries can be any positive measure of correspondence. In this example, we use the flying mileages between ten American cities. The cities are shown in Table 10.3.

Table 10.3   City labels

City	Label	City	Label
Atlanta	Atl	Miami	Mia
Chicago	Chi	New York	NY
Denver	Den	San Francisco	SF
Houston	Hou	Seattle	Sea
Los Angeles	LA	Washington, DC	DC

Figure 10.27 contains the flying mileages between the cities. Notice that there is only one variable for both rows and columns and that the table is symmetric; the distance from Los Angeles to Miami is the same as the distance from Miami to Los Angeles. Moreover, the distance between any city and itself is 0. The active margin reflects the total flying mileage from each city to all other cities.

Figure 10.27   Flying mileages between 10 American cities

	Atl	Chi	Den	Hou	LA	Mia	NY	SF	Sea	DC	Active Margin
Atl	0	587	1212	701	1936	604	748	2139	2182	543	10652
Chi	587	0	920	940	1745	1188	713	1858	1737	597	10285
Den	1212	920	0	879	831	1726	1631	949	1021	1494	10663
Hou	701	940	879	0	1374	968	1420	1645	1891	1220	11038
LA	1936	1745	831	1374	0	2339	2451	347	959	2300	14282
Mia	604	1188	1726	968	2339	0	1092	2594	2734	923	14168
NY	748	713	1631	1420	2451	1092	0	2571	2408	205	13239
SF	2139	1858	949	1645	347	2594	2571	0	678	2442	15223
Sea	2182	1737	1021	1891	959	2734	2408	678	0	2329	15939
DC	543	597	1494	1220	2300	923	205	2442	2329	0	12053
Active Margin	10652	10285	10663	11038	14282	14168	13239	15223	15939	12053	127542

In general, distances are dissimilarities; large values indicate a large difference between the categories. However, correspondence analysis requires an association measure; thus, we need to convert dissimilarities into similarities. In other words, a large table entry must correspond to a small difference between the categories. Subtracting every table entry from the largest table entry converts the dissimilarities into similarities. Thus, the new distance of 0 between Sea and Mia indicates that they are most distant (least similar), whereas the distance of 2529 between NY and DC indicates that they are the least distant (most similar) pair of cities.

Row and Column Scores

By using flying mileages instead of driving mileages, the terrain of the United States does not impact the distances. Consequently, all similarities should be representable in two dimensions. We center both the rows and columns and use principal normalization. Because of the symmetry of the correspondence table and the principal normalization, the row and column scores are equal and the total inertia is in both, so it does not matter whether we inspect the row or column scores. Figure 10.28 shows the orientation of the scores in two dimensions. Two dimensions account for 95% of the total inertia.

Figure 10.28   Points for 10 cities

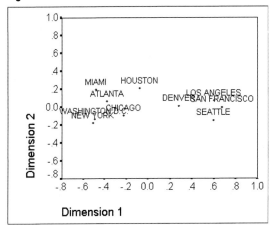

The locations of the cities are very similar to their actual geographical locations. Cities which are further south have larger values along the second dimension, whereas cities which are further west have larger values along the first dimension. Houston has a some-what larger value on the second dimension than expected; as a result, Houston is further south than Miami. However, the overall representation is quite accurate.

11 Homogeneity Analysis Examples

Homogeneity analysis quantifies nominal (categorical) data by assigning numerical values to the cases (objects) and categories. Homogeneity analysis is also known by the acronym HOMALS, for *hom*ogeneity analysis by means of *a*lternating *l*east *s*quares.

The values assigned to cases (objects) are called **object scores**. The values assigned to the categories are called **category quantifications**. A category quantification is the average of the object scores for all objects in a particular category. The purpose of homogeneity analysis is to find quantifications that are optimal in the sense that the categories are separated from each other as much as possible. This implies that objects in the same category are plotted close to each other and objects in different categories are plotted as far apart as possible. The term **homogeneity** also refers to the fact that the analysis will be most successful when the variables are homogeneous; that is, when they partition the objects (cases) into homogeneous groups.

Alternating least squares is an iterative method in which least-squares estimates of object scores and new quantifications given the object score estimates are alternately computed. It is the optimization technique used for estimation in homogeneity analysis, nonlinear principal components analysis, nonlinear canonical correlation analysis, and categorical regression with optimal scaling.

Homogeneity analysis is also known in the literature as multiple correspondence analysis or dual scaling. It gives comparable results to correspondence analysis when there are only two variables. Like correspondence analysis, homogeneity analysis analyzes bivariate relationships between variables. Unlike correspondence analysis, homogeneity analysis is not limited to two variables.

An Example

To explore how homogeneity analysis works, we will use data from Hartigan (1975). This data set contains information on the characteristics of screws, bolts, nuts, and tacks. Table 11.1 shows the variables, along with their variable labels, and the value labels assigned to the categories of each variable in the Hartigan hardware data set. Variables *threadn*, *brassn* and *objectn* have no variable labels.

Table 11.1 Hartigan hardware data set

Variable name	Variable label	Value labels
threadn		Yes_Thread, No_Thread
headn	Head form	Flat, Cup, Cone, Round, Cylinder
indheadn	Indentation of head	None, Star, Slit
bottomn	Bottom shape	sharp, flat
lengthn	Length in half inches	1/2_in, 1_in, 1_1/2_ in, 2_in, 2_1/2_in
brassn		Yes_Br, Not_Br
objectn		tack, nail1, nail2, nail3, nail4, nail5, nail6, nail7, nail8, screw1, screw2, screw3, screw4, screw5, bolt1, bolt2, bolt3, bolt4, bolt5, bolt6, tack1, tack2, nailb, screwb

This example includes all of the variables in the homogeneity analysis with the exception of *objectn*, which is used only to label a plot of the object scores.

Multiple Dimensions

Homogeneity analysis can compute a solution for several dimensions. The maximum number of dimensions equals either the number of categories minus the number of variables with no missing data, or the number of observations minus one, whichever is smaller. However, you should rarely use the maximum number of dimensions. A smaller number of dimensions is easier to interpret, and after a certain number of dimensions, the amount of additional association accounted for becomes negligible. A one-, two-, or three-dimensional solution in homogeneity analysis is very common.

The eigenvalues measure how much of the categorical information is accounted for by each dimension and are similar to the total variance accounted for. However, because the quantifications differ for each dimension, the total variance accounted for is defined on a different set of quantified variables for each dimension. For this example, a two-dimensional solution produces eigenvalues of 0.62 and 0.37 for dimensions 1 and 2, respectively. The largest possible eigenvalue for each dimension is 1.

The two dimensions together provide an interpretation in terms of distances. If a variable discriminates well, the objects will be close to the categories to which they belong. Ideally, objects in the same category will be close to each other (that is, they should have similar scores), and categories of different variables will be close if they belong to the same objects (that is, two objects that have similar scores for one variable should also score close to each other for the other variables in the solution).

Object Scores

After examining the frequency table and eigenvalues, you should look at the object scores. The default object scores plot, shown in Figure 11.1, is useful for spotting outliers. In Figure 11.1, there is one object at the bottom of the plot that might be considered an outlier. We'll consider later what happens if we drop this object.

Figure 11.1   Object scores plot

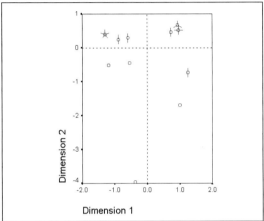

The plot shown in Figure 11.1 groups the object scores and displays them as **sunflowers**. Each **petal** on the sunflower represents a number of cases. This provides an easy way to see at a glance if many cases fall close together. Sunflowers with many petals indicate that a large number of cases fall in that area, while sunflowers with few petals indicate that a smaller number of cases fall in that area.

The distance from an object to the origin reflects variation from the "average" response pattern. This average response pattern corresponds to the most frequent category for each variable. Objects with many characteristics corresponding to the most frequent categories lie near the origin. In contrast, objects with unique characteristics are located far from the origin.

With a large data set, a sunflower plot is probably sufficient for most purposes. With smaller data sets like the one in this example, however, it would be nice to see exactly where each case (object) falls on the plot. It is difficult to see specific relationships among individual objects unless you can tell which object is number 1, which object is number 2, and so on. You can specify one or more variables to label the object scores plot. Each labeling variable produces a separate plot labeled with the values of that variable.

We'll take a look at the plot of object scores labeled by the variable *objectn*. This is just a case identification variable and was not used in any computations. Figure 11.2 shows the plot of object scores labeled with *objectn*.

Figure 11.2   Object scores labeled by variable objectn

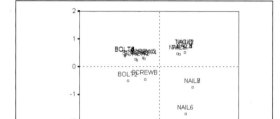

Examining the plot, we see that the first dimension (the horizontal axis) discriminates the screws and bolts (which have threads) from the nails and tacks (which don't have threads). This is easily seen on the plot since screws and bolts are on one end of the horizontal axis and tacks and nails are on the other. To a lesser extent, the first dimension also separates the bolts (which have flat bottoms) from all the others (which have sharp bottoms).

The second dimension (the vertical axis) seems to separate *screw1* and *nail6* from all other objects. What *screw1* and *nail6* have in common are their values on variable *lengthn*—they are the longest objects in the data. Moreover, *screw1* lies much farther from the origin than the other objects, suggesting that, taken as a whole, many of the characteristics of this object are not shared by the other objects.

If an analysis involves more than two dimensions, SPSS produces three-dimensional plots of the first three dimensions. Other dimensions can be displayed by editing the chart. See the *SPSS Base User's Guide* for information on editing charts and using the chart gallery.

Discrimination Measures

Before examining the rest of the object score plots, let's see if the discrimination measures agree with what we've said so far. For each variable, a discrimination measure, which can be regarded as a squared component loading, is computed for each dimension. This measure is also the variance of the quantified variable in that dimension. It has a maximum value of 1, which is achieved if the object scores fall into mutually exclusive groups and all object scores within a category are identical. (*Note*: This measure may have a value greater than 1 if there are missing data.) Large discrimination measures correspond to a large spread among the categories of the variable, and consequently indicate a high degree of discrimination between the categories of a variable along that dimension.

The average of the discrimination measures for any dimension equals the eigenvalue (the total variance accounted for) for that dimension. Consequently, the dimensions are ordered according to average discrimination. The first dimension has the largest average discrimination, the second dimension has the second largest average discrimination, and so on for all dimensions in the solution.

As noted on the object scores plot, Figure 11.3 shows that the first dimension is related to variables *threadn* and *bottomn* (labeled *Bottom shape*). These variables have large discrimination measures on the first dimension and small discrimination measures on the second dimension. Thus for both of these variables, the categories are spread far apart along the first dimension only. Variable *lengthn* (labeled *Length in ha*) has a large value on the second dimension, but a small value on the first dimension. As a result, *lengthn* is closest to the second dimension, agreeing with the observation from the object scores plot that the second dimension seems to separate the longest objects from the rest. *indheadn* (labeled *Indentation*) and *headn* (labeled *Head form*) have relatively large values on both dimensions, indicating discrimination in both the first and second dimensions.

Figure 11.3 Plot of discrimination measures

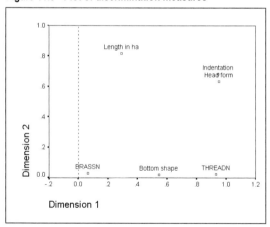

Variable *brassn*, located very close to the origin, does not discriminate at all in the first two dimensions. This makes sense, since all of the objects can be made of brass or not made of brass. Moreover, variable *lengthn* only discriminates in the second dimension for the same reason.

Figure 11.4   Category quantifications

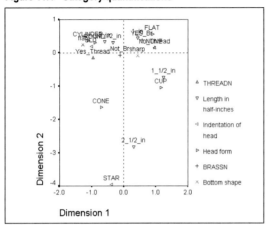

Category Quantifications

Recall that a discrimination measure is the variance of the quantified variable along a particular dimension. The discrimination measures plot contains these variances, indicating which variables discriminate along which dimension. However, the same variance could correspond to all of the categories being spread moderately far apart or to most of the categories being close together, with a few categories differing from this group. The discrimination plot cannot differentiate between these two conditions.

Category quantification plots provide an alternative method of displaying discrimination of variables which can identify category relationships. In this plot, the coordinates of each category on each dimension are displayed. Thus, you can determine which categories are similar for each variable. The category quantifications are plotted in Figure 11.4.

Variable *lengthn* has 5 categories, three of which group together near the top of the plot. The remaining two categories are in the lower half of the plot, with the *2_1/2_in* category very far from the group. The large discrimination for *lengthn* along dimension 2 is a result of this one category being very different from the other categories of *lengthn*. Similarly, for *headn*, the category *STAR* is vary far from the other categories and yields a large discrimination measure along the second dimension. These patterns cannot be illustrated in a plot of discrimination measures.

The category quantifications are the average object scores for objects in the same category. For example, in Figure 11.5, which is an overlay of Figure 11.2 and Figure 11.4 (with some categories omitted), you can see that the category *2_1/2_in* is centered in the space between the two objects that are in that category, *screw1* and *nail6*. Furthermore, categories that contain the same objects should appear close together. In Figure 11.5, you see that for the most part this is true. For example, the two categories that overlap are no indentation and no thread. The group of objects located near this point includes a variety of nails and all of the tacks, all of which have a flat head and no thread.

Figure 11.5   Object scores and category quantifications

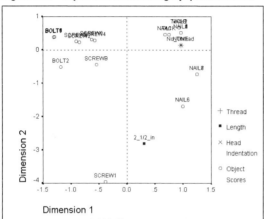

The spread of the category quantifications for a variable reflects the variance and thus indicates how well that variable is discriminated in each dimension. This is illustrated in Figure 11.6, in which some of the category labels have been omitted. Focusing on dimension 1, the categories for *threadn* are far apart. However, along dimension 2, the categories for this variable are very close. Thus, *threadn* discriminates better in dimension 1 than in dimension 2. In contrast, the categories for *headn* are spread far apart along both dimensions, suggesting that this variable discriminates well in both dimensions.

Figure 11.6   Selected category quantifications

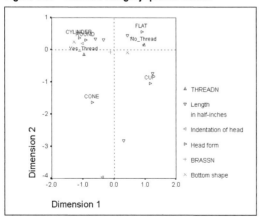

In addition to determining the dimensions along which a variable discriminates and how that variable discriminates, the category quantification plot also compares variable discrimination. A variable with categories that are far apart discriminates better than a variable with categories that are close together. In Figure 11.4, for example, along dimension 1, the two categories of *brassn* are much closer to each other than the two categories of *threadn*, indicating that *threadn* discriminates better than *brassn* along this dimension. However, along dimension 2, the distances are very similar, suggesting that these variables discriminate to the same degree along this dimension. The discrimination measures plot discussed previously identifies these same relationships by using variances to reflect the spread of the categories.

A More Detailed Look at Object Scores

A greater insight into the data can be gained by examining the object score plots labeled by each variable. Ideally, similar objects should form exclusive groups, and these groups should be far from each other. Figure 11.7, Figure 11.8, Figure 11.9, and Figure 11.10 present object scores labeled by *threadn*, *headn*, *lengthn*, and *brassn*. Figure 11.7 shows that the first dimension separates *Yes_Thread* and *No_Thread* perfectly. All of the objects with threads have negative object scores, whereas all of the non-threaded objects have positive scores. Although the two categories do not form compact groups, the perfect differentiation between the categories is generally considered a good result.

Figure 11.7   Object scores labeled with variable threadn

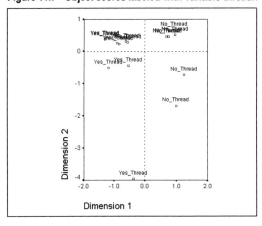

Figure 11.8   Object scores labeled with variable headn

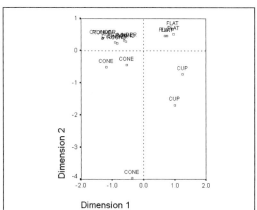

Figure 11.9   Object scores labeled with variable lengthn

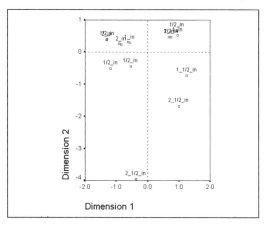

154   Chapter 11

Figure 11.10 Object scores labeled with variable brassn

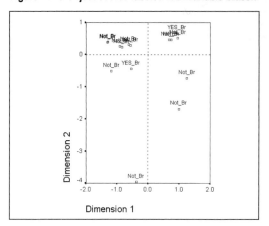

Figure 11.8 shows that *headn* discriminates in both dimensions. The *FLAT* objects group together in the upper right corner of the plot, whereas the *CUP* objects group together in the lower right. *CONE* objects all lie in the lower left. However, these objects are more spread out than the other groups, and thus are not as homogeneous. Finally, *CYLINDER* objects cannot be separated from *ROUND* objects, both of which lie in the upper left of the plot.

Figure 11.9 shows that *lengthn* does not discriminate in the first dimension. The categories of *lengthn* display no grouping when projected onto a horizontal line. However, *lengthn* does discriminate in the second dimension. The shorter objects correspond to positive scores, and the longer objects correspond to large, negative scores.

Figure 11.10 shows that *brassn* has categories that can't be separated very well in the first or second dimensions. The object scores are widely spread throughout the space. The brass objects cannot be differentiated from the non-brass objects.

Omission of Outliers

Outliers are objects that have too many unique features. As noted in Figure 11.1, *screw1* might be considered an outlier. If this object is deleted and the analysis run again, we see that the solution changes considerably. The eigenvalues for a two-dimensional solution are 0.64 and 0.35. As shown in the discrimination plot in Figure 11.11, *indheadn* no longer discriminates in the second dimension, whereas *brassn* changes from no discrimination in either dimension to discrimination in the second dimension. Discrimination for the other variables is largely unchanged.

Figure 11.11 Discrimination measures

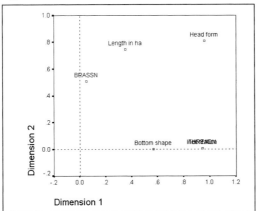

The object score plot labeled by *brassn* is shown in Figure 11.12. The four brass objects all appear near the bottom of the plot (three objects occupy identical locations), indicating high discrimination along the second dimension. As was the case for *threadn* in the previous analysis, the objects do not form compact groups, but the differentiation of objects by categories is perfect.

Figure 11.12 Object scores labeled with variable brassn

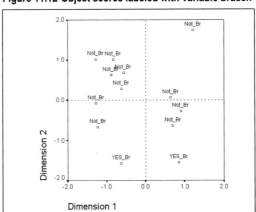

The object score plot labeled by *indheadn* is shown in Figure 11.13. The first dimension discriminates perfectly between the non-indented objects and the indented objects, as in the previous analysis. In contrast to the previous analysis, however, the second dimension cannot now distinguish the two *indheadn* categories.

Thus, omission of *screw1*, which is the only object with a star-shaped head, dramatically affects the interpretation of the second dimension. This dimension now differentiates objects based on *brassn, headn,* and *lengthn*.

Figure 11.13 Object scores labeled with variable indheadn

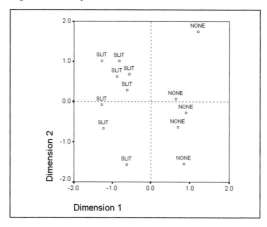

Syntax Reference

Introduction

This syntax reference guide describes the SPSS command language underlying SPSS Categories. Most of the features of these commands are implemented in the dialog boxes and can be used directly from the dialog boxes. Or you can paste the syntax into a syntax window and edit it or build a command file, which you can save and reuse. The features that are available only in command syntax are summarized following the discussion of the dialog box interface in the corresponding chapter on each statistical procedure.

A Few Useful Terms

All terms in the SPSS command language fall into one or more of the following categories:

Keyword. A word already defined by SPSS to identify a command, subcommand, or specification. Most keywords are, or resemble, common English words.

Command. A specific instruction that controls the execution of SPSS.

Subcommand. Additional instructions for SPSS commands. A command can contain more than one subcommand, each with its own specifications.

Specifications. Instructions added to a command or subcommand. Specifications may include subcommands, keywords, numbers, arithmetic operators, variable names, special delimiters, and so forth.

Each command begins with a command keyword (which may contain more than one word). The command keyword is followed by at least one blank space and then any additional specifications. Each command ends with a command terminator, which is a period. For example:

Syntax Diagrams

Each SPSS command described in this manual includes a syntax diagram that shows all of the subcommands, keywords, and specifications allowed for that command. These syntax diagrams are also available in the online Help system for easy reference when entering commands in a syntax window. By remembering the following rules, you can use the syntax diagram as a quick reference for any command:

- Elements shown in all capital letters are keywords defined by SPSS to identify commands, subcommands, functions, operators, and other specifications.
- Elements in lower case describe specifications you supply.

- Elements in boldface type are defaults. A default indicated with two asterisks (**) is in effect when the keyword is not specified. (Boldface is not used in the online Help system syntax diagrams.)
- Parentheses, apostrophes, and quotation marks are required where indicated.
- Elements enclosed in square brackets ([ ]) are optional.
- Braces ({ }) indicate a choice among elements. You can specify any one of the elements enclosed within the aligned braces.
- Ellipses indicate that an element can be repeated.
- Most abbreviations are obvious; for example, varname stands for variable name and varlist stands for a list of variables.
- The command terminator is not shown in the syntax diagrams.

Syntax Rules

Keep in mind the following simple rules when writing and editing commands in a syntax window:

- Each command must begin on a new line and end with a period.
- Subcommands are separated by slashes. The slash before the first subcommand in a command is optional in most commands.
- SPSS keywords are not case-sensitive, and three-letter abbreviations can be used for most keywords.
- Variable names must be spelled out in full.
- You can use as many lines as you want to specify a single command. However, text included within apostrophes or quotation marks must be contained on a single line.
- You can add space or break lines at almost any point where a single blank is allowed, such as around slashes, parentheses, arithmetic operators, or between variable names.
- Each line of syntax cannot exceed 80 characters.
- The period must be used as the decimal indicator, regardless of your language settings.

For example,

```
FREQUENCIES
 VARIABLES=JOBCAT SEXRACE
 /PERCENTILES=25 50 75
 /BARCHART.
```

and

```
freq var=jobcat sexrace /percent=25 50 75 /bar.
```

are both acceptable alternatives that generate the same results. The second example uses three-letter abbreviations and lower case, and the command is on one line.

INCLUDE Files

If your SPSS commands are contained in a command file that is specified on the SPSS INCLUDE command, the syntax rules are slightly different:

- Each command must begin in the first column of a new line.
- Continuation lines within a command must be indented at least one space.
- The period at the end of the command is optional.

If you generate command syntax by pasting dialog box choices into a syntax window, the format of the commands is suitable for both INCLUDE files and commands run in a syntax window.

ANACOR

```
ANACOR   TABLE={row var (min, max) BY column var (min, max)}
              {ALL (# of rows, # of columns)                }

[/DIMENSION={2**  }]

             {value}

[/NORMALIZATION={CANONICAL**}]
                {PRINCIPAL  }
                {RPRINCIPAL }
                {CPRINCIPAL }
                {value      }

[/VARIANCES=[SINGULAR] [ROWS] [COLUMNS]]


[/PRINT=[TABLE**] [PROFILES] [SCORES**] [CONTRIBUTIONS**]

        [DEFAULT] [PERMUTATION] [NONE]]


[/PLOT=[NDIM=({1, 2**       })]

             {value, value}
             {ALL, MAX     }

      [ROWS**[(n)]][COLUMNS**[(n)]][DEFAULT[(n)]]

      [TRROWS] [TRCOLUMNS] [JOINT[(n)]] [NONE]]

[/MATRIX OUT=[SCORE({*   })] [VARIANCE({*   })]]
                    {file}             {file}
```

**Default if subcommand or keyword is omitted.

Example:

```
ANACOR   TABLE=MENTAL(1,4) BY SES(1,6)
 /PRINT=SCORES CONTRIBUTIONS
 /PLOT=ROWS COLUMNS.
```

Overview

ANACOR performs correspondence analysis, which is an isotropic graphical representation of the relationships between the rows and columns of a two-way table.

Options

Number of Dimensions. You can specify how many dimensions ANACOR should compute.

Method of Normalization. You can specify one of five different methods for normalizing the row and column scores.

Computation of Variances and Correlations. You can request computation of variances and correlations for singular values, row scores, or column scores.

Data Input. You can analyze the usual individual casewise data or aggregated data from table cells.

Display Output. You can control which statistics are displayed and plotted. You can also control how many value label characters are used on the plots.

Writing Matrices. You can write matrix data files containing row and column scores and variances for use in further analyses.

Basic Specification

- The basic specification is ANACOR and the TABLE subcommand. By default, ANACOR computes a two-dimensional solution, displays the TABLE, SCORES, and CONTRIBUTIONS statistics, and plots the row scores and column scores of the first two dimensions.

Subcommand Order

- Subcommands can appear in any order.

Operations

- If a subcommand is specified more than once, only the last occurrence is executed.

Limitations

- The data within table cells cannot contain negative values. ANACOR will treat such values as 0.

Example

```
ANACOR TABLE=MENTAL(1,4) BY SES(1,6)
 /PRINT=SCORES CONTRIBUTIONS
 /PLOT=ROWS COLUMNS.
```

- Two variables, *MENTAL* and *SES*, are specified on the TABLE subcommand. *MENTAL* has values ranging from 1 to 4 and *SES* has values ranging from 1 to 6.
- The row and column scores and the contribution of each row and column to the inertia of each dimension are displayed.
- Two plots are produced. The first one plots the first two dimensions of row scores and the second one plots the first two dimensions of column scores.

TABLE Subcommand

TABLE specifies the row and column variables along with their value ranges for individual casewise data. For table data, TABLE specifies the keyword ALL and the number of rows and columns.

- The TABLE subcommand is required.

Casewise Data

- Each variable is followed by a value range in parentheses. The value range consists of the variable's minimum value, a comma, and its maximum value.
- Values outside of the specified range are not included in the analysis.
- Values do not have to be sequential. Empty categories receive scores of 0 and do not affect the rest of the computations.

Example

```
DATA LIST FREE/VAR1 VAR2.
BEGIN DATA
3  1
6  1
3  1
4  2
4  2
6  3
6  3
6  3
3  2
4  2
6  3
END DATA.
ANACOR TABLE=VAR1(3,6) BY VAR2(1,3).
```

- DATA LIST defines two variables, *VAR1* and *VAR2*.
- *VAR1* has three levels, coded 3, 4, and 6, while *VAR2* also has three levels, coded 1, 2, and 3.
- Since a range of (3,6) is specified for *VAR1*, ANACOR defines four categories, coded 3, 4, 5, and 6. The empty category, 5, for which there is no data, receives zeros for all statistics but does not affect the analysis.

Table Data

- The cells of a table can be read and analyzed directly by using the keyword ALL after TABLE.
- The columns of the input table must be specified as variables on the DATA LIST command. Only columns are defined, not rows.
- ALL is followed by the number of rows in the table, a comma, and the number of columns in the table, in parentheses.
- The number of rows and columns specified can be smaller than the actual number of rows and columns if you want to analyze only a subset of the table.

- The variables (columns of the table) are treated as the column categories, and the cases (rows of the table) are treated as the row categories.
- Rows cannot be labeled when you specify TABLE=ALL. If labels in your output are important, use the WEIGHT command method to enter your data (see "Analyzing Aggregated Data" on p. 169).

Example

```
DATA LIST /COL01 TO COL07 1-21.
BEGIN DATA
 50 19 26  8 18  6  2
 16 40 34 18 31  8  3
 12 35 65 66123 23 21
 11 20 58110223 64 32
 14 36114185714258189
  0  6 19 40179143 71
END DATA.
ANACOR TABLE=ALL(6,7).
```

- DATA LIST defines the seven columns of the table as the variables.
- The TABLE=ALL specification indicates that the data are the cells of a table. The (6,7) specification indicates that there are six rows and seven columns.

DIMENSION Subcommand

DIMENSION specifies the number of dimensions you want ANACOR to compute.

- If you do not specify the DIMENSION subcommand, ANACOR computes two dimensions.
- DIMENSION is followed by an integer indicating the number of dimensions.
- In general, you should choose as few dimensions as needed to explain most of the variation. The minimum number of dimensions that can be specified is 1. The maximum number of dimensions that can be specified is equal to the number of levels of the variable with the least number of levels, minus 1. For example, in a table where one variable has 5 levels and the other has 4 levels, the maximum number of dimensions that can be specified is 4 – 1, or 3. Empty categories (categories with no data, all zeros, or all missing data) are not counted toward the number of levels of a variable.
- If more than the maximum allowed number of dimensions is specified, ANACOR reduces the number of dimensions to the maximum.

NORMALIZATION Subcommand

The NORMALIZATION subcommand specifies one of five methods for normalizing the row and column scores. Only the scores and variances are affected; contributions and profiles are not changed.

The following keywords are available:

CANONICAL   *For each dimension, rows are the weighted average of columns divided by the matching singular value, and columns are the weighted average of rows divided by the matching singular value. This is the default if the*

NORMALIZATION subcommand is not specified. DEFAULT is an alias for CANONICAL. Use this normalization method if you are primarily interested in differences or similarities between variables.

PRINCIPAL *Distances between row points and column points are approximations of chi-square distances.* The distances represent the distance between the row or column and its corresponding average row or column profile. Use this normalization method if you want to examine both differences between categories of the row variable and differences between categories of the column variable (but not differences between variables).

RPRINCIPAL *Distances between row points are approximations of chi-square distances.* This method maximizes distances between row points. This is useful when you are primarily interested in differences or similarities between categories of the row variable.

CPRINCIPAL *Distances between column points are approximations of chi-square distances.* This method maximizes distances between column points. This is useful when you are primarily interested in differences or similarities between categories of the column variable.

The fifth method has no keyword. Instead, any value in the range –2 to +2 is specified after NORMALIZATION. A value of 1 is equal to the RPRINCIPAL method, a value of 0 is equal to CANONICAL, and a value of –1 is equal to the CPRINCIPAL method. The inertia is spread over both row and column scores. This method is useful for interpreting joint plots.

VARIANCES Subcommand

Use VARIANCES to display variances and correlations for the singular values, the row scores, and/or the column scores. If VARIANCES is not specified, variances and correlations are not included in the output.

The following keywords are available:

SINGULAR *Variances and correlations of the singular values.*

ROWS *Variances and correlations of the row scores.*

COLUMNS *Variances and correlations of the column scores.*

PRINT Subcommand

Use PRINT to control which of several correspondence statistics are displayed. If PRINT is not specified, the numbers of rows and columns, all nontrivial singular values, proportions of inertia, and the cumulative proportion of inertia accounted for are displayed.

The following keywords are available:

TABLE *A crosstabulation of the input variables showing row and column marginals.*

PROFILES	*The row and column profiles.* PRINT=PROFILES is analogous to the CELLS=ROW COLUMN subcommand in CROSSTABS.
SCORES	*The marginal proportions and scores of each row and column.*
CONTRIBUTIONS	*The contribution of each row and column to the inertia of each dimension, and the proportion of distance to the origin accounted for in each dimension.*
PERMUTATION	*The original table permuted according to the scores of the rows and columns for each dimension.*
NONE	*No output other than the singular values.*
DEFAULT	*TABLE, SCORES, and CONTRIBUTIONS.* These statistics are displayed if you omit the PRINT subcommand.

PLOT Subcommand

Use PLOT to produce plots of the row scores, column scores, row and column scores, transformations of the row scores, and transformations of the column scores. If PLOT is not specified, a plot of the row scores in the first two dimensions and a plot of the column scores in the first two dimensions are produced.

The following keywords are available:

TRROWS	*Plot of transformations of the row category values into row scores.*
TRCOLUMNS	*Plot of transformations of the column category values into column scores.*
ROWS	*Plot of row scores.*
COLUMNS	*Plot of column scores.*
JOINT	*A combined plot of the row and column scores.* This plot is not available when NORMALIZATION=PRINCIPAL.
NONE	*No plots.*
DEFAULT	*ROWS and COLUMNS.*

- The keywords ROWS, COLUMNS, JOINT, and DEFAULT can be followed by an integer value in parentheses to indicate how many characters of the value label are to be used on the plot. The value can range from 1 to 20; the default is 3. Spaces between words count as characters.
- TRROWS and TRCOLUMNS plots use the full value labels up to 20 characters.
- If a label is missing for any value, the actual values are used for all values of that variable.
- Value labels should be unique.
- The first letter of a label on a plot marks the place of the actual coordinate. Be careful that multiple-word labels are not interpreted as multiple points on a plot.

In addition to the plot keywords, the following can be specified:

NDIM   *Dimension pairs to be plotted.* NDIM is followed by a pair of values in parentheses. If NDIM is not specified, plots are produced for dimension 1 by dimension 2.

- The first value indicates the dimension that is plotted against all higher dimensions. This value can be any integer from 1 to the number of dimensions minus 1.
- The second value indicates the highest dimension to be used in plotting the dimension pairs. This value can be any integer from 2 to the number of dimensions.
- Keyword ALL can be used instead of the first value to indicate that all dimensions are paired with higher dimensions.
- Keyword MAX can be used instead of the second value to indicate that plots should be produced up to and including the highest dimension fit by the procedure.

Example

```
ANACOR TABLE=MENTAL(1,4) BY SES(1,6)
/PLOT NDIM(1,3) JOINT(5).
```

- The NDIM (1,3) specification indicates that plots should be produced for two dimension pairs—dimension 1 versus dimension 2 and dimension 1 versus dimension 3.
- JOINT requests combined plots of row and column scores. The (5) specification indicates that the first five characters of the value labels are to be used on the plots.

Example

```
ANACOR TABLE=MENTAL(1,4) BY SES(1,6)
/PLOT NDIM(ALL,3) JOINT(5).
```

- This plot is the same as above except for the ALL specification following NDIM. This indicates that all possible pairs up to the second value should be plotted, so JOINT plots will be produced for dimension 1 versus dimension 2, dimension 2 versus dimension 3, and dimension 1 versus dimension 3.

MATRIX Subcommand

Use MATRIX to write row and column scores and variances to matrix data files.

MATRIX is followed by keyword OUT, an equals sign, and one or both of the following keywords:

SCORE (file)   *Write row and column scores to a matrix data file.*

VARIANCE (file)   *Write variances to a matrix data file.*

- You can specify the file with either an asterisk (*), to replace the working data file with the matrix file, or the name of an external file.
- If you specify both SCORE and VARIANCE on the same MATRIX subcommand, you must specify two different files.

The variables in the SCORE matrix data file and their values are:

ROWTYPE_   *String variable containing the value ROW for all of the rows and COLUMN for all of the columns.*

LEVEL	*String variable containing the values (or value labels, if present) of each original variable.*
VARNAME_	*String variable containing the original variable names.*
DIM1...DIMn	*Numeric variables containing the row and column scores for each dimension.* Each variable is labeled *DIMn*, where *n* represents the dimension number.

The variables in the VARIANCE matrix data file and their values are:

ROWTYPE_	*String variable containing the value COV for all of the cases in the file.*
SCORE	*String variable containing the values SINGULAR, ROW, and COLUMN.*
LEVEL	*String variable containing the system-missing value for SINGULAR and the sequential row or column number for ROW and COLUMN.*
VARNAME_	*String variable containing the dimension number.*
DIM1...DIMn	*Numeric variable containing the covariances for each dimension.* Each variable is labeled *DIMn*, where *n* represents the dimension number.

See the *SPSS Base Syntax Reference Guide* for more information on matrix data files.

Analyzing Aggregated Data

To analyze aggregated data, such as data from a crosstabulation where cell counts are available but the original raw data are not, you can use the TABLE=ALL option or the WEIGHT command before ANACOR.

Example

To analyze a 3×3 table such as the one shown in Table 1 below, you could use these commands:

```
DATA LIST FREE/ BIRTHORD ANXIETY COUNT.
BEGIN DATA
1 1 48
1 2 27
1 3 22
2 1 33
2 2 20
2 3 39
3 1 29
3 2 42
3 3 47
END DATA.
WEIGHT BY COUNT.
ANACOR TABLE=BIRTHORD (1,3) BY ANXIETY (1,3).
```

- The WEIGHT command weights each case by the value of *COUNT*, as if there are 48 sub-jects with *BIRTHORD*=1 and *ANXIETY*=1, 27 subjects with *BIRTHORD*=1 and *ANXIETY*=2, and so on.
- ANACOR can then be used to analyze the data.
- If any of the table cell values equals 0, the WEIGHT command issues a warning, but the ANACOR analysis is done correctly.
- The table cell values (the WEIGHT values) cannot be negative. WEIGHT changes system-missing and negative values to 0.
- For large aggregated tables, you can use the TABLE=ALL option or the transformation lan-guage to enter the table "as is."

Table 1   3 x 3 table

		Anxiety		
		High	**Med**	**Low**
	First	48	27	22
Birth order	**Second**	33	20	39
	Other	29	42	47

Annotated Example

This example of ANACOR uses the crosstabular data on staff category and smoking habits from Greenacre (1984).

```
DATA LIST FREE /STAFF SMOKE FREQ.
WEIGHT BY FREQ.
VALUE LABELS
 STAFF 1 'SENIOR MANAGERS' 2 'JUNIOR MANAGERS'
 3 'SENIOR EMPLOYEES' 4 'JUNIOR EMPLOYEES' 5 'SECRETARIES'
 /SMOKE 1 'none' 2 'light' 3 'medium' 4 'heavy'.
BEGIN DATA
1 1   4   1 2  2   1 3  3   1 4  2
2 1   4   2 2  3   2 3  7   2 4  4
3 1 25    3 2 10   3 3 12   3 4  4
4 1 18    4 2 24   4 3 33   4 4 13
5 1 10    5 2  6   5 3  7   5 4  2
END DATA.
ANACOR TABLE=STAFF(1,5) BY SMOKE(1,4)
 /DIMENSION=2
 /NORMALIZATION=PRINCIPAL
 /PRINT=SCORES
 /PLOT TRROWS TRCOLUMNS ROWS(15) COLUMNS(15).
```

- The DATA LIST command specifies three variables in freefield format. The data from this example are taken from a crosstabulation. Variable *STAFF* represents the category values of the row variable, variable *SMOKE* represents the category values of the column vari-able, and variable *FREQ* is the cell count.
- The WEIGHT command counts each "case" as many times as the value of the cell count variable *FREQ*.

- The VALUE LABELS command provides descriptive labels for each category of variables *STAFF* and *SMOKE*. Since value labels are used in plots generated by ANACOR, it is usually helpful to assign short, unique labels. It is also a good idea to try to distinguish value labels for the different variables. In this example, the value labels for *STAFF* appear in upper case, and the labels for *SMOKE* are in lower case to further distinguish between variables on the plots.

- The TABLE subcommand on ANACOR specifies the row and column variables, along with their value ranges in parentheses.

- The DIMENSION subcommand tells ANACOR to compute two dimensions. (This is the default if the DIMENSION subcommand is omitted.)

- The NORMALIZATION subcommand indicates that the PRINCIPAL method should be used. The distances between categories of the row variable and between categories of the column variable are approximations of chi-square distances. (The distances between variables, however, are not.)

- The PRINT subcommand requests a display of marginal proportions and scores for each row and column. This subcommand produces the output shown in Figure 2. The singular values (eigenvalues) shown in Figure 1 are displayed automatically, even if you specify the keyword NONE on the PRINT subcommand.

- The PLOT subcommand requests plots of values calculated by ANACOR. The keywords TRROWS and TRCOLUMNS produce the plots of transformed row and column scores shown in Figure 4 and Figure 5. The keywords ROWS and COLUMNS produce the two-dimensional plots of row scores and column scores shown in Figure 6 and Figure 7. (With the principal normalization method, combined plots are not appropriate, and the keyword JOINT is not available for the PLOT subcommand. Joint plots are available with all other normalization techniques.) The optional integer values in parentheses after the keywords ROWS and COLUMNS specify the number of characters from the value labels that should be used on the plots.

The singular values shown in Figure 1 can be interpreted as correlations between the row and column scores displayed in Figure 2. For example, the singular value for dimension 1, which is 0.273, is the correlation between the row and column scores for dimension 1. If you replace the category values with the scores and calculate the Pearson correlation coefficient, the resulting r value is the same as the singular value (see Figure 3).

Figure 1   Singular values

Dimension	Singular Value	Inertia	Proportion Explained	Cumulative Proportion
1	.27342	.07476	.878	.878
2	.10009	.01002	.118	.995
3	.02034	.00041	.005	1.000
		---------	----------	----------
Total		.08519	1.000	1.000

Figure 2   Row and column scores

```
Row Scores:

STAFF            Marginal      Dim
                 Profile        1            2

     1 SENIOR M    .057      -.066         .194
     2 JUNIOR M    .093       .259         .243
     3 SENIOR E    .264      -.381         .011
     4 JUNIOR E    .456       .233        -.058
     5 SECRETAR    .130      -.201        -.079

Column Scores:

SMOKE            Marginal      Dim
                 Profile        1            2

     1 none        .316      -.393         .030
     2 light       .233       .099        -.141
     3 medium      .321       .196        -.007
     4 heavy       .130       .294         .198
```

Figure 3   Correlation between row and column scores

```
RECODE
 STAFF (1=-.066) (2=.259) (3=-.381) (4=.233) (5=-.201) INTO STAFFP
 /SMOKE (1=-.393) (2=.099) (3=.196) (4=.294) INTO SMOKEP.
CORRELATION STAFFP SMOKEP.



                    - -  Correlation Coefficients  - -

                  STAFFP      SMOKEP

STAFFP            1.0000        .2734
                 (  193)      (  193)
                 P=  .        P=  .000

SMOKEP             .2734      1.0000
                 (  193)      (  193)
                 P=  .000     P=  .


(Coefficient / (Cases) / 2-tailed Significance)

" . " is printed if a coefficient cannot be computed
```

Figure 4 and Figure 5 show the separate plots of transformed row and column scores. From Figure 4, we can see that the first dimension differentiates between juniors—both managers and employees—and other groups. The second dimension separates managers from employees and secretaries. In Figure 5, dimension 1 distinguishes smokers from nonsmokers.

Figure 4   Plots of transformed row scores

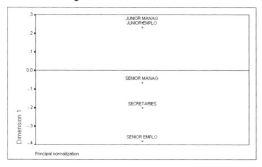 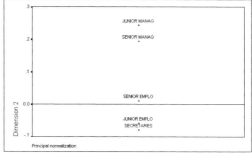

Figure 5   Plots of transformed column scores

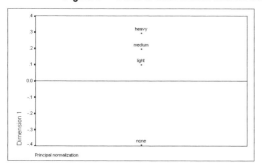 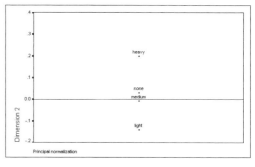

In Figure 6, the two dimensions are combined. The plot of row scores shows that dimension 1 separates seniors from juniors (both employees and managers) and dimension 2 distinguishes between managers and employees. The plot of column scores (see Figure 7) shows that dimension 1 separates smokers from nonsmokers, and dimension 2 differentiates between categories of smokers.

Figure 6   Two-dimensional plot of row scores

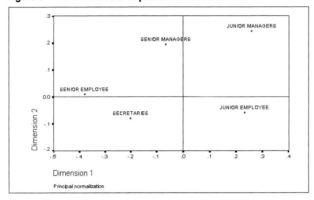

Figure 7   Two-dimensional plot of column scores

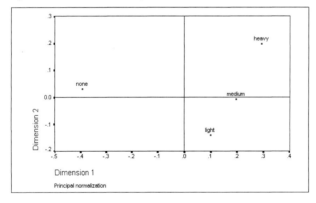

Figure 8 shows the joint plot of row and column scores produced with canonical normalization. This plot shows the relationship between the two variables. From this plot, we can see that heavy smoking is most common among managers (both junior and senior) and nonsmoking is most prevalent among senior employees. Junior employees tend to be either medium or light smokers, and secretaries tend to be either nonsmokers or light to medium smokers.

Figure 8   Joint plot with canonical normalization

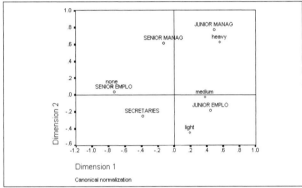

CATREG

```
CATREG [VARIABLES =] varlist (max)

/ANALYSIS depvar[({ORDI**})] WITH indvarlist[({ORDI**})]

{NOMI  }                        {NOMI  }

{NUME  }                        {NUME  }

[/INITIAL = {NUMERICAL**}]

{RANDOM      }

[/MAXITER = {100** }]

{value }

[/CONVERGENCE = {.00001**}]

{value }

[/MISSING = {LISTWISE**}]

{MODEIMPU  }

[/PRINT = [R**] [COEFF**] [FREQ**] [HISTORY] [ANOVA**]

[CORR] [OCORR] [QUANT] [TRANS[(value)]]
[DEFAULT] [NONE]]

[/PLOT = QUANT({varlist}) [value]]

{ALL }

[/SAVE = [ {TRANS**  } ]]

{rootname}

[/OUTFILE = `filename'].
```

** Default if subcommand or keyword is omitted.

Overview

CATREG (*Cat*egorical *re*gression with optimal scaling using alternating least squares) quantifies categorical variables using optimal scaling, resulting in an optimal linear regression equation for the transformed variables. The variables can be of mixed optimal scaling levels and no distributional assumptions about the variables are made.

Options

Transformation type. You can specify the transformation type (nominal, ordinal, numerical) at which you want to analyze each variable.

Initial solution. You can specify the kind of initial solution through the INITIAL subcommand.

Tuning the algorithm. You can control the values of algorithm-tuning parameters with the MAX-ITER and CONVERGENCE subcommands.

Missing data. You can specify the treatment of missing data with the MISSING subcommand.

Display output. You can request optional output through the PRINT subcommand.

Quantification plot. For each variable, you can request a plot of the quantifications against the category numbers.

Writing transformed data. You can write the quantifications to an outfile for use in further analyses.

Saving scores. You can save the transformed variables in the working data file.

Basic Specification

- The basic specification is the command CATREG with the VARIABLES and ANALYSIS subcommands. By default, CATREG assumes all variables are ordinal and displays tables listing fit statistics, regression coefficients, descriptive statistics, and analysis of variance results.

Subcommand Order

- The VARIABLES and ANALYSIS subcommands must appear.
- The VARIABLES subcommand must be the first subcommand specified.
- Other subcommands, if specified, can be in any order.

Operations

- Variables specified in the ANALYSIS subcommand must be found in the VARIABLES subcommand.
- In the ANALYSIS subcommand, exactly one variable must be specified as a dependent variable and at least one variable must be specified as an independent variable after the keyword WITH.

- If more than one dependent variable is specified in the ANALYSIS subcommand, CATREG is not executed.
- The words WITH and TO may not be used as variable names.
- If a subcommand is specified more than once, the last one is executed.
- CATREG treats every positive integer as a valid category indicator. To avoid unnecessary output, use the AUTORECODE or RECODE command to recode a categorical variable with nonsequential values or with a large number of categories. For continuous variables, recoding is not recommended, since the characteristic of equal intervals in the data will not be maintained. (See the *SPSS Base Syntax Reference Guide* or the *SPSS Base User's Guide* for more information on AUTORECODE and RECODE).

Limitations

- String variables are not allowed; use AUTORECODE to recode nominal string variables.
- CATREG-missing values for a variable are values less than 1 or greater than or equal to *max*+1, where *max* is the largest valid category number defined for the variable on the VARIABLES subcommand. If one of the category values of a variable has been coded 0 or some negative value and you want to treat it as a valid category, use AUTORECODE or RECODE to recode that variable.
- The data must be positive integers. Fractional values are truncated after the decimal. Thus, note that a value larger than 0 but less than 1 becomes 0 and is regarded as a missing value. On the other hand, if a variable takes a value larger than its *max* but less than (*max* + 1), then the value is still valid because of the truncation.
- CATREG ignores user-missing value specifications. User-missing values larger than or equal to 1 are treated as valid category values (after truncation if necessary) and are included in the analysis. If you do not want the category included, use COMPUTE or RECODE to change the value to a CATREG-missing value.
- There must be at least three valid cases.
- The number of valid cases must be greater than the number of independent variables plus one.
- The maximum number of independent variables is 200.

Example

```
CATREG VARIABLES = TEST1 TEST3 (2) TEST2 TEST4 TEST5 (3) TEST6 (4)
                   TEST7 TO TEST9 (5) STATUS01 STATUS02 (4)
       /ANALYSIS TEST4 (ORDI)
           WITH TEST1 TO TEST2 (NUME) TEST5 TEST7 (NOMI) TEST8 (ORDI)
               STATUS01 STATUS02 (NOMI)
       /INITIAL = RANDOM
       /MAXITER = 100
       /CONVERGENCE = .000001
       /MISSING = MODEIMPU
       /PRINT = R COEFF FREQ ANOVA QUANT TRANS
       /PLOT = QUANT (TEST2 TO TEST7 TEST4)
       /SAVE
       /OUTFILE = 'c:\data\qdata.sav'.
```

- VARIABLES defines the variables and their maximum number of categories. The keyword TO refers to the order of the variables in the working data file.

- The ANALYSIS subcommand defines variables used in the analysis. It is specified that *TEST4* is the dependent variable, to be treated as ordinal and that the variables *TEST1*, *TEST2*, *TEST3*, *TEST5*, *TEST7*, *TEST8*, *STATUS01* and *STATUS02* are the independent variables to be used in the analysis. (The keyword TO refers to the order of the variables in the VARIABLES subcommand.) The variables *TEST1*, *TEST2*, and *TEST3* are treated as numerical, the variables *TEST5*, *TEST7*, *STATUS01*, and *STATUS02* as nominal and variable *TEST8* as ordinal.

- Because there are nominal variables, a random initial solution is requested by the INITIAL subcommand.

- MAXITER specifies the maximum number of iterations to be 100. This is the default, so this subcommand could be omitted here.

- CONVERGENCE sets the convergence criterion to a value smaller than the default value.

- To include cases with CATREG-missing values, the MISSING subcommand specifies that for each variable missing values are replaced with the most frequent category (the mode).

- PRINT lists the correlations, the coefficients, the descriptive statistics, the ANOVA table, the category quantifications, and the transformed data list of all cases.

- PLOT is used to request quantification plots for the variables *TEST2*, *TEST5*, *TEST7* and *TEST4*.

- The SAVE subcommand adds the transformed variables to the working data file. The names of these new variables are *TRANS1_1, ..., TRANS9_1*.

- The OUTFILE subcommand writes the transformed data to a data file called *qdata.sav* in the directory c:\data.

VARIABLES Subcommand

VARIABLES specifies the variables that may be analyzed in the current CATREG procedure.

- The VARIABLES subcommand is required and precedes all other subcommands. The actual keyword VARIABLES can be omitted.
- Each variable or variable list is followed by the maximum category number in parentheses. This value can be any positive integer, but in practice, if it is 1, then the procedure stops because of the 0 variance of such variable.
- Each maximum category number applies to all variables preceding the number but after the previous number if given.
- The keyword TO on the VARIABLES subcommand refers to the order of variables in the working data file.

ANALYSIS Subcommand

ANALYSIS specifies the dependent variable, the keyword WITH, and the independent variables (in that order).

- All the variables on ANALYSIS must be specified on the VARIABLES subcommand.
- The ANALYSIS subcommand is required and follows the VARIABLES subcommand.
- The first variable list contains exactly one variable as the dependent variable, whereas the variable list following WITH contains at least one variable as an independent variable. For each variable, you may add an optional keyword in parentheses indicating the transformation type of the variable.
- The keyword TO in the independent variable list honors the order of variables in the VARIABLES subcommand.

The following keywords can be specified to indicate the transformation type:

NOMI   *Nominal*. Categories are treated as unordered. Objects in the same category obtain the same quantification.

ORDI   *Ordinal*. This is the default for variables listed without any effective transformation type; that is, those without a transformation type specification after them. Categories are treated as ordered. The order of the categories of the observed variable is preserved in the optimally transformed variable.

NUME   *Numerical*. Categories are treated as equally spaced (interval level). The order of the categories and the differences between category numbers of the observed variables are preserved in the optimally scaled variable. When all variables are scaled at the numerical level, the CATREG analysis is analogous to standard multiple regression analysis.

- Keywords indicating transformation type can apply to a variable list as well as to a single variable. The default ORDI is not applied to a variable without a keyword if a subsequent variable on the list has a keyword.

INITIAL Subcommand

INITIAL specifies the method used to compute the initial solution/configuration.

- The specification on INITIAL is keyword NUMERICAL or RANDOM.
- If INITIAL is not specified, NUMERICAL is the default.

The following keywords can be specified:

NUMERICAL   *Treat all variables as numerical.* This is usually best to use when there are only numerically and/or ordinally scaled variables.

RANDOM   *Compute a random initial solution.* This should be used only when some or all of the variables are scaled at the nominal level.

MAXITER Subcommand

MAXITER specifies the maximum number of iterations CATREG can go through in its computations. Note that the output starts from the iteration number 0, which is the initial value before any iteration, when INITIAL=NUMERICAL is in effect.

- If MAXITER is not specified, CATREG will iterate up to 100 times.
- The specification on MAXITER is a positive integer indicating the maximum number of iterations.

CONVERGENCE Subcommand

CONVERGENCE specifies a convergence criterion value. CATREG stops iterating if the difference in fit between the last two iterations is less than this value.

- If CONVERGENCE is not specified, the convergence value is 0.00001.
- The specification on CONVERGENCE is any value between 0.01 and 0.000001, inclusive.

MISSING Subcommand

CATREG ignores user-missing value specifications. User-missing values between 1 and the maximum value specified on the VARIABLES subcommand are treated as valid category values and are included in the analysis. Missing values in CATREG are values outside the valid range. By default, cases with CATREG-missing values on any of the variables are excluded from the analysis. The MISSING subcommand allows you to have CATREG-missing values on a variable replaced with the most frequent category (mode) of the variable.

The following keywords can be specified:

LISTWISE   *Exclude cases with* CATREG-*missing value.* Only cases with valid values for all variables are included. This is the default when MISSING is not specified.

MODEIMPU   *Replace* CATREG-*missing value with mode.* All cases are included and the imputations are treated as valid observations. When there are multiple modes, the smallest mode is used.

PRINT Subcommand

The PRINT subcommand controls the display of output. The output of the CATREG procedure is always based on the transformed variables. However, the correlations of the original predictor variables can be requested by the keyword OCORR. The default keywords are R, COEFF, FREQ, and ANOVA. If a keyword is duplicated or contradicted (for example, /PRINT = R R NONE), then the last occurence is executed.

The following keywords can be specified for PRINT:

R   *Multiple R. R includes R^2 and adjusted R^2.*

COEFF   *Standardized regression coefficients (beta).* COEFF includes the standard errors of the beta's, zero-order, part, and partial correlation, Pratt's relative importance measure for the transformed predictors, the tolerance before and after transformation and *F*. If the tolerance for a transformed predictor is lower than 0.0001, or if the tolerance is 0, then the computation for this variable is not done.

FREQ   A table with *descriptive statistics* (transformation type, number of missing values, mode) including *marginal frequencies* for the variables in the analysis.

HISTORY   *History of iterations.* For each iteration (including 0), the multiple *R*, and the regression error (square root of $(1 - R^2)$) are shown. The increase in multiple *R* is listed from iteration number 1.

ANOVA   *Analysis of variance table.* This option includes regression and residual sums of squares, mean squares and *F*.

CORR   *Correlations of the transformed predictors.*

OCORR   *Correlations of the original predictors.*

QUANT   *Category quantifications.*

TRANS (n)   *Transformed data list. n* is a non-negative integer. If *n* is specified, only the first *n* cases are shown in the list, assuming that *n* is less than the total number of cases. When *n* is 0, the table is empty and does not appear. If *n* is not specified or if *n* is larger than or equal to the total number of cases, then all cases are shown.

DEFAULT   *R, COEFF, FREQ, and ANOVA.*

NONE   *No PRINT output is shown.*

PLOT Subcommand

This subcommand produces quantification plots (optimal quantifications against original category numbers). The following keyword must be specified:

QUANT(varlist)(l)   *Quantification plots.* A list of variables must be given in parentheses following the keyword. A keyword **ALL** is allowed. Also, after the variables list, you can specify an optional parameter (l) in parentheses to control the length of all category value label lengths.

- If the plot keyword QUANT is omitted or if the variable list is empty, no plot is created.
- The category value label length parameter (l) must be an integer between 0 and 20, inclusive. If l = 0, instead of value labels, variable values are displayed on the horizontal axis. If the length parameter is omitted, the first 20 characters of the value label are used for each category.
- For categories without a value label, the value is used. However, the length of the value is truncated in accordance with the length parameter. For example, a category coded as 100 with no value label appears as 10 along the category axis if the length parameter is 2.
- The keyword TO in the variable list honors the order of the variables in the ANALYSIS subcommand.

SAVE Subcommand

The SAVE subcommand is used to add the transformed variables to the working data file. If on the MISSING subcommand LISTWISE is specified, excluded cases are represented by a dot on every variable.

- A variable rootname can be specified on the SAVE subcommand to which CATREG adds a number corresponding to the position of the variables on the ANALYSIS subcommand. That is, the dependent variable has the position number 1, and the independent variables have the position numbers 2, 3, ... as they are listed. Only one rootname can be specified and it can contain up to five characters (if more than one rootname is specified, the first name is used. If a rootname contains more than five characters, the first five characters are used) .
- If a rootname is not specified, unique variable names are automatically generated. The formula is *TRANSm_n*, where *m* increments from 1 to create unique variable names using the source variable's position numbers in the ANALYSIS subcommand and *n* increments from 1 to create unique rootnames for CATREG procedures with the SAVE subcommand. For example, the first set of default names, if they do not exist in the data file, would be *TRANS1_1*, *TRANS2_1*, *TRANS3_1*, and so forth. The next set of default names, if they do not exist in the data file, would be *TRANS1_2*, *TRANS2_2*, *TRANS3_2*, and so forth. If, for example, *TRANS2_2* already exists in the data file, then the default names would be *TRANS1_3*, *TRANS2_3*, *TRANS3_3*, and so forth.
- As *m* and/or *n* increase, the prefix *TRANS* is truncated to keep variable names within eight characters. For example, the variable after *TRANS9_1* would be *TRAN10_1*. The initial character *T* is required.

OUTFILE Subcommand

The OUTFILE subcommand is used to write the transformed data to an external data file. If on the MISSING subcommand LISTWISE is specified, excluded cases are represented by a dot on every variable.

- The specification on OUTFILE is a filename enclosed by single quotation marks.
- A working data file, in principle, should not be replaced by this subcommand, and the asterisk (*) file specification is not supported.

CORRESPONDENCE

```
CORRESPONDENCE

 /TABLE = rowvar (min, max) BY colvar (min, max)
             {ALL (# of rows, # of columns )

[/SUPPLEMENTARY = [rowvar (valuelist)] [colvar (valuelist)]]

[/EQUAL = [rowvar (valuelist)... (valuelist)]
           [colvar (valuelist)... (valuelist)]]

[/MEASURE = {CHISQ**}]
             {EUCLID}

[/STANDARDIZE = {RMEAN}]
                 {CMEAN}
                 {RCMEAN**}
                 {RSUM}
                 {CSUM}

[/DIMENSION = {2**}]
               {value}

[/NORMALIZATION = {SYMMETRICAL**}]
                   {PRINCIPAL}
                   {RPRINCIPAL}
                   {CPRINCIPAL}
                   {value}

[/PRINT = [TABLE**] [RPROF] [CPROF] [RPOINTS**] [CPOINTS**]
           [RCONF] [CCONF] [PERMUTATION[(n)]] [DEFAULT] [NONE]]

[/PLOT = [NDIM({1**, 2**})]
               {value, value}
               {ALL, MAX}
         [RPOINTS[(n)]] [CPOINTS[(n)] [TRROWS[(n)]]
         [TRCOLUMNS[(n)]] [BIPLOT**[(n)]] [NONE]]

[/OUTFILE = {SCORE(filename)                               }]
            {                          VARIANCE(filename)}
            {SCORE(filename)           VARIANCE(filename)}}
```

**Default if subcommand or keyword is omitted.

Overview

CORRESPONDENCE displays the relationships between rows and columns of a two-way table graphically by a scatterplot matrix. It computes the row and column scores and statistics and produces plots based on the scores. Also, confidence statistics are computed.

185

Options

Number of Dimensions. You can specify how many dimensions CORRESPONDENCE should compute.

Supplementary Points. You can specify supplementary rows and columns.

Equality Restrictions. You can restrict rows and columns to have equal scores.

Measure. You can specify the distance measure to be Chi-Square of Euclidean.

Standardization. You can specify one of five different standardization methods.

Method of Normalization. You can specify one of five different methods for normalizing the row and column scores.

Confidence Statistics. You can request computation of confidence statistics (standard deviations and correlations) for row and column scores. For singular values, confidence statistics are always computed.

Data Input. You can analyze individual casewise data, aggregated data, or table data.

Display Output. You can control which statistics are displayed and plotted.

Writing Matrices. You can write a matrix data file containing the row and column scores, and a matrix data file containing confidence statistics (variances and covariances) for the singular values, row scores, and column scores.

Basic Specification

- The basic specification is CORRESPONDENCE and the TABLE subcommand. By default, CORRESPONDENCE computes a two-dimensional solution, displays the correspondence table, the summary table, an overview of the row and column points, and a scatterplot matrix of biplots of the row and column scores for the first two dimensions.

Subcommand Order

- The TABLE subcommand must appear first.
- All other subcommands can appear in any order.

Syntax Rules

- Only one keyword can be specified on the MEASURE subcommand.
- Only one keyword can be specified on the STANDARDIZE subcommand.
- Only one keyword can be specified on the NORMALIZATION subcommand.
- Only one parameter can be specified on the DIMENSION subcommand.

Operations

- If a subcommand is specified more than once, only the last occurrence is executed.

Limitations

- The table input data and the aggregated input data cannot contain negative values. CORRESPONDENCE will treat such values as 0.
- Rows and columns that are specified as supplementary cannot be equalized.

Example

```
CORRESPONDENCE TABLE=MENTAL(1,4) BY SES(1,6)
/PRINT=RPOINTS CPOINTS
/PLOT=RPOINTS CPOINTS.
```

- Two variables, *MENTAL* and *SES*, are specified on the TABLE subcommand. *MENTAL* has values ranging from 1 to 4 and *SES* has values ranging from 1 to 6.
- The summary table and overview tables of the row and column points are displayed.
- Two scatterplot matrices are produced. The first one plots the first two dimensions of row scores and the second one plots the first two dimensions of column scores.

TABLE Subcommand

TABLE specifies the row and column variables along with their integer value ranges. The two variables are separated by the keyword BY.

- The TABLE subcommand is required.

Casewise Data

- Each variable is followed by an integer value range in parentheses. The value range consists of the variable's minimum value and its maximum value.
- Values outside of the specified range are not included in the analysis.
- Values do not have to be sequential. Empty categories yield a zero in the input table, and do not affect the statistics for other categories.

Example

```
DATA LIST FREE/VAR1 VAR2.
BEGIN DATA
3  1
6  1
3  1
4  2
4  2
6  3
6  3
6  3
3  2
4  2
6  3
END DATA.
CORRESPONDENCE TABLE=VAR1(3,6) BY VAR2(1,3).
```

- DATA LIST defines two variables, *VAR1* and *VAR2*.

- *VAR1* has three levels, coded 3, 4, and 6. *VAR2* also has three levels, coded 1, 2, and 3.

- Since a range of (3,6) is specified for *VAR1*, CORRESPONDENCE defines four categories, coded 3, 4, 5, and 6. The empty category, 5, for which there is no data, receives system missing values for all statistics and does not affect the analysis.

Table Data

- The cells of a table can be read and analyzed directly by using the keyword ALL after TABLE.

- The columns of the input table must be specified as variables on the DATA LIST command. Only columns are defined, not rows.

- ALL is followed by the number of rows in the table, a comma, and the number of columns in the table, in parentheses.

- The row variable is named *ROW* and the column variable is named *COLUMN*.

- The number of rows and columns specified can be smaller than the actual number of rows and columns if you want to analyze only a subset of the table.

- The variables (columns of the table) are treated as the column categories, and the cases (rows of the table) are treated as the row categories.

- Row categories can be assigned values (category codes) when you specify TABLE=ALL by the optional variable ROWCAT_. This variable must be defined as a numeric variable with unique values corresponding to the row categories. If *ROWCAT_* is not present, the row index numbers are used as row category values.

Example

```
DATA LIST /ROWCAT_ 1 COL1 3-4 COL2 6-7 COL3 9-10.
BEGIN DATA
1 50 19 26
2 16 40 34
3 12 35 65
4 11 20 58
END DATA.
VALUE LABELS ROWCAT_ 1 'ROW1' 2 'ROW2' 3 'ROW3' 4 'ROW4'.
CORRESPONDENCE TABLE=ALL(4,3).
```

- DATA LIST defines the row category naming variable *ROWCAT_* and the three columns of the table as the variables.

- The TABLE=ALL specification indicates that the data are the cells of a table. The (4,3) specification indicates that there are four rows and three columns.

- The column variable is named *COLUMN* with categories labeled *COL1*, *COL2*, and *COL3*.

- The row variable is named *ROW* with categories labeled *ROW1*, *ROW2*, *ROW3*, and *ROW4*.

DIMENSION Subcommand

DIMENSION specifies the number of dimensions you want CORRESPONDENCE to compute.

- If you do not specify the DIMENSION subcommand, CORRESPONDENCE computes two dimensions.

- DIMENSION is followed by a positive integer indicating the number of dimensions. If this parameter is omitted, a value of 2 is assumed.

- In general, you should choose as few dimensions as needed to explain most of the variation. The minimum number of dimensions that can be specified is 1. The maximum number of dimensions that can be specified equals the minimum of the number of active rows and the number of active columns, minus 1. An active row or column is a nonsupplementary row or column that is used in the analysis. For example, in a table where the number of rows is 5 (2 of which are supplementary) and the number of columns is 4, the number of active rows (3) is smaller than the number of active columns (4). Thus, the maximum number of dimensions that can be specified is $(5 - 2) - 1$, or 2. Rows and columns that are restricted to have equal scores count as 1 toward the number of active rows or columns. For example, in a table with 5 rows and 4 columns where 2 columns are restricted to have equal scores, the number of active rows is 5 and the number of active columns is 4-1, or 3. The maximum number of dimensions that can be specified is (3 - 1), or 2. Empty rows and columns (rows or columns with no data, all zeros, or all missing data) are not counted toward the number of rows and columns.

- If more than the maximum allowed number of dimensions is specified, CORRESPONDENCE reduces the number of dimensions to the maximum.

SUPPLEMENTARY Subcommand

The SUPPLEMENTARY subcommand specifies the rows and columns that you want to treat as supplementary (also called passive or illustrative).

- For casewise data, the specification on SUPPLEMENTARY is a variable name, followed by a value list in parentheses. The values must be in the value range specified on the TABLE subcommand for the row or column variable.
- For table data, the specification on SUPPLEMENTARY is *ROW* and/or *COLUMN*, followed by a value list in parentheses. The values represent the row or column indices of the table input data.
- The maximum number of supplementary rows or columns is the number of active rows or columns minus 2.
- Supplementary rows and columns cannot be equalized.

Example

```
CORRESPONDENCE TABLE=MENTAL(1,8) BY SES(1,6)
/SUPPLEMENTARY MENTAL(3) SES(2,6).
```

- SUPPLEMENTARY specifies the third level of *MENTAL* and the second and sixth levels of *SES* to be supplementary.

Example

```
CORRESPONDENCE TABLE=ALL(8,6)
/SUPPLEMENTARY ROW(3) COLUMN(2,6).
```

- SUPPLEMENTARY specifies the third level of the row variable and the second and sixth levels of the column variable to be supplementary.

EQUAL Subcommand

The EQUAL subcommand specifies the rows or columns that you want to restrict to have equal scores.

- For casewise data, the specification on EQUAL is a variable name, followed by a list of at least two values in parentheses. The values must be in the value range specified on the TABLE subcommand for the row or column variable.
- For table data, the specification on EQUAL is *ROW* and/or *COLUMN*, followed by a value list in parentheses. The values represent the row or column indices of the table input data.
- Rows or columns that are restricted to have equal scores cannot be supplementary.
- The maximum number of equal rows or columns is the number of active rows or columns minus 1.

Example

```
CORRESPONDENCE TABLE=MENTAL(1,8) BY SES(1,6)
/EQUAL MENTAL(1,2) (6,7) SES(1,2,3).
```

- EQUAL specifies the first and second level of *MENTAL*, the sixth and seventh level of *MENTAL*, and the first, second, and third levels of *SES* to have equal scores.

MEASURE Subcommand

The MEASURE subcommand specifies the measure of distance between the row and column profiles.

- Only one keyword can be used in a given analysis.

The following keywords are available:

CHISQ *Chi-square distance.* This is the weighted distance, where the weight is the mass of the rows or columns. This is the default specification for MEASURE and is the necesary specification for standard Correspondence Analysis.

EUCLID *Euclidean distance.* The distance is the square root of the sum of squared differences between the values for two rows or columns.

STANDARDIZE Subcommand

When MEASURE=EUCLID, the STANDARDIZE subcommand specifies the method of standardization.

- Only one keyword can be used.
- If MEASURE is CHISQ, the standardization is automatically set to RCMEAN and corresponds to standard Correspondence Analysis.

The following keywords are available:

RMEAN The row means are removed.

CMEAN The column means are removed.

RCMEAN Both the row and column means are removed. This is the default specification.

RSUM First the row totals are equalized and then the row means are removed.

CSUM First the column totals are equalized and then the column means are removed.

NORMALIZATION Subcommand

The NORMALIZATION subcommand specifies one of five methods for normalizing the row and column scores. Only the scores and confidence statistics are affected; contributions and profiles are not changed.

The following keywords are available:

SYMMETRICAL *For each dimension, rows are the weighted average of columns divided by the matching singular value, and columns are the weighted average of rows divided by the matching singular value.* This is the default if the NORMALIZATION subcommand is not specified. Use this normalization method if you are primarily interested in differences or similarities between rows and columns.

PRINCIPAL
: *Distances between row points and column points are approximations of chi-square distances or of Euclidean distances (depending on MEASURE).* The distances represent the distance between the row or column and its corresponding average row or column profile. Use this normalization method if you want to examine both differences between categories of the row variable and differences between categories of the column variable (but not differences between variables).

RPRINCIPAL
: *Distances between row points are approximations of chi-square distances or of Euclidean distances (depending on MEASURE).* This method maximizes distances between row points. The row points are weighted averages of the column points. This is useful when you are primarily interested in differences or similarities between categories of the row variable.

CPRINCIPAL
: *Distances between column points are approximations of chi-square distances or of Euclidean distances (depending on MEASURE).* This method maximizes distances between column points. The column points are weighted averages of the row points. This is useful when you are primarily interested in differences or similarities between categories of the column variable.

The fifth method allows the user to specify any value in the range –1 to +1 inclusive. A value of 1 is equal to the RPRINCIPAL method, a value of 0 is equal to the SYMMETRICAL method, and a value of –1 is equal to the CPRINCIPAL method. By specifying a value between -1 and 1, the user can spread the inertia over both row and column scores to varying degrees. This method is useful for making tailor-made biplots.

PRINT Subcommand

Use PRINT to control which of several correspondence statistics are displayed. The summary table (singular values, inertia, proportion of inertia accounted for, cumulative proportion of inertia accounted for, and confidence statistics for the maximum number of dimensions) is always produced. If PRINT is not specified, the input table, the summary table, the overview of row points table, and the overview of column points table are displayed.

The following keywords are available:

TABLE
: *A crosstabulation of the input variables showing row and column marginals.*

RPROFILES
: *The row profiles.* PRINT=RPROFILES is analogous to the CELLS=ROW subcommand in CROSSSTABS.

CPROFILES
: *The column profiles.* PRINT=CPROFILES is analogous to the CELLS= COLUMN subcommand in CROSSSTABS.

RPOINTS
: *Overview of Row Points (mass, scores, inertia, contribution of the points to the inertia of the dimension, and the contribution of the dimensions to the inertia of the points).*

CPOINTS	*Overview of Column Points (mass, scores, inertia, contribution of the points to the inertia of the dimension, and the contribution of the dimensions to the inertia of the points).*
RCONF	*Confidence statistics (standard deviations and correlations) for the active row points.*
CCONF	*Confidence statistics (standard deviations and correlations) for the active column points.*
PERMUTATION(n)	*The original table permuted according to the scores of the rows and columns.* PERMUTATION can be followed by a number in parentheses indicating the maximum number of dimensions for which you want permuted tables. The default number of dimensions is 1.
NONE	*No output other than the* SUMMARY *table.*
DEFAULT	*TABLE, RPOINTS, CPOINTS and the* SUMMARY *tables.* These statistics are displayed if you omit the PRINT subcommand.

PLOT Subcommand

Use PLOT to produce plots of the row scores, column scores, row and column scores, transformations of the row scores, and transformations of the column scores. If PLOT is not specified or is specified without keywords, a biplot is produced.

The following keywords are available:

TRROWS(n)	*Line chart of transformations of the row category values into row scores.*
TRCOLUMNS(n)	*Line chart of transformations of the column category values into column scores.*
RPOINTS(n)	*Scatterplot matrix of row scores.*
CPOINTS(n)	*Scatterplot matrix of column scores.*
BIPLOT(n)	*Biplot matrix of the row and column scores.* This is the default plot. This plot is not available when NORMALIZATION=PRINCIPAL. From the chart editor, you can create a two-dimensional biplot of any pair of dimensions in the biplot matrix. You can also create a three-dimensional biplot of any three dimensions in the biplot matrix.
NONE	*No plots.*

- All keywords can be followed by an integer value in parentheses to indicate how many characters of the value label are to be used in the plot. The value can range from 0 to 20. Spaces between words count as characters. A value of 0 corresponds to using the values instead of the value labels.
- If a label is missing for a value, the actual value is used. However, the length of the value is truncated in accordance with the length parameter. For example, a category coded as 100 with no value label appears as 10 if the length parameter is 2.

- TRROWS and TRCOLUMNS produce line charts. RPOINTS and CPOINTS produce scatter-plot matrices. BIPLOT produces a biplot matrix. For line charts, the value labels are used to label the category axis. For scatterplot matrices and biplot matrices, the value labels are used to label the points in the plot.

In addition to the plot keywords, the following can be specified:

NDIM   *Dimensions to be plotted.* NDIM is followed by a pair of values in parentheses. If NDIM is not specified, NDIM(1,2) is assumed.

- The first value must be any integer from 1 to the number of dimensions minus 1.
- The second value can be any integer from 2 to the number of dimensions. The second value must exceed the first. Alternatively, the keyword MAX can be used instead of a value to indicate the highest dimension of the solution.
- For TRROWS and TRCOLUMNS, the first and second values indicate the range of dimensions for which the plots are created.
- For RPOINTS, CPOINTS, and BIPLOT, the first and second values indicate the range of dimensions included in the scatterplot matrix or biplot matrix.

Example

```
CORRESPONDENCE TABLE=MENTAL(1,4) BY SES(1,6)
/PLOT NDIM(1,3) BIPLOT(5).
```

- BIPLOT and NDIM(1,3) request a biplot matrix of the first three dimensions.
- The 5 following BIPLOT indicates that only the first five characters of each label are to be shown in the biplot matrix.

Example

```
CORRESPONDENCE TABLE=MENTAL(1,4) BY SES(1,6)
/DIMENSION = 3
/PLOT NDIM(1,MAX) TRROWS.
```

- Three transformation plots of row categories into row points are produced, one for each dimension from 1 to the highest dimension of the analysis (in this case, 3).

OUTFILE Subcommand

Use OUTFILE to write row and column scores and/or confidence statistics (variances and co-variances) for the singular values and row and column scores to matrix data files.

OUTFILE must be followed by one or both of the following keywords:

SCORE (filename)   *Write row and column scores to a matrix data file.*

VARIANCE (filename)   *Write variances and covariances to a matrix data file.*

- You must specify the name of an external file.
- If you specify both SCORE and VARIANCE on the same OUTFILE subcommand, you must specify two different file names.

- For VARIANCE, supplementary and equality constrained rows and columns are not produced in the matrix file.

The variables in the SCORE matrix data file and their values are:

ROWTYPE_   *String variable containing the value ROW for all of the rows and COLUMN for all of the columns.*

LEVEL_   *String variable containing the values (or value labels, if present) of each original variable.*

VARNAME_   *String variable containing the original variable names.*

DIM1...DIMn   *Numerical variables containing the row and column scores for each dimension.* Each variable is labeled *DIMn*, where *n* represents the dimension number.

The variables in the VARIANCE matrix data file and their values are:

ROWTYPE_   *String variable containing the value COV for all of the cases in the file.*

SCORE_   *String variable containing the value SINGULAR, the row variable's name (or label), and the column variable's name (or label).*

LEVEL_   *String variable containing the row variable's values (or labels), the column variable's values (or labels), and a blank value for score_ = SINGULAR.*

VARNAME_   *String variable containing the dimension number.*

DIM1...DIMn   *Numerical variables containing the variances and covariances for each dimension.* Each variable is named *DIMn*, where *n* represents the dimension number.

See the *SPSS Base Syntax Reference Guide* for more information on matrix data files.

Analyzing Aggregated Data

To analyze aggregated data, such as data from a crosstabulation where cell counts are available but the original raw data are not, you can use the WEIGHT command before CORRESPONDENCE.

Example

To analyze a 3×3 table such as the one shown in Table 1 below, you could use these commands:

```
DATA LIST FREE/ BIRTHORD ANXIETY COUNT.
BEGIN DATA
1 1 48
1 2 27
1 3 22
2 1 33
2 2 20
2 3 39
3 1 29
3 2 42
3 3 47
END DATA.
WEIGHT BY COUNT.
CORRESPONDENCE TABLE=BIRTHORD (1,3) BY ANXIETY (1,3).
```

- The WEIGHT command weights each case by the value of *COUNT*, as if there are 48 subjects with *BIRTHORD*=1 and *ANXIETY*=1, 27 subjects with *BIRTHORD*=1 and *ANXIETY*=2, and so on.
- CORRESPONDENCE can then be used to analyze the data.
- If any of the table cell values equals 0, the WEIGHT command issues a warning, but the CORRESPONDENCE analysis is done correctly.
- The table cell values (the WEIGHT values) cannot be negative.

Table 1   3 x 3 table

		Anxiety		
		High	**Med**	**Low**
	First	48	27	22
Birth order	**Second**	33	20	39
	Other	29	42	47

HOMALS

```
HOMALS  VARIABLES=varlist(max)

 [/ANALYSIS=varlist]

 [/NOBSERVATIONS=value]

 [/DIMENSION={2**  }]

           {value}

 [/MAXITER={100**}]

         {value}

 [/CONVERGENCE={.00001**}]

             {value   }

 [/PRINT=[DEFAULT**] [FREQ**] [EIGEN**] [DISCRIM**]

    [QUANT**] [OBJECT] [HISTORY] [ALL] [NONE]]

 [/PLOT=[NDIM=({1, 2        }**)]

              {value, value}
              {ALL, MAX     }

    [QUANT**[(varlist)][(n)]] [OBJECT**[(varlist)][(n)]]

    [DEFAULT**[(n)]] [DISCRIM[(n)]] [ALL[(n)]] [NONE]]

 [/SAVE=[rootname] [(value)]]

 [/MATRIX=OUT({*   })]
             {file}
```

**Default if subcommand or keyword is omitted.

Example:

```
HOMALS  VARIABLES=ACOLA(2) BCOLA(2) CCOLA(2) DCOLA(2)
 /PRINT=FREQ EIGEN QUANT OBJECT.
```

Overview

HOMALS (*hom*ogeneity analysis by means of *a*lternating *l*east *s*quares) estimates category quantifications, object scores, and other associated statistics that separate categories (levels) of nominal variables as much as possible and divide cases into homogeneous subgroups.

Options

Data and Variable Selection. You can use a subset of the variables in the analysis and restrict the analysis to the first *n* observations.

197

Number of Dimensions. You can specify how many dimensions HOMALS should compute.

Iterations and Convergence. You can specify the maximum number of iterations and the value of a convergence criterion.

Display Output. The output can include all available statistics, just the default frequencies, eigenvalues, discrimination measures and category quantifications, or just the specific statistics you request. You can also control which statistics are plotted and specify the number of characters used in plot labels.

Saving Scores. You can save object scores in the working data file.

Writing Matrices. You can write a matrix data file containing category quantifications for use in further analyses.

Basic Specification

- The basic specification is HOMALS and the VARIABLES subcommand. By default, HOMALS analyzes all of the variables listed for all cases and computes two solutions. Frequencies, eigenvalues, discrimination measures, and category quantifications are displayed and category quantifications and object scores are plotted.

Subcommand Order

- Subcommands can appear in any order.

Syntax Rules

- If ANALYSIS is specified more than once, HOMALS is not executed. For all other subcommands, if a subcommand is specified more than once, only the last occurrence is executed.

Operations

- HOMALS treats every value in the range 1 to the maximum value specified on VARIABLES as a valid category. If the data are not sequential, the empty categories (categories with no valid data) are assigned zeros for all statistics. You may want to use RECODE or AUTORECODE before HOMALS to get rid of these empty categories and avoid the unnecessary output. (See the *SPSS Base Syntax Reference Guide* for more information on AUTORECODE and RECODE.)

Limitations

- String variables are not allowed; use AUTORECODE to recode string variables into numeric variables.
- The data (category values) must be positive integers. Zeros and negative values are treated as system-missing, which means that they are excluded from the analysis. Fractional values are truncated after the decimal and are included in the analysis. If one of the levels of a variable has been coded 0 or a negative value and you want to treat it as a valid category, use the AUTORECODE or RECODE command to recode the values of that variable.
- HOMALS ignores user-missing value specifications. Positive user-missing values less than the maximum value specified on the VARIABLES subcommand are treated as valid category values and are included in the analysis. If you do not want the category included, use COMPUTE or RECODE to change the value to something outside of the valid range. Values outside of the range (less than 1 or greater than the maximum value) are treated as system-missing and are excluded from the analysis.

Example

```
HOMALS  VARIABLES=ACOLA(2) BCOLA(2) CCOLA(2) DCOLA(2)
  /PRINT=FREQ EIGEN QUANT OBJECT.
```

- The four variables are analyzed using all available observations. Each variable has two categories, 1 and 2.
- The PRINT subcommand lists the frequencies, eigenvalues, category quantifications, and object scores.
- By default, plots of the category quantifications and the object scores are produced.

VARIABLES Subcommand

VARIABLES specifies the variables that will be used in the analysis.

- The VARIABLES subcommand is required. The actual word VARIABLES can be omitted.
- After each variable or variable list, specify in parentheses the maximum number of categories (levels) of the variables.
- The number specified in parentheses indicates the number of categories *and* the maximum category value. For example, *VAR1(3)* indicates that *VAR1* has three categories coded 1, 2, and 3. However, if a variable is not coded with consecutive integers, the number of categories used in the analysis will differ from the number of observed categories. For example, if a three-category variable is coded {2, 4, 6}, the maximum category value is 6. The analysis treats the variable as having six categories, three of which (categories 1, 3, and 5) are not observed and receive quantifications of 0.
- To avoid unnecessary output, use the AUTORECODE or RECODE command before HOMALS to recode a variable that does not have sequential values. (See the *SPSS Base Syntax Reference Guide* for more information on AUTORECODE and RECODE.)

Example

```
DATA LIST FREE/V1 V2 V3.
BEGIN DATA
3 1 1
6 1 1
3 1 3
3 2 2
3 2 2
6 2 2
6 1 3
6 2 2
3 2 2
6 2 1
END DATA.
AUTORECODE V1 /INTO NEWVAR1.
HOMALS VARIABLES=NEWVAR1 V2(2) V3(3).
```

- DATA LIST defines three variables, *V1*, *V2*, and *V3*.

- *V1* has two levels, coded 3 and 6, *V2* has two levels, coded 1 and 2, and *V3* has three levels, coded 1, 2, and 3.

- The AUTORECODE command creates *NEWVAR1* containing recoded values of *V1*. Values of 3 are recoded to 1; values of 6 are recoded to 2.

- The maximum category value for both *NEWVAR1* and *V2* is 2. A maximum value of 3 is specified for *V3*.

ANALYSIS Subcommand

ANALYSIS limits the analysis to a specific subset of the variables named on the VARIABLES subcommand.

- If ANALYSIS is not specified, all variables listed on the VARIABLES subcommand are used.

- ANALYSIS is followed by a variable list. The variables on the list must be specified on the VARIABLES subcommand.

- Variables listed on the VARIABLES subcommand but not on the ANALYSIS subcommand can still be used to label object scores on the PLOT subcommand.

Example

```
HOMALS VARIABLES=ACOLA(2) BCOLA(2) CCOLA(2) DCOLA(2)
  /ANALYSIS=ACOLA BCOLA
  /PRINT=OBJECT QUANT
  /PLOT=OBJECT(CCOLA).
```

- The VARIABLES subcommand specifies four variables.

- The ANALYSIS subcommand limits analysis to the first two variables. The PRINT subcommand lists the object scores and category quantifications from this analysis.

- The plot of the object scores is labeled with variable *CCOLA*, even though this variable is not included in the computations.

NOBSERVATIONS Subcommand

NOBSERVATIONS specifies how many cases are used in the analysis.

- If NOBSERVATIONS is not specified, all available observations in the working data file are used.
- NOBSERVATIONS is followed by an integer indicating that the first n cases are to be used.

DIMENSION Subcommand

DIMENSION specifies the number of dimensions you want HOMALS to compute.

- If you do not specify the DIMENSION subcommand, HOMALS computes two dimensions.
- The specification on DIMENSION is a positive integer indicating the number of dimensions.
- The minimum number of dimensions is 1.
- The maximum number of dimensions is equal to the smaller of the 2 values below:

    The total number of valid variable categories (levels) minus the number of variables without missing values.

    The number of observations minus 1.

MAXITER Subcommand

MAXITER specifies the maximum number of iterations HOMALS can go through in its computations.

- If MAXITER is not specified, HOMALS will iterate up to 100 times.
- The specification on MAXITER is a positive integer indicating the maximum number of iterations.

CONVERGENCE Subcommand

CONVERGENCE specifies a convergence criterion value. HOMALS stops iterating if the difference in total fit between the last two iterations is less than the CONVERGENCE value.

- If CONVERGENCE is not specified, the default value is 0.00001.
- The specification on CONVERGENCE is a positive value.

PRINT Subcommand

PRINT controls which statistics are included in your display output. The default display includes the frequencies, eigenvalues, discrimination measures, and category quantifications.

The following keywords are available:

FREQ   *Marginal frequencies for the variables in the analysis.*

HISTORY	*History of the iterations.*
EIGEN	*Eigenvalues.*
DISCRIM	*Discrimination measures for the variables in the analysis.*
OBJECT	*Object scores.*
QUANT	*Category quantifications for the variables in the analysis.*
DEFAULT	*FREQ, EIGEN, DISCRIM, and QUANT.* These statistics are also displayed when you omit the PRINT subcommand.
ALL	*All available statistics.*
NONE	*No statistics.*

PLOT Subcommand

PLOT can be used to produce plots of category quantifications, object scores, and discrimination measures.

- If PLOT is not specified, plots of the object scores and of the quantifications are produced.
- No plots are produced for a one-dimensional solution.

The following keywords can be specified on PLOT:

DISCRIM	*Plots of the discrimination measures.*
OBJECT	*Plots of the object scores.*
QUANT	*Plots of the category quantifications.*
DEFAULT	*QUANT and OBJECT.*
ALL	*All available plots.*
NONE	*No plots.*

- Keywords OBJECT and QUANT can each be followed by a variable list in parentheses to indicate that plots should be labeled with those variables. For QUANT, the labeling variables must be specified on both the VARIABLES and ANALYSIS subcommands. For OBJECT, the variables must be specified on the VARIABLES subcommand but need not appear on the ANALYSIS subcommand. This means that variables not used in the computations can be used to label OBJECT plots. If the variable list is omitted, the default object and quantification plots are produced.
- Object score plots labeled with variables which appear on the ANALYSIS subcommand use category labels corresponding to all categories within the defined range. Objects in a category which is outside the defined range are labeled with the label corresponding to the category immediately following the defined maximum category value.
- Object score plots labeled with variables not included on the ANALYSIS subcommand use all category labels, regardless of whether or not the category value is inside the defined range.

- All keywords except NONE can be followed by an integer value in parentheses to indicate how many characters of the variable or value label are to be used on the plot. (If you specify a variable list after OBJECT or QUANT, specify the value in parentheses after the list.) The value can range from 1 to 20; the default is to use twelve characters. Spaces between words count as characters.
- DISCRIM plots use variable labels; all other plots use value labels.
- If a variable label is not supplied, the variable name is used for that variable. If a value label is not supplied, the actual value is used.
- Variable and value labels should be unique.
- When points overlap, the points involved are described in a summary following the plot.

Example

```
HOMALS VARIABLES COLA1 (4) COLA2 (4) COLA3 (4) COLA4 (2)
 /ANALYSIS COLA1 COLA2 COLA3 COLA4
 /PLOT OBJECT(COLA4).
```

- Four variables are included in the analysis.
- OBJECT requests a plot of the object scores labeled with the values of *COLA4*. Any object whose *COLA4* value is not 1 or 2, is labeled 3 (or the value label for category 3, if supplied).

Example

```
HOMALS VARIABLES COLA1 (4) COLA2 (4) COLA3 (4) COLA4 (2)
 /ANALYSIS COLA1 COLA2 COLA3
 /PLOT OBJECT(COLA4).
```

- Three variables are included in the analysis.
- OBJECT requests a plot of the object scores labeled with the values of *COLA4*, a variable not included in the analysis. Objects are labeled using all values of *COLA4*.

In addition to the plot keywords, the following can be specified:

NDIM   *Dimension pairs to be plotted.* NDIM is followed by a pair of values in parentheses. If NDIM is not specified, plots are produced for dimension 1 versus dimension 2.

- The first value indicates the dimension that is plotted against all higher dimensions. This value can be any integer from 1 to the number of dimensions minus 1.
- The second value indicates the highest dimension to be used in plotting the dimension pairs. This value can be any integer from 2 to the number of dimensions.
- Keyword ALL can be used instead of the first value to indicate that all dimensions are paired with higher dimensions.
- Keyword MAX can be used instead of the second value to indicate that plots should be produced up to and including the highest dimension fit by the procedure.

Example

```
HOMALS COLA1 COLA2 COLA3 COLA4 (4)
 /PLOT NDIM(1,3) QUANT(5).
```

- The NDIM(1,3) specification indicates that plots should be produced for two dimension pairs—dimension 1 versus dimension 2 and dimension 1 versus dimension 3.
- QUANT requests plots of the category quantifications. The (5) specification indicates that the first five characters of the value labels are to be used on the plots.

Example

```
HOMALS COLA1 COLA2 COLA3 COLA4 (4)
 /PLOT NDIM(ALL,3) QUANT(5).
```

- This plot is the same as above except for the ALL specification following NDIM. This indicates that all possible pairs up to the second value should be plotted, so QUANT plots will be produced for dimension 1 versus dimension 2, dimension 2 versus dimension 3, and dimension 1 versus dimension 3.

SAVE Subcommand

SAVE lets you add variables containing the object scores computed by HOMALS to the working data file.

- If SAVE is not specified, object scores are not added to the working data file.
- A variable rootname can be specified on the SAVE subcommand to which HOMALS adds the number of the dimension. Only one rootname can be specified and it can contain up to six characters.
- If a rootname is not specified, unique variable names are automatically generated. The variable names are *HOMn_m*, where *n* is a dimension number and *m* is a set number. If three dimensions are saved, the first set of names is *HOM1_1*, *HOM2_1*, and *HOM3_1*. If another HOMALS is then run, the variable names for the second set are *HOM1_2*, *HOM2_2*, *HOM3_2*, and so on.
- Following the rootname, the number of dimensions for which you want to save object scores can be specified in parentheses. The number cannot exceed the value on the DIMENSION subcommand.
- If the number of dimensions is not specified, the SAVE subcommand saves object scores for all dimensions.
- If you replace the working data file by specifying an asterisk (*) on a MATRIX subcommand, the SAVE subcommand is not executed.

Example

```
HOMALS CAR1 CAR2 CAR3 CAR4(5)
 /DIMENSION=3
 /SAVE=DIM(2).
```

- Four variables, each with five categories, are analyzed.
- The DIMENSION subcommand specifies that results for three dimensions will be computed.
- SAVE adds the object scores from the first two dimensions to the working data file. The names of these new variables will be *DIM00001* and *DIM00002*, respectively.

MATRIX Subcommand

The MATRIX subcommand is used to write category quantifications to a matrix data file.

- The specification on MATRIX is keyword OUT and a file enclosed in parentheses.
- You can specify the file with either an asterisk (*), to indicate that the working data file is to be replaced, or with the name of an external file.
- The matrix data file has one case for each value of each original variable.

The variables of the matrix data file and their values are:

ROWTYPE_   *String variable containing value QUANT for all cases.*

LEVEL   *String variable LEVEL containing the values (or value labels if present) of each original variable.*

VARNAME_   *String variable containing the original variable names.*

DIM1...DIMn   *Numeric variable containing the category quantifications for each dimension.* Each variable is labeled *DIMn*, where *n* represents the dimension number.

See the *SPSS Base Syntax Reference Guide* for more information on matrix data files.

OVERALS

```
OVERALS VARIABLES=varlist (max)

/ANALYSIS=varlist[({ORDI**})]

              {SNOM }
              {MNOM }
              {NUME }

 /SETS= n (# of vars in set 1, ..., # of vars in set n)

[/NOBSERVATIONS=value]

[/DIMENSION={2** }]
            {value}

[/INITIAL={NUMERICAL**}]

          {RANDOM }

[/MAXITER={100**}]

         {value}

[/CONVERGENCE={.00001**}]

             {value }

[/PRINT=[DEFAULT] [FREQ**] [QUANT] [CENTROID**]
        [HISTORY] [WEIGHTS**]
        [OBJECT] [FIT] [NONE]]

[/PLOT=[NDIM=({1,2 }**)]

             {value, value}
             {ALL, MAX }

   [DEFAULT[(n)]] [OBJECT**[(varlist)][(n)]]

   [QUANT[(varlist)][(n)]] [LOADINGS**[(n)]]

   [TRANS[(varlist)]]Æ[CENTROID[(varlist)][(n)]]
   [NONE]]

[/SAVE=[rootname][(value)]]

[/MATRIX=OUT({* })]
          {file}
```

**Default if subcommand or keyword is omitted.

Example:

```
OVERALS VARIABLES=PRETEST1 PRETEST2 POSTEST1 POSTEST2(20)
               SES(5) SCHOOL(3)
 /ANALYSIS=PRETEST1 TO POSTEST2 (NUME) SES (ORDI) SCHOOL (SNOM)
 /SETS=3(2,2,2)
 /PRINT=OBJECT FIT
 /PLOT=QUANT(PRETEST1 TO SCHOOL).
```

Overview

OVERALS performs nonlinear canonical correlation analysis on two or more sets of variables. Variables can have different optimal scaling levels, and no assumptions are made about the distribution of the variables or the linearity of the relationships.

Options

Optimal Scaling Levels. You can specify the level of optimal scaling at which you want to analyze each variable.

Number of Dimensions. You can specify how many dimensions OVERALS should compute.

Iterations and Convergence. You can specify the maximum number of iterations and the value of a convergence criterion.

Display Output. The output can include all available statistics, just the default statistics, or just the specific statistics you request. You can also control whether some of these statistics are plotted.

Saving Scores. You can save object scores in the working data file.

Writing Matrices. You can write a matrix data file containing quantification scores, centroids, weights, and loadings for use in further analyses.

Basic Specification

- The basic specification is command OVERALS, the VARIABLES subcommand, the ANALYSIS subcommand, and the SETS subcommand. By default, OVERALS estimates a two-dimensional solution and displays a table listing optimal scaling levels of each variable by set, eigenvalues and loss values by set, marginal frequencies, centroids and weights for all variables, and plots of the object scores and component loadings.

Subcommand Order

- The VARIABLES subcommand, ANALYSIS subcommand, and SETS subcommand must appear in that order before all other subcommands.
- Other subcommands can appear in any order.

Operations

- If the ANALYSIS subcommand is specified more than once, OVERALS is not executed. For all other subcommands, if a subcommand is specified more than once, only the last occurrence is executed.
- OVERALS treats every value in the range 1 to the maximum value specified on VARIABLES as a valid category. To avoid unnecessary output, use the AUTORECODE or RECODE command to recode a categorical variable with nonsequential values or with a large number of categories.

For variables treated as numeric, recoding is not recommended because the characteristic of equal intervals in the data will not be maintained. (See the *SPSS Base Syntax Reference Guide* for more information on AUTORECODE and RECODE.)

Limitations

- String variables are not allowed; use AUTORECODE to recode nominal string variables.
- The data must be positive integers. Zeros and negative values are treated as system-missing, which means that they are excluded from the analysis. Fractional values are truncated after the decimal and are included in the analysis. If one of the levels of a categorical variable has been coded 0 or some negative value and you want to treat it as a valid category, use the AUTORECODE or RECODE command to recode the values of that variable.
- OVERALS ignores user-missing value specifications. Positive user-missing values less than the maximum value specified on the VARIABLES subcommand are treated as valid category values and are included in the analysis. If you do not want the category included, use COMPUTE or RECODE to change the value to something outside of the valid range. Values outside of the range (less than 1 or greater than the maximum value) are treated as system-missing and are excluded from the analysis.
- If one variable in a set has missing data, all variables in that set are missing for that object (case).
- Each set must have at least three valid (non-missing, non-empty) cases.

Example

```
OVERALS VARIABLES=PRETEST1 PRETEST2 POSTEST1 POSTEST2(20)
              SES(5) SCHOOL(3)
 /ANALYSIS=PRETEST1 TO POSTEST2 (NUME) SES (ORDI) SCHOOL (SNOM)
 /SETS=3(2,2,2)
 /PRINT=OBJECT FIT
 /PLOT=QUANT(PRETEST1 TO SCHOOL).
```

- VARIABLES defines the variables and their maximum values.
- ANALYSIS specifies that all of the variables from *PRETEST1* to *POSTEST2* are to be analyzed at the numerical level of optimal scaling, *SES* at the ordinal level, and *SCHOOL* as a single nominal. These are all of the variables that will be used in the analysis.
- SETS specifies that there are three sets of variables to be analyzed and two variables in each set.
- PRINT lists the object and fit scores.
- PLOT plots the single- and multiple-category coordinates of all of the variables in the analysis.

VARIABLES Subcommand

VARIABLES specifies all of the variables in the current OVERALS procedure.

- The VARIABLES subcommand is required and precedes all other subcommands. The actual word VARIABLES can be omitted.
- Each variable or variable list is followed by the maximum value in parentheses.

ANALYSIS Subcommand

ANALYSIS specifies the variables to be used in the analysis and the optimal scaling level at which each variable is to be analyzed.

- The ANALYSIS subcommand is required and follows the VARIABLES subcommand.
- The specification on ANALYSIS is a variable list and an optional keyword in parentheses indicating the level of optimal scaling.
- The variables on ANALYSIS must also be specified on the VARIABLES subcommand.
- Only active variables are listed on the ANALYSIS subcommand. **Active variables** are those used in the computation of the solution. **Passive variables**, those listed on the VARIABLES subcommand but not on the ANALYSIS subcommand, are ignored in the OVERALS solution. Object score plots can still be labeled by passive variables.

The following keywords can be specified to indicate the optimal scaling level:

MNOM *Multiple nominal.* The quantifications can be different for each dimension. When all variables are multiple nominal and there is only one variable in each set, OVERALS gives the same results as HOMALS.

SNOM *Single nominal.* OVERALS gives only one quantification for each category. Objects in the same category (cases with the same value on a variable) obtain the same quantification. When all variables are SNOM, ORDI, or NUME, and there is only one variable per set, OVERALS will give the same results as PRINCALS.

ORDI *Ordinal.* This is the default for variables listed without optimal scaling levels. The order of the categories of the observed variable is preserved in the quantified variable.

NUME *Numerical.* Interval or ratio scaling level. OVERALS assumes that the observed variable already has numerical values for its categories. When all variables are quantified at the numerical level and there is only one variable per set, the OVERALS analysis is analogous to classical principal components analysis.

These keywords can apply to a variable list as well as to a single variable. Thus, the default ORDI is not applied to a variable without a keyword if a subsequent variable on the list has a keyword.

SETS Subcommand

SETS specifies how many sets of variables there are and how many variables are in each set.

- SETS is required and must follow the ANALYSIS subcommand.
- SETS is followed by an integer to indicate the number of variable sets. Following this integer is a list of values in parentheses indicating the number of variables in each set.
- There must be at least two sets.

- The sum of the values in parentheses must equal the number of variables specified on the ANALYSIS subcommand. The variables in each set are read consecutively from the ANALYSIS subcommand.

For example,

/SETS=2(2,3)

indicates that there are two sets. The first two variables named on ANALYSIS are the first set, and the last three variables named on ANALYSIS are the second set.

NOBSERVATIONS Subcommand

NOBSERVATIONS specifies how many cases are used in the analysis.

- If NOBSERVATIONS is not specified, all available observations in the working data file are used.
- NOBSERVATIONS is followed by an integer, indicating that the first n cases are to be used.

DIMENSION Subcommand

DIMENSION specifies the number of dimensions you want OVERALS to compute.

- If you do not specify the DIMENSION subcommand, OVERALS computes two dimensions.
- DIMENSION is followed by an integer indicating the number of dimensions.
- If all the variables are SNOM (single nominal), ORDI (ordinal), or NUME (numerical), the maximum number of dimensions you can specify is the total number of variables on the ANALYSIS subcommand.
- If some or all of the variables are MNOM (multiple nominal), the maximum number of dimensions you can specify is the number of MNOM variable levels (categories) plus the number of non-MNOM variables, minus the number of MNOM variables.
- The maximum number of dimensions must be less than the number of observations minus 1.
- If the number of sets is two and all variables are SNOM, ORDI, or NUME, the number of dimensions should not be more than the number of variables in the smaller set.
- If the specified value is too large, OVERALS tries to adjust the number of dimensions to the allowable maximum. It might not be able to adjust if there are MNOM variables with missing data.

INITIAL Subcommand

The INITIAL subcommand specifies the method used to compute the initial configuration.

- The specification on INITIAL is keyword NUMERICAL or RANDOM. If the INITIAL subcommand is not specified, NUMERICAL is the default.

NUMERICAL   *Treat all variables except multiple nominal as numerical.* This is usually best to use when there are no SNOM variables.

      RANDOM   *Compute a random initial configuration.* This should be used only when some or all of the variables are SNOM.

MAXITER Subcommand

MAXITER specifies the maximum number of iterations OVERALS can go through in its computations.

- If MAXITER is not specified, OVERALS will iterate up to 100 times.
- The specification on MAXITER is an integer indicating the maximum number of iterations.

CONVERGENCE Subcommand

CONVERGENCE specifies a convergence criterion value. OVERALS stops iterating if the difference in fit between the last two iterations is less than the CONVERGENCE value.

- If CONVERGENCE is not specified, the CONVERGENCE value is 0.00001.
- The specification on CONVERGENCE is any value greater than 0.000001. (Values less than this might seriously affect performance.)

PRINT Subcommand

PRINT controls which statistics are included in your display output. The default output includes a table listing optimal scaling levels of each variable by set, eigenvalues and loss values by set by dimension, and the output produced by keywords FREQ, CENTROID, and WEIGHTS.

The following keywords are available:

FREQ	*Marginal frequencies for the variables in the analysis.*
HISTORY	*History of the iterations.*
FIT	*Multiple fit, single fit, and single loss per variable.*
CENTROID	*Category quantification scores, the projected centroids, and the centroids.*
OBJECT	*Object scores.*
QUANT	*Category quantifications and the single and multiple coordinates.*
WEIGHTS	*Weights and component loadings.*
DEFAULT	*FREQ, CENTROID, and WEIGHTS.*
NONE	*Summary loss statistics.*

PLOT Subcommand

PLOT can be used to produce plots of transformations, object scores, coordinates, centroids, and component loadings.

- If PLOT is not specified, plots of the object scores and component loadings are produced.

The following keywords can be specified on PLOT:

LOADINGS   *Plot of the component loadings.*

OBJECT   *Plot of the object scores.*

TRANS   *Plot of category quantifications.*

QUANT   *Plot of all category coordinates.*

CENTROID   *Plot of all category centroids.*

DEFAULT   *OBJECT and LOADINGS.*

NONE   *No plots.*

- Keywords OBJECT, QUANT, and CENTROID can each be followed by a variable list in parentheses to indicate that plots should be labeled with these variables. For QUANT and CENTROID, the variables must be specified on both the VARIABLES and the ANALYSIS subcommands. For OBJECT, the variables must be specified on VARIABLES but need not appear on ANALYSIS. This means that variables not used in the computations can still be used to label OBJECT plots. If the variable list is omitted, the default plots are produced.
- Object score plots use category labels corresponding to all categories within the defined range. Objects in a category which is outside the defined range are labeled with the label corresponding to the category immediately following the defined maximum category.
- If TRANS is followed by a variable list, only plots for those variables are produced. If a variable list is not specified, plots are produced for each variable.
- All of the keywords except NONE can be followed by an integer in parentheses to indicate how many characters of the variable or value label are to be used on the plot. (If you specified a variable list after OBJECT, CENTROID, TRANS, or QUANT, you can specify the value in parentheses after the list.) The value can range from 1 to 20. If the value is omitted, twelve characters are used. Spaces between words count as characters.
- If a variable label is missing, the variable name is used for that variable. If a value label is missing, the actual value is used.
- You should make sure that your variable and value labels are unique by at least one letter in order to distinguish them on the plots.
- When points overlap, the points involved are described in a summary following the plot.

In addition to the plot keywords, the following can be specified:

NDIM   *Dimension pairs to be plotted.* NDIM is followed by a pair of values in parentheses. If NDIM is not specified, plots are produced for dimension 1 versus dimension 2.

- The first value indicates the dimension that is plotted against all higher dimensions. This value can be any integer from 1 to the number of dimensions minus 1.
- The second value indicates the highest dimension to be used in plotting the dimension pairs. This value can be any integer from 2 to the number of dimensions.
- Keyword ALL can be used instead of the first value to indicate that all dimensions are paired with higher dimensions.
- Keyword MAX can be used instead of the second value to indicate that plots should be produced up to and including the highest dimension fit by the procedure.

Example

```
OVERALS COLA1 COLA2 JUICE1 JUICE2 (4)
 /ANALYSIS=COLA1 COLA2 JUICE1 JUICE2 (SNOM)
 /SETS=2(2,2)
 /PLOT NDIM(1,3) QUANT(5).
```

- The NDIM(1,3) specification indicates that plots should be produced for two dimension pairs—dimension 1 versus dimension 2 and dimension 1 versus dimension 3.
- QUANT requests plots of the category quantifications. The (5) specification indicates that the first five characters of the value labels are to be used on the plots.

Example

```
OVERALS COLA1 COLA2 JUICE1 JUICE2 (4)
 /ANALYSIS=COLA1 COLA2 JUICE1 JUICE2 (SNOM)
 /SETS=2(2,2)
 /PLOT NDIM(ALL,3) QUANT(5).
```

- This plot is the same as above except for the ALL specification following NDIM. This indicates that all possible pairs up to the second value should be plotted, so QUANT plots will be produced for dimension 1 versus dimension 2, dimension 2 versus dimension 3, and dimension 1 versus dimension 3.

SAVE Subcommand

SAVE lets you add variables containing the object scores computed by OVERALS to the working data file.

- If SAVE is not specified, object scores are not added to the working data file.
- A variable rootname can be specified on the SAVE subcommand to which OVERALS adds the number of the dimension. Only one rootname can be specified and it can contain up to six characters.
- If a rootname is not specified, unique variable names are automatically generated. The variable names are *OVEn_m*, where n is a dimension number and m is a set number. If three dimensions are saved, the first set of names are *OVE1_1*, *OVE2_1*, and *OVE3_1*. If another OVERALS is then run, the variable names for the second set are *OVE1_2*, *OVE2_2*, *OVE3_2*, and so on.
- Following the name, the number of dimensions for which you want object scores saved can be listed in parentheses. The number cannot exceed the value of the DIMENSION subcommand.

- The prefix should be unique for each OVERALS command in the same session. If it is not, OVERALS replaces the prefix with *DIM*, *OBJ*, or *OBSAVE*. If all of these already exist, SAVE is not executed.
- If the number of dimensions is not specified, the SAVE subcommand saves object scores for all dimensions.
- If you replace the working data file by specifying an asterisk (*) on a MATRIX subcommand, the SAVE subcommand is not executed.

Example

```
OVERALS CAR1 CAR2 CAR3(5) PRICE (10)
 /SET=2(3,1)
 /ANALYSIS=CAR1 TO CAR3(SNOM) PRICE(NUME)
 /DIMENSIONS=3
 /SAVE=DIM(2).
```

- Three single nominal variables, *CAR1*, *CAR2*, and *CAR3*, each with 5 categories, and one numerical level variable, with 10 categories, are analyzed.
- The DIMENSIONS subcommand requests results for three dimensions.
- SAVE adds the object scores from the first two dimensions to the working data file. The names of these new variables will be *DIM00001* and *DIM00002*, respectively.

MATRIX Subcommand

The MATRIX subcommand is used to write category quantifications, coordinates, centroids, weights, and component loadings to a matrix data file.

- The specification on MATRIX is keyword OUT and a file enclosed in parentheses.
- You can specify the file with either an asterisk (*), to indicate that the working data file is to be replaced, or with the name of an external file.
- All values are written to the same file.
- The matrix data file has one case for each value of each original variable.

The variables of the matrix data file and their values are:

ROWTYPE_   *String variable containing value QUANT for the category quantifications, SCOOR_ for the single-category coordinates, MCOOR_ for multiple-category coordinates, CENTRO_ for centroids, PCENTRO_ for projected centroids, WEIGHT_ for weights, and LOADING_ for the component scores.*

LEVEL   *String variable containing the values (or value labels if present) of each original variable for category quantifications. For cases with ROWTYPE_=LOADING_ or WEIGHT_, the value of LEVEL is blank.*

VARNAME_   *String variable containing the original variable names.*

VARTYPE_   *String variable containing values MULTIPLE, SINGLE N, ORDINAL, or NUMERICAL, depending on the level of optimal scaling specified for the variable.*

SET_   *The set number of the original variable.*

DIM1...DIMn   *Numeric variables containing the category quantifications, the single-category coordinates, multiple-category coordinates, weights, centroids, projected centroids, and component loadings for each dimension.* Each one of these variables is labeled *DIMn*, where *n* represents the dimension number. If any of these values cannot be computed, they are assigned 0 in the file.

See the *SPSS Base Syntax Reference Guide* for more information on matrix data files.

PRINCALS

```
PRINCALS VARIABLES=varlist(max)

[/ANALYSIS=varlist[({ORDI**})]]

                      {SNOM }
                      {MNOM }
                      {NUME }

[/NOBSERVATIONS=value]

[/DIMENSION={2** }]

            {value}

[/MAXITER={100**}]

            {value}

[/CONVERGENCE={.00001**}]

              {value }

[/PRINT=[DEFAULT] [FREQ**] [EIGEN**] [LOADINGS**] [QUANT]

         [HISTORY] [CORRELATION] [OBJECT] [ALL] [NONE]]

[/PLOT=[NDIM=({ 1, 2 }**)]

            {value, value}
            { ALL, MAX }

         [DEFAULT[(n)]] [OBJECT**[(varlist)][(n)]]

         [QUANT**[(varlist)][(n)]] [LOADINGS[(n)]]

         [ALL[(n)]] [NONE]]

[/SAVE=[rootname] [(value)]]

[/MATRIX=OUT({ * })]
             {file}
```

**Default if subcommand or keyword is omitted.

Example:

```
PRINCALS VARIABLES=ACOLA BCOLA(2) PRICEA PRICEB(5)
/ANALYSIS=ACOLA BCOLA(SNOM) PRICEA PRICEB(NUME)
/PRINT=EIGEN QUANT OBJECT.
```

Overview

PRINCALS (*prin*cipal *c*omponents analysis by means of *a*lternating *l*east *s*quares) analyzes a set of variables for major dimensions of variation. The variables can be of mixed optimal scaling levels, and the relationships among observed variables are not assumed to be linear.

Options

Optimal Scaling Level. You can specify the optimal scaling level for each variable to be used in the analysis.

Number of Cases. You can restrict the analysis to the first n observations.

Number of Dimensions. You can specify how many dimensions PRINCALS should compute.

Iterations and Convergence. You can specify the maximum number of iterations and the value of a convergence criterion.

Display Output. The output can include all available statistics, just the default statistics, or just the specific statistics you request. You can also control whether some of these statistics are plotted.

Saving Scores. You can save object scores in the working data file.

Writing Matrices. You can write a matrix data file containing category quantifications and loadings for use in further analyses.

Basic Specification

- The basic specification is command PRINCALS and the VARIABLES subcommand. PRINCALS performs the analysis assuming an ordinal level of optimal scaling for all variables and uses all cases to compute a two-dimensional solution. By default, marginal frequencies, eigenvalues, and summary measures of fit and loss are displayed, and quantifications and object scores are plotted.

Subcommand Order

- The VARIABLES subcommand must precede all others.
- Other subcommands can appear in any order.

Operations

- If the ANALYSIS subcommand is specified more than once, PRINCALS is not executed. For all other subcommands, only the last occurrence of each subcommand is executed.
- PRINCALS treats every value in the range 1 to the maximum value specified on VARIABLES as a valid category. Use the AUTORECODE or RECODE command if you want to recode a categorical variable with nonsequential values or with a large number of categories to avoid unnecessary output. For variables treated as numeric, recoding is *not* recommended because the intervals between consecutive categories will not be maintained.

Limitations

- String variables are not allowed; use AUTORECODE to recode nominal string variables into numeric ones before using PRINCALS.

- The data must be positive integers. Zeros and negative values are treated as system-missing and are excluded from the analysis. Fractional values are truncated after the decimal and are included in the analysis. If one of the levels of a categorical variable has been coded 0 or some negative value and you want to treat it as a valid category, use the AUTORECODE or RECODE command to recode the values of that variable. (See the *SPSS Base Syntax Reference Guide* for more information on AUTORECODE and RECODE.)

- PRINCALS ignores user-missing value specifications. Positive user-missing values less than the maximum value on the VARIABLES subcommand are treated as valid category values and are included in the analysis. If you do not want the category included, you can use COMPUTE or RECODE to change the value to something outside of the valid range. Values outside of the range (less than 1 or greater than the maximum value) are treated as system-missing.

Example

```
PRINCALS VARIABLES=ACOLA BCOLA(2) PRICEA PRICEB(5)
 /ANALYSIS=ACOLA BCOLA(SNOM) PRICEA PRICEB(NUME)
 /PRINT=QUANT OBJECT.
```

- VARIABLES defines the variables and their maximum number of levels.

- The ANALYSIS subcommand specifies that variables *ACOLA* and *BCOLA* are single nominal (SNOM) and that variables *PRICEA* and *PRICEB* are numeric (NUME).

- The PRINT subcommand lists the category quantifications and object scores.

- By default, plots of the category quantifications and the object scores are produced.

VARIABLES Subcommand

VARIABLES specifies all of the variables that will be used in the current PRINCALS procedure.

- The VARIABLES subcommand is required and precedes all other subcommands. The actual word VARIABLES can be omitted.

- Each variable or variable list is followed by the maximum number of categories (levels) in parentheses.

- The number specified in parentheses indicates the number of categories *and* the maximum category value. For example, *VAR1(3)* indicates that *VAR1* has three categories coded 1, 2, and 3. However, if a variable is not coded with consecutive integers, the number of categories used in the analysis will differ from the number of observed categories. For example, if a three category variable is coded {2, 4, 6}, the maximum category value is 6. The analysis treats the variable as having six categories, three of which are not observed and receive quantifications of 0.

- To avoid unnecessary output, use the AUTORECODE or RECODE command before PRINCALS to recode a categorical variable that was coded with nonsequential values.

As noted in "Limitations" above, recoding is *not* recommended with variables treated as numeric. (See the *SPSS Base Syntax Reference Guide* for more information on AUTORECODE and RECODE.)

Example

```
DATA LIST FREE/V1 V2 V3.
BEGIN DATA
3 1 1
6 1 1
3 1 3
3 2 2
3 2 2
6 2 2
6 1 3
6 2 2
3 2 2
6 2 1
END DATA.
AUTORECODE V1 /INTO NEWVAR1.
PRINCALS VARIABLES=NEWVAR1 V2(2) V3(3).
```

- DATA LIST defines three variables, *V1*, *V2*, and *V3*.
- *V1* has two levels, coded 3 and 6, *V2* has two levels, coded 1 and 2, and *V3* has three levels, coded 1, 2, and 3.
- The AUTORECODE command creates *NEWVAR1* containing recoded values of *V1*. Values of 3 are recoded to 1 and values of 6 are recoded to 2.
- A maximum value of 2 can then be specified on the PRINCALS VARIABLES subcommand as the maximum category value for both *NEWVAR1* and *V2*. A maximum value of 3 is specified for *V3*.

ANALYSIS Subcommand

ANALYSIS specifies the variables to be used in the computations and the optimal scaling level used by PRINCALS to quantify each variable or variable list.

- If ANALYSIS is not specified, an ordinal level of optimal scaling is assumed for all variables.
- The specification on ANALYSIS is a variable list and an optional keyword in parentheses to indicate the optimal scaling level.
- The variables on the variable list must also be specified on the VARIABLES subcommand.
- Variables listed on the VARIABLES subcommand but not on the ANALYSIS subcommand can still be used to label object scores on the PLOT subcommand.

The following keywords can be specified to indicate the optimal scaling level:

MNOM   *Multiple nominal*. The quantifications can be different for each dimension. When all variables are multiple nominal, PRINCALS gives the same results as HOMALS.

SNOM   *Single nominal*. PRINCALS gives only one quantification for each category. Objects in the same category (cases with the same value on a variable) obtain the same quantification. When DIMENSION=1 and all variables are SNOM, this solution is the same as that of the first HOMALS dimension.

ORDI   *Ordinal*. This is the default for variables listed without optimal scaling levels and for all variables if the ANALYSIS subcommand is not used. The order of the categories of the observed variable is preserved in the quantified variable.

NUME   *Numerical*. Interval or ratio level of optimal scaling. PRINCALS assumes that the observed variable already has numerical values for its categories. When all variables are at the numerical level, the PRINCALS analysis is analogous to classical principal components analysis.

These keywords can apply to a variable list as well as to a single variable. Thus, the default ORDI is not applied to a variable without a keyword if a subsequent variable on the list has a keyword.

NOBSERVATIONS Subcommand

NOBSERVATIONS specifies how many cases are used in the analysis.

- If NOBSERVATIONS is not specified, all available observations in the working data file are used.
- NOBSERVATIONS is followed by an integer indicating that the first *n* cases are to be used.

DIMENSION Subcommand

DIMENSION specifies the number of dimensions you want PRINCALS to compute.

- If you do not specify the DIMENSION subcommand, PRINCALS computes two dimensions.
- DIMENSION is followed by an integer indicating the number of dimensions.
- If all of the variables are SNOM (single nominal), ORDI (ordinal), or NUME (numerical), the maximum number of dimensions you can specify is the smaller of the number of observations minus 1 *or* the total number of variables.
- If some or all of the variables are MNOM (multiple nominal), the maximum number of dimensions is the smaller of the number of observations minus 1 *or* the total number of valid MNOM variable levels (categories) plus the number of SNOM, ORDI, and NUME variables, minus the number of MNOM variables without missing values.
- PRINCALS adjusts the number of dimensions to the maximum if the specified value is too large.
- The minimum number of dimensions is 1.

MAXITER Subcommand

MAXITER specifies the maximum number of iterations PRINCALS can go through in its computations.

- If MAXITER is not specified, PRINCALS will iterate up to 100 times.
- MAXITER is followed by an integer indicating the maximum number of iterations allowed.

CONVERGENCE Subcommand

CONVERGENCE specifies a convergence criterion value. PRINCALS stops iterating if the difference in total fit between the last two iterations is less than the CONVERGENCE value.

- If CONVERGENCE is not specified, the default value is 0.00001.
- The specification on CONVERGENCE is a convergence criteria value.

PRINT Subcommand

PRINT controls which statistics are included in your output. The default output includes frequencies, eigenvalues, loadings, and summary measures of fit and loss.

PRINT is followed by one or more of the following keywords:

FREQ	*Marginal frequencies for the variables in the analysis.*
HISTORY	*History of the iterations.*
EIGEN	*Eigenvalues.*
CORRELATION	*Correlation matrix for the transformed variables in the analysis.* No correlation matrix is produced if there are any missing data.
OBJECT	*Object scores.*
QUANT	*Category quantifications and category coordinates for SNOM, ORDI, and NUME variables, and category quantifications in each dimension for MNOM variables.*
LOADINGS	*Component loadings for SNOM, ORDI, and NUME variables.*
DEFAULT	*FREQ, EIGEN, LOADINGS, and QUANT.*
ALL	*All of the available statistics.*
NONE	*Summary measures of fit.*

PLOT Subcommand

PLOT can be used to produce plots of category quantifications, object scores, and component loadings.

- If PLOT is not specified, plots of the object scores and of the quantifications are produced.
- No plots are produced for a one-dimensional solution.

PLOT is followed by one or more of the following keywords:

LOADINGS	*Plots of the component loadings of SNOM, ORDI, and NUME variables.*
OBJECT	*Plots of the object scores.*
QUANT	*Plots of the category quantifications for MNOM variables, and plots of the single-category coordinates for SNOM, ORDI, and NUME variables.*

DEFAULT   *QUANT and OBJECT.*

ALL   *All available plots.*

NONE   *No plots.*

- Keywords OBJECT and QUANT can each be followed by a variable list in parentheses to indicate that plots should be labeled with these variables. For QUANT, the variables must be specified on both the VARIABLES and ANALYSIS subcommands. For OBJECT, the variables must be specified on VARIABLES, but need not appear on the on ANALYSIS subcommand. This means that variables not included in the computations can still be used to label OBJECT plots. If the variable list is omitted, only the default plots are produced.

- Object score plots labeled with variables which appear on the ANALYSIS subcommand use category labels corresponding to all categories within the defined range. Objects in a category which is outside the defined range are labeled with the label corresponding to the next category greater than the defined maximum category.

- Object score plots labeled with variables not included on the ANALYSIS subcommand use all category labels, regardless of whether or not the category value is inside the defined range.

- All of the keywords except NONE can be followed by an integer in parentheses to indicate how many characters of the variable or value label are to be used on the plot. (If you specify a variable list after OBJECT or QUANT, you can specify the value in parentheses after the list.) The value can range from 1 to 20. If the value is omitted, twelve characters are used. Spaces between words count as characters.

- The LOADINGS plots and one of the QUANT plots use variable labels; all other plots that use labels use value labels.

- If a variable label is missing, the variable name is used for that variable. If a value label is missing, the actual value is used.

- You should make sure that your variable and value labels are unique by at least one letter in order to distinguish them on the plots.

- When points overlap, the points involved are described in a summary following the plot.

Example

```
PRINCALS VARIABLES COLA1 (4) COLA2 (4) COLA3 (4) COLA4 (2)
 /ANALYSIS COLA1 COLA2 (SNOM) COLA3 (ORDI) COLA4 (ORDI)
 /PLOT OBJECT(COLA4).
```

- Four variables are included in the analysis.
- OBJECT requests a plot of the object scores labeled with the values of *COLA4*. Any object whose *COLA4* value is not 1 or 2, is labeled 3 (or the value label for category 3, if defined).

Example

```
PRINCALS VARIABLES COLA1 (4) COLA2 (4) COLA3 (4) COLA4 (2)
 /ANALYSIS COLA1 COLA2 (SNOM) COLA3 (ORDI)
 /PLOT OBJECT(COLA4).
```

- Three variables are included in the analysis.

- OBJECT requests a plot of the object scores labeled with the values of *COLA4*, a variable not included in the analysis. Objects are labeled using all values of *COLA4*.

In addition to the plot keywords, the following can be specified:

NDIM   *Dimension pairs to be plotted.* NDIM is followed by a pair of values in parentheses. If NDIM is not specified, plots are produced for dimension 1 versus dimension 2.

- The first value indicates the dimension that is plotted against all higher dimensions. This value can be any integer from 1 to the number of dimensions minus 1.
- The second value indicates the highest dimension to be used in plotting the dimension pairs. This value can be any integer from 2 to the number of dimensions.
- Keyword ALL can be used instead of the first value to indicate that all dimensions are paired with higher dimensions.
- Keyword MAX can be used instead of the second value to indicate that plots should be produced up to and including the highest dimension fit by the procedure.

Example

```
PRINCALS COLA1 COLA2 COLA3 COLA4 (4)
 /PLOT NDIM(1,3) QUANT(5).
```

- The NDIM(1,3) specification indicates that plots should be produced for two dimension pairs—dimension 1 versus dimension 2 and dimension 1 versus dimension 3.
- QUANT requests plots of the category quantifications. The (5) specification indicates that the first five characters of the value labels are to be used on the plots.

Example

```
PRINCALS COLA1 COLA2 COLA3 COLA4 (4)
 /PLOT NDIM(ALL,3) QUANT(5).
```

- This plot is the same as above except for the ALL specification following NDIM. This indicates that all possible pairs up to the second value should be plotted, so QUANT plots will be produced for dimension 1 versus dimension 2, dimension 2 versus dimension 3, and dimension 1 versus dimension 3.

SAVE Subcommand

SAVE lets you add variables containing the object scores computed by PRINCALS to the working data file.

- If SAVE is not specified, object scores are not added to the working data file.
- A variable rootname can be specified on the SAVE subcommand to which PRINCALS adds the number of the dimension. Only one rootname can be specified, and it can contain up to six characters.
- If a rootname is not specified, unique variable names are automatically generated. The variable names are *PRIn_m*, where *n* is a dimension number and *m* is a set number. If three dimensions are saved, the first set of names is *PRI1_1*, *PRI2_1*, and *PRI3_1*. If another PRINCALS is then run, the variable names for the second set are *PRI1_2*, *PRI2_2*, *PRI3_2*, and so on.

- Following the name, the number of dimensions for which you want to save object scores can be listed in parentheses. The number cannot exceed the value of the DIMENSION subcommand.
- If the number of dimensions is not specified, the SAVE subcommand saves object scores for all dimensions.
- If you replace the working data file by specifying an asterisk (*) on a MATRIX subcommand, the SAVE subcommand is not executed.
- The prefix should be unique for each PRINCALS command in the same session. If it is not, PRINCALS replaces the prefix with *DIM*, *OBJ*, or *OBSAVE*. If all of these already exist, SAVE is not executed.

Example

```
PRINCALS CAR1 CAR2 CAR3(5) PRICE (10)
/ANALYSIS=CAR1 TO CAR3(SNOM) PRICE(NUM)
/DIMENSIONS=3
/SAVE=DIM(2).
```

- Three nominal variables, *CAR1*, *CAR2*, and *CAR3*, each with 5 categories, and one numerical (interval level) variable, with 10 categories, are analyzed in this PRINCALS example.
- The DIMENSIONS subcommand requests results for three dimensions.
- SAVE adds the object scores from the first two dimensions to the working data file. The names of these new variables will be *DIM00001* and *DIM00002*, respectively.

MATRIX Subcommand

The MATRIX subcommand is used to write category quantifications, single-category coordinates, and component loadings to a matrix data file.

- The specification on MATRIX is keyword OUT and the file enclosed in parentheses.
- You can specify the file with either an asterisk (*), to indicate that the working data file is to be replaced, or with the name of an external file.
- The category quantifications, coordinates, and component loadings are written to the same file.
- The matrix data file has one case for each value of each original variable.

The variables of the matrix data file and their values are:

ROWTYPE_	*String variable rowtype_ containing value QUANT for the category quantifications, SCOOR_ for single-category coordinates, MCOOR_ for multiple-category coordinates, and LOADING_ for the component scores.*
LEVEL	*String variable containing the values (or value labels if present) of each original variable for category quantifications.* For cases with *ROWTYPE_=LOADING_*, the value of *LEVEL* is blank.
VARNAME_	*String variable containing the original variable names.*

VARTYPE_   *String variable containing values MULTIPLE, SINGLE N, ORDINAL, or NUMERICAL, depending on the optimal scaling level specified for the variable.*

DIM1...DIMn   *Numeric variables containing category quantifications, the single-category coordinates, and component loadings for each dimension. Each variable is labeled DIMn, where n represents the dimension number. The single-category coordinates and component loadings are written only for SNOM, ORDI, and NUME variables.*

See the *SPSS Base Syntax Reference Guide* for more information on matrix data files.

Bibliography

Barlow, R. E., D. J. Bartholomew, D. J. Bremner, and H. D. Brunk. 1972. *Statistical inference under order restrictions*. New York: John Wiley and Sons.

Bell, E. H. 1961. *Social foundations of human behavior: Introduction to the study of sociology*. New York: Harper & Row.

Benzecri, J. P. 1969. Statistical analysis as a tool to make patterns emerge from data. In: *Methodologies of pattern recognition*, S. Watanabe, ed. New York: Academic Press.

Bishop, Y. M., S. E. Feinberg, and P. W. Holland. 1975. *Discrete multivariate analysis*. Cambridge, Mass.: MIT Press.

Breiman, L., and J. H. Friedman. 1985. Estimating optimal transformations for multiple regression and correlation. *Journal of the American Statistical Association*, 80: 580–598.

Buja, A. 1990. Remarks on functional canonical variates, alternating least squares methods and ACE. *Annals of Statistics*, 18: 1032-1069.

Carroll, J. D. 1968. Generalization of canonical correlation analysis to three or more sets of variables. *Proceedings of the 76th annual convention of the American Psychological Association*, 3: 227–228.

Carroll, J. D., and P. E. Green. 1988. An INDSCAL-based approach to multiple correspondence analysis. *Journal of Marketing Research*, 55: 193–203.

De Leeuw, J. 1982. Nonlinear principal components analysis. In: *COMPSTAT Proceedings in Computational Statistics*, 77–89. Vienna: Physica Verlag.

_____. 1984. *Canonical analysis of categorical data*. 2nd ed. Leiden: DSWO Press.

_____. 1984. The Gifi system of nonlinear multivariate analysis. In: *Data analysis and informatics*, E. Diday et al., eds. III: 415–424.

De Leeuw, J., and J. Van Rijckevorsel. 1980. HOMALS and PRINCALS—Some generalizations of principal components analysis. In: *Data analysis and informatics*, E. Diday et al., eds. Amsterdam: North-Holland.

De Leeuw, J., F. W. Young, and Y. Takane. 1976. Additive structure in qualitative data: An alternating least squares method with optimal scaling features. *Psychometrika*, 41: 471–503.

Eckart, C., and G. Young. 1936. The approximation of one matrix by another one of lower rank. *Psychometrika*, I: 211–218.

Fisher, R. A. 1938. *Statistical methods for research workers*. Edinburgh: Oliver and Boyd.

_____. 1940. The precision of discriminant functions. *Annals of Eugenics*, 10: 422–429.

Gabriel, K. R. 1971. The biplot graphic display of matrices with application to principal components analysis. *Biometrika*, 58: 453–467.

Gifi, A. 1985. *PRINCALS*. Research Report UG-85-02. Leiden: Department of Data Theory, University of Leiden.

_____. 1990. *Nonlinear multivariate analysis*. Chichester: John Wiley and Sons (First edition 1981, Department of Data Theory, University of Leiden).

Gilula, Z., and S. J. Haberman. 1988. The analysis of multivariate contingency tables by restricted canonical and restricted association models. *Journal of the American Statistical Association*, 83: 760–771.

Gower, J. C. and J. J. Meulman. 1993. The treatment of categorical information in physical anthropology. *International Journal of Anthropology*, 8: 43–51.

Green, P. E., and Y. Wind. 1973. *Multiattribute decisions in marketing: A measurement approach*. Hinsdale, Ill.: Dryden Press.

Greenacre, M. J. 1984. *Theory and applications of correspondence analysis*. London: Academic Press.

Guttman, L. 1941. The quantification of a class of attributes: A theory and method of scale construction. In: *The prediction of personal adjustment*, P. Horst et al., eds. New York: Social Science Research Council.

_____. 1968. A general nonmetric technique for finding the smallest coordinate space for configurations of points. *Psychometrika*, 33: 469–506.

Hartigan, J. A. 1975. *Clustering algorithms*. New York: John Wiley and Sons.

Hastie, T. J. and R. J. Tibshirani. 1990. *Generalized additive models*. London: Chapman and Hall.

Heiser, W. J. 1981. *Unfolding analysis of proximity data*. Leiden: Department of Data Theory, University of Leiden.

Heiser, W. J., and J. J. Meulman. 1994. Homogeneity analysis: exploring the distribution of variables and their nonlinear relationships. In: *Correspondence analysis in the social sciences: Recent developments and applications*, M. Greenacre and J. Blasius, eds. New York: Academic Press, 179–209.

_____. 1995. Nonlinear methods for the analysis of homogeneity and heterogeneity. In: W. J. Krzanowski (Ed.), *Recent advances in descriptive multivariate analysis*. Oxford: Oxford University Press, 51–89.

Horst, P. 1935. Measuring complex attitudes. *Journal of Social Psychology*, 6: 369–374.

_____. 1963. *Matrix algebra for social scientists*. New York: Holt, Rinehart and Winston.

Israels, A. 1987. *Eigenvalue techniques for qualitative data*. Leiden: DSWO Press.

Kennedy, R., C. Riquier, and B. Sharp. 1996. Practical applications of correspondence analysis to categorical data in market research. *Journal of Targeting, Mearurement, and Analysis for Marketing*, 5(1): 56–70

Kruskal, J. B. 1964. Multidimensional scaling by optimizing goodness of fit to a nonmetric hypothesis. *Psychometrika*, 29: 1–28.

_____. 1964. Nonmetric multidimensional scaling: A numerical method. *Psychometrika*, 29: 115–129.

_____. 1965. Analysis of factorial experiments by estimating monotone transformations of the data. *Journal of the Royal Statistical Society Series B*, 27: 251–263.

_____. 1978. Factor analysis and principal components analysis: bilinear methods. In: *International encyclopedia of statistics*: 307-330, W. H. Kruskal and J. M. Tanur, eds. New York: The Free Press.

Kruskal, J. B., and R. N. Shepard. 1974. A nonmetric variety of linear factor analysis. *Psychometrika*, 39: 123–157.

Krzanowski W. J. and F. H. C. Marriott. 1994. *Multivariate analysis: Part I, distributions, ordination and inference*, Edward Arnold, London, 1994.

Lebart L., A. Morineau, and K. M. Warwick. 1984. *Multivariate descriptive statistical analysis*. New York: John Wiley and Sons.

Lingoes, J. C. 1968. The multivariate analysis of qualitative data. *Multivariate Behavioral Research*, 3: 61–94.

Meulman, J. 1982. *Homogeneity analysis of incomplete data*. Leiden: DSWO Press.

_____. 1986. *A distance approach to nonlinear multivariate analysis*. Leiden: DSWO Press.

_____. 1992. The integration of multidimensional scaling and multivariate analysis with optimal transformations of the variables. *Psychometrika*, 57: 539–565.

_____. 1993. Principal coordinates analysis with optimal transformations of the variables: minimizing the sum of squares of the smallest eigenvalues. *British Journal of Mathematical and Statistical Psychology*, 46: 287–300.

_____. 1996. Fitting a distance model to homogeneous subsets of variables: Points of view analysis of categorical data. *Journal of Classification*, 13: 249–266.

Meulman, J. J. and W. J. Heiser. 1997. Graphical display of interaction in multiway contingency tables by use of homogeneity analysis. In: *Visual display of categorical data*, M. Greenacre and J. Blasius, eds. New York: Academic Press (in press).

Meulman, J. J. and P. Verboon. 1993. Points of view analysis revisited: fitting multidimensional structures to optimal distance components with cluster restrictions on the variables. *Psychometrika*, 58: 7P35.

Nishisato, S. 1980. *Analysis of categorical data: Dual scaling and its applications*. Toronto: University of Toronto Press.

_____. 1994, *Elements of dual scaling: An introduction to practical data analysis*. Hillsdale: Lawrence Erlbaum Associates, Inc.

Ramsay, J. O. 1989. Monotone regression splines in action. *Statistical Science*, 4: 425–441.

Rao, C. R. 1973. *Linear statistical inference and its applications*. New York: John Wiley and Sons.

_____. 1980. Matrix approximations and reduction of dimensionality in multivariate statistical analysis. In: *Multivariate Analysis*, Vol. 5, P. R. Krishnaiah, ed. Amsterdam: North-Holland.

Roskam, E. E. 1968. *Metric analysis of ordinal data in psychology*. Voorschoten, VAM.

Shepard, R. N. 1962a. The analysis of proximities: Multidimensional scaling with an unknown distance function I. *Psychometrika*, 27: 125–140.

_____. 1962b. The analysis of proximities: Multidimensional scaling with an unknown distance function II. *Psychometrika*, 27: 219–246.

_____. 1966. Metric structures in ordinal data. *Journal of Mathematical Psychology*, 3: 287–315.

Tenenhaus, M., and F. W. Young. 1985. An analysis and synthesis of multiple correspondence analysis, optimal scaling, dual scaling, homogeneity analysis, and other methods for quantifying categorical multivariate data. *Psychometrika*, 50: 91–119.

Tucker, L. R. 1960. Intra-individual and inter-individual multidimensionality. In: *Psychological Scaling: Theory & Applications*, H. Gulliksen and S. Messick, eds. New York: Wiley.

Van der Burg, E. 1988. *Nonlinear canonical correlation and some related techniques*. Leiden: DSWO Press.

Van der Burg, E., and J. De Leeuw. 1983. Nonlinear canonical correlation. *British Journal of Mathematical and Statistical Psychology*, 36: 54–80.

Van der Burg, E., J. De Leeuw, and R. Verdegaal. 1988. Homogeneity analysis with k sets of variables: An alternating least squares method with optimal scaling features. *Psychometrika*, 53: 177–197.

Van der Ham, Th., J. J. Meulman, D. C. Van Strien, and H. Van Engeland. 1997. Empirically based subgrouping of eating disorders in adolescents: a longitudinal perspective. *British Journal of Psychiatry*, 170: 363–368.

Van der Kooij, A. J., and J. J. Meulman. 1997. MURALS: Multiple regression and optimal scaling using alternating least squares. In: *Softstat '97*: 99–106, F. Faulbaum and W. Bandilla, eds. Stuttgart: Gustav Fisher.

Van Rijckevorsel, J. 1987. *The application of fuzzy coding and horseshoes in multiple correspondence analysis*. Leiden: DSWO Press.

Verboon, P., and I. A. Van der Lans. 1994. Robust canonical discriminant analysis. *Psychometrika*, 59: 485–507.

Verdegaal, R. 1985. *Meer sets analyse voor kwalitatieve gegevens* (in Dutch). Leiden: Department of Data Theory, University of Leiden.

Vlek, C. and P. J. Stallen. 1981. Judging risks and benefits in the small and in the large. *Organizational Behavior and Human Performance*, 28: 235–271.

Wagenaar, W. A. 1988. *Paradoxes of gambling behaviour*. London: Lawrence Erlbaum Associates.

Winsberg, S., and J. O. Ramsay. 1983. Monotone spline transformations for dimension reduction. *Psychometrika*, 48: 575–595.

Wolter, K. M. 1985. *Introduction to variance estimation*. Berlin: Springer-Verlag.

Young, F. W. 1981. Quantitative analysis of qualitative data. *Psychometrika*, 40: 357–387.

Young, F. W., J. De Leeuw, and Y. Takane. 1976. Regression with qualitative and quantitative variables: An alternating least squares method with optimal scaling features. *Psychometrika*, 41: 505–528.

Young, F. W., Y. Takane, and J. De Leeuw. 1978. The principal components of mixed measurement level multivariate data: An alternating least squares method with optimal scaling features. *Psychometrika*, 43: 279–281.

Subject Index

active row
    in Correspondence Analysis procedure, 129
aggregated data
    in Correspondence Analysis procedure, 169–170
alternating least squares, 83, 101, 145
analyzing aggregated data
    in Correspondence Analysis procedure, 195
analyzing table data
    in Correspondence Analysis procedure, 188
aspect ratio, 19

biplots, 12, 133, 134–135, 142
    in Correspondence Analysis procedure, 51, 193

canonical correlations, 106
cases
    excluding from Homogeneity Analysis procedure, 201
    excluding from Nonlinear Canonical Correlation Analysis procedure, 210
    excluding from Nonlinear Principal Components Analysis procedure, 220
casewise data, 164
Categorical Regression. *See* Regression with Optimal Scaling procedure
categorizing variables, 73–74
category quantifications
    in Homogeneity Analysis procedure, 56, 145, 150–152
    in Nonlinear Canonical Correlation Analysis procedure, 40
    in Nonlinear Principal Components Analysis procedure, 31, 84
    in Regression with Optimal Scaling procedure, 24
CATREG. *See* Regression with Optimal Scaling procedure

centroid plots
    in Nonlinear Canonical Correlation Analysis procedure, 212
centroids
    in Correspondence Analysis procedure, 125
    in Nonlinear Canonical Correlation Analysis procedure, 40, 101, 112–114, 117–118
chi-square distances
    in Correspondence Analysis procedure, 122, 191
coding categories, 7–9
column scores
    in Correspondence Analysis procedure, 126–127, 144, 171–175
component loadings
    in Nonlinear Canonical Correlation Analysis procedure, 40, 108
    in Nonlinear Principal Components Analysis procedure, 31, 90–91, 93, 95–96, 97
confidence statistics
    in Correspondence Analysis procedure, 49, 136–137
contributions
    in Correspondence Analysis procedure, 130–133, 139–140
correlations
    in Correspondence Analysis procedure, 171
    part, 66
    partial, 65
    zero-order, 65
Correspondence Analysis procedure, 3, 12–14, 43, 119–144, 185–196
    active row, 129
    aggregated data, 169–170
    centroids, 125
    chi-square distance, 122
    column principal normalization, 133
    column scores, 126–127, 144, 171–175
    compared to crosstabulation, 12–13, 119
    compared to Homogeneity Analysis procedure, 14, 15
    confidence statistics, 136–137
    contributions, 130–133, 139–140
    correlations, 171

custom normalization, 135, 165–166
dimensions, 129–130, 138, 168, 189
distance measure, 191
distances, 124–125, 127
equality constraints, 119, 129, 190
inertia, 126, 127, 129–130
interaction variables, 13–14
labeling plots, 167–168
mass, 125
matrix output, 168–169
normalization, 122–123, 133–135, 191
permutations, 135–136
plots, 43, 121–124, 193
principal normalization, 133, 140–141, 144
profiles, 124–125
row principal normalization, 122–123, 133
row scores, 126–127, 144, 171–175
singular values, 130, 171–172
standardization, 119–120, 191
statistics, 43
supplementary points, 120, 127–129, 189
symmetrical normalization, 133, 142
transformed column scores, 173
transformed row scores, 173
correspondence tables, 12, 119, 143
crosstabulation
    compared to Correspondence Analysis procedure,
        119

dimension reduction, 2
dimensions, 15–18
    in 3D scatterplots, 16
    in Correspondence Analysis procedure, 48,
        129–130, 138, 168, 189
    in Homogeneity Analysis procedure, 146, 203
    in Nonlinear Canonical Correlation Analysis
        procedure, 105, 212–213
    in Nonlinear Principal Components Analysis
        procedure, 87, 91, 94, 96, 223
    saving in Nonlinear Canonical Correlation
        Analysis procedure, 213–214
    saving in Nonlinear Principal Components
        Analysis procedure, 223–224
discrimination measures
    in Homogeneity Analysis procedure, 56, 148–149,
        154–155
dissimilarities, 143

distance measures
    in Correspondence Analysis procedure, 48, 191
distances
    in Correspondence Analysis procedure, 124–125,
        127

eigenvalues
    in Homogeneity Analysis procedure, 56, 146
    in Nonlinear Canonical Correlation Analysis
        procedure, 104, 106, 115
    in Nonlinear Principal Components Analysis
        procedure, 31, 87
equality constraints
    in Correspondence Analysis procedure, 119, 129,
        187, 190
Euclidean distance
    in Correspondence Analysis procedure, 191

fit
    in Nonlinear Canonical Correlation Analysis
        procedure, 40
    multiple, 107, 115
    single, 107, 115

HOMALS. *See* Homogeneity Analysis procedure
Homogeneity Analysis procedure, 3, 14–15, 53
    category quantifications, 145, 150–152
    compared to Correspondence Analysis procedure,
        14, 15, 145
    compared to crosstabulation, 14
    compared to factor analysis, 15
    compared to principal components analysis, 15
    dimensions, 146, 203
    discrimination measures, 148–149, 154–155
    eigenvalues, 146
    excluding cases, 201
    labeling plots, 202
    matrix output, 205
    object scores, 145, 147–148, 152–154, 155–156
    plots, 53
    saving object scores, 204
    statistics, 53
    value labels, 203
    variable labels, 203
    variance, 148

importance
    in Regression with Optimal Scaling procedure, 66, 78
INCLUDE files, 161
inertia
    in Correspondence Analysis procedure, 49, 126, 127, 129
initial configuration
    in Nonlinear Canonical Correlation Analysis procedure, 40, 103
    in Regression with Optimal Scaling procedure, 24, 181
isotropic scaling, 19

linear canonical correlation analysis
    compared to nonlinear canonical correlation analysis, 101
linear regression, 60–62
    model fit, 60
    residuals, 61
low-resolution charts, 19

mass
    in Correspondence Analysis procedure, 125
matrix output
    in Correspondence Analysis procedure, 168–169
    in Homogeneity Analysis procedure, 205
    in Nonlinear Canonical Correlation Analysis procedure, 214–215
    in Nonlinear Principal Components Analysis procedure, 224–225
measurement level
    compared to optimal scaling level, 3–4
missing values, 8
    in Regression with Optimal Scaling procedure, 24, 178, 181
model fit
    in Regression with Optimal Scaling procedure, 64
multicollinearity
    in Regression with Optimal Scaling procedure, 62–63, 67
multiple category coordinates
    in Nonlinear Canonical Correlation Analysis procedure, 101, 111–112

in Nonlinear Principal Components Analysis procedure, 88
multiple correlation
    in Nonlinear Canonical Correlation Analysis procedure, 105
multiple correspondence analysis, 14, 145

Nonlinear Canonical Correlation Analysis procedure, 3, 11–12, 35
    centroid plots, 212
    centroids, 101, 112–114, 117–118
    compared to canonical correlation analysis, 11–12
    compared to Homogeneity Analysis procedure, 12
    compared to Nonlinear Principal Components Analysis procedure, 12
    compared to Regression with Optimal Scaling procedure, 12
    component loadings, 108
    dimensions, 105, 212–213
    eigenvalues, 104, 106, 115
    excluding cases, 210
    fit, 104–107
    initial configuration, 103
    loss, 104–107
    matrix output, 214–215
    multiple category coordinates, 101, 111–112
    multiple correlation, 105
    multiple fit, 107, 115
    object scores, 103–104
    optimal scaling level, 209
    outliers, 103–104
    plots, 35
    projected centroids, 102, 112–114, 117–118
    quantifications, 111–112
    saving dimensions, 213–214
    saving object scores, 213–214
    sets, 101
    single category coordinates, 102, 111–112
    single fit, 107, 115
    single loss, 107
    statistics, 35
    transformation plots, 109–110, 115–117, 212
    value labels, 212–213
    variable labels, 212–213
    weights, 102
Nonlinear Principal Components Analysis procedure, 3, 10–11, 27
    category quantifications, 84

compared to classical principal components analysis, 10–11, 83
compared to factor analysis, 11
compared to Homogeneity Analysis procedure, 11
component loadings, 90–91, 93, 95–96, 97
dimensions, 87, 91, 94, 96, 223
eigenvalues, 87
excluding cases, 220
labeling plots, 222–223
matrix output, 224–225
object scores, 84, 89–90, 92–93, 94–95, 96
optimal scaling level, 83, 84–86, 219–220
plots, 27
quantifications, 88–89
saving dimensions, 223–224
saving object scores, 223–224
statistics, 27
variable labels, 222–223
normalization, 122–124, 133–135
    canonical, 175
    column principal, 133
    custom, 135
    custom in Correspondence Analysis procedure, 165–166
    in Correspondence Analysis procedure, 48, 191
    principal, 133, 140–141
    row principal, 122–124, 133
    symmetrical, 133, 142

object scores
    in Homogeneity Analysis procedure, 56, 145, 147–148, 152–154, 155–156
    in Nonlinear Canonical Correlation Analysis procedure, 40, 103–104
    in Nonlinear Principal Components Analysis procedure, 84, 89–90, 92–93, 94–95, 96
    saving in Homogeneity Analysis procedure, 204
    saving in Nonlinear Canonical Correlation Analysis procedure, 213–214
    saving in Nonlinear Principal Components Analysis procedure, 223–224
optimal scaling
    categories, 83
    objects, 83
optimal scaling level, 3–5, 102
    compared to measurement level, 3–4
    in Nonlinear Canonical Correlation Analysis procedure, 209

    in Nonlinear Principal Components Analysis procedure, 83, 84–86, 219–220
    multiple nominal, 14, 85–86
    nominal, 3, 4, 5, 8, 12, 68, 69, 74
    numerical, 3, 4, 5, 8–9, 67, 68, 85–86, 94–96
    ordinal, 3, 4, 5, 8, 67, 79, 84–86, 96–99
    single nominal, 84–86
outliers
    in Nonlinear Canonical Correlation Analysis procedure, 103–104
OVERALS. See Nonlinear Canonical Correlation Analysis procedure

partial residual plots, 71
perceptual mapping, 2
permutations
    in Correspondence Analysis procedure, 135–136
plots
    in Correspondence Analysis procedure, 51, 121–124, 193
    in Homogeneity Analysis procedure, 14–15, 56
    in Nonlinear Canonical Correlation Analysis procedure, 40
    in Nonlinear Principal Components Analysis procedure, 31
    in Regression with Optimal Scaling procedure, 25, 74–78, 183
Pratt's relative importance measure
    in Regression with Optimal Scaling procedure, 182
PRINCALS. See Nonlinear Principal Components Analysis procedure
profiles
    in Correspondence Analysis procedure, 124–125
projected centroids
    in Nonlinear Canonical Correlation Analysis procedure, 102, 112–114, 117–118

quantifications
    in Nonlinear Canonical Correlation Analysis procedure, 111–112
    in Nonlinear Principal Components Analysis procedure, 88–89

regression coefficients
  in Regression with Optimal Scaling procedure, 24
Regression with Optimal Scaling procedure, 2–3,
      9–10, 21, 59–82, 176–184
  compared to linear regression, 10
  compared to loglinear modeling, 10
  compared to Nonlinear Canonical Correlation
      Analysis procedure, 10
  compared to standard linear regression, 59
  correlations, 65–66
  importance, 66, 78
  initial configuration, 181
  intercorrelations, 62–63
  linearity, 80–82
  missing values, 181
  model fit, 64
  multicollinearity, 62–63, 67
  optimal scaling level
  optimality, 79–80
  plots, 21, 67–69, 75–78, 183
  residuals, 70–72
  response variable, 62, 74
  standardized regression coefficients, 64, 74, 78
  statistics, 21
  transformation type, 74–79
residuals
  in Regression with Optimal Scaling procedure,
      70–72
row scores
  in Correspondence Analysis procedure, 126–127,
      144, 171–175

scatterplot matrices, 17–18, 92
sets
  in Nonlinear Canonical Correlation Analysis
      procedure, 101
similarities, 143
single category coordinates
  in Nonlinear Canonical Correlation Analysis
      procedure, 102, 111–112
  in Nonlinear Principal Components Analysis
      procedure, 88
single loss, 107
singular values, 130
  in Correspondence Analysis procedure, 171–172

standardization
  in Correspondence Analysis procedure, 48,
      119–120, 191
standardized regression coefficients, 60–61
  in Regression with Optimal Scaling procedure, 64,
      74
sunflower plots, 147
supplementary points
  in Correspondence Analysis procedure, 120,
      127–129, 189
syntax
  diagrams, 159–160
  INCLUDE files, 161
  rules, 159–160
table data, 164–165
transformation plots, 5–7
  creating, 6–7
  in Nonlinear Canonical Correlation Analysis
      procedure, 109–110, 115–117, 212
  in Nonlinear Principal Components Analysis
      procedure, 97–99
transformation type, 59
  nominal, 62, 68, 69, 74
  numerical, 62, 67, 68
  ordinal, 62, 67, 79
  See also optimal scaling level
transformed column scores
  in Correspondence Analysis procedure, 173
transformed row scores
  in Correspondence Analysis procedure, 173

value labels
  as point labels in Correspondence Analysis
      procedure, 167
  as point labels in Homogeneity Analysis procedure,
      202
  as point labels in Nonlinear Canonical Correlation
      Analysis procedure, 212–213
  as point labels in Nonlinear Principal Components
      Analysis procedure, 222–223
  in Homogeneity Analysis procedure, 203
variable labels
  as plot labels in Homogeneity Analysis procedure,
      202
  as plot labels in Nonlinear Canonical Correlation
      Analysis procedure, 212–213

as plot labels in Nonlinear Principal Components
        Analysis procedure, 222–223
    in Homogeneity Analysis procedure, 203
    in Nonlinear Principal Components Analysis
        procedure, 222–223
variance
    in Homogeneity Analysis procedure, 148
    in Nonlinear Canonical Correlation Analysis
        procedure, 107
weights
    in Nonlinear Canonical Correlation Analysis
        procedure, 40, 102

Syntax Index

aggregate data
  ANACOR command, 169–170
ALL (keyword)
  ANACOR command, 164–165, 168
  CORRESPONDENCE command, 188
  HOMALS command, 202
  OVERALS command, 213
  PRINCALS command, 221–223
ANACOR (command), 162–175
  aggregate data, 169–170
  DIMENSION subcommand, 165, 171, 171
  MATRIX subcommand, 168–169
  NORMALIZATION subcommand, 165–166
  PLOT subcommand, 167–168, 171
  PRINT subcommand, 166–167, 171
  TABLE subcommand, 164–165, 171
  value labels, 167, 170–171
  VARIANCES subcommand, 166
  with WEIGHT command, 169–170
ANALYSIS (subcommand)
  CATREG command, 179, 180
  HOMALS command, 200
  OVERALS command, 209
  PRINCALS command, 219–220
  with SETS subcommand, 209–210
  with VARIABLES subcommand, 200, 209
analyzing aggregated data
  in Correspondence Analysis, 195
ANOVA (keyword)
  CATREG command, 182
AUTORECODE (command)
  with HOMALS command, 198–199
  with OVERALS command, 208
  with PRINCALS command, 218–219
AUTORECODE command
  with CATREG command, 178

BIPLOT (keyword)
  CORRESPONDENCE command, 193

CANONICAL (keyword)
  ANACOR command, 165–166
CATREG (command), 176–184
  ANALYSIS subcommand, 179, 180
  CONVERGENCE subcommand, 179, 181
  INITIAL subcommand, 179, 181
  MAXITER subcommand, 179, 181
  MISSING subcommand, 179, 181
  OUTFILE subcommand, 179, 184
  PLOT subcommand, 179, 183
  PRINT subcommand, 179, 182
  SAVE subcommand, 179, 183
  VARIABLES subcommand, 179, 180
  with AUTORECODE command, 178
CCONF (keyword)
  CORRESPONDENCE command, 193
CENTROID (keyword)
  OVERALS command, 211, 212–213
CHISQ (keyword)
  CORRESPONDENCE command, 191
CMEAN (keyword)
  CORRESPONDENCE command, 191
COEFF (keyword)
  CATREG command, 182
COLUMNS (keyword)
  ANACOR command, 166, 167–168
CONTRIBUTIONS (keyword)
  ANACOR command, 167
CONVERGENCE (subcommand)
  CATREG command, 179, 181
  HOMALS command, 201
  OVERALS command, 211
  PRINCALS command, 221
CORR (keyword)
  CATREG command, 182
CORRELATION (keyword)
  PRINCALS command, 221
CORRESPONDENCE (command), 185–196
  DIMENSION subcommand, 189
  EQUAL subcommand, 190
  MEASURE subcommand, 191
  NORMALIZATION subcommand, 191
  OUTFILE subcommand, 194
  PLOT subcommand, 193

PRINT subcommand, 192
STANDARDIZE subcommand, 191
SUPPLEMENTARY subcommand, 189
TABLE subcommand, 187
CPOINTS (keyword)
CORRESPONDENCE command, 193
CPRINCIPAL (keyword)
ANACOR command, 166
CORRESPONDENCE command, 192
CPROFILES (keyword)
CORRESPONDENCE command, 192
CSUM (keyword)
CORRESPONDENCE command, 191

DEFAULT (keyword)
ANACOR command, 167, 167–168
CATREG command, 182
CORRESPONDENCE command, 193
HOMALS command, 202
OVERALS command, 211, 212–213
PRINCALS command, 221, 222–223
DIM variable
ANACOR command, 169
HOMALS command, 205
OVERALS command, 215
PRINCALS command, 225
DIMENSION (subcommand)
ANACOR command, 165, 171
CORRESPONDENCE command, 189
HOMALS command, 201
OVERALS command, 210
PRINCALS command, 220
with SAVE subcommand, 204, 213, 223–224
DIMn variable
CORRESPONDENCE command, 195
DISCRIM (keyword)
HOMALS command, 202

EIGEN (keyword)
HOMALS command, 202
PRINCALS command, 221
EQUAL (subcommand)
CORRESPONDENCE command, 190
EUCLID (keyword)
CORRESPONDENCE command, 191

FIT (keyword)
OVERALS command, 211
FREQ (keyword)
CATREG command, 182
HOMALS command, 201
OVERALS command, 211
PRINCALS command, 221

HISTORY (keyword)
CATREG command, 182
HOMALS command, 202
OVERALS command, 211
PRINCALS command, 221
HOMALS
value labels, 203
HOMALS (command), 197
ANALYSIS subcommand, 200
compared to OVERALS, 209
CONVERGENCE subcommand, 201
DIMENSION subcommand, 201
MATRIX subcommand, 205
MAXITER subcommand, 201
NOBSERVATIONS subcommand, 201
PLOT subcommand, 202
PRINT subcommand, 201
SAVE subcommand, 204
variable labels, 203
VARIABLES subcommand, 199
with AUTORECODE command, 198–199
with RECODE command, 198
Homogeneity, 203

INITIAL (subcommand)
CATREG command, 179, 181
OVERALS command, 210–211

JOINT (keyword)
ANACOR command, 167–168

LEVEL variable
ANACOR command, 169
HOMALS command, 205

OVERALS command, 214
PRINCALS command, 224
LEVEL_ variable
CORRESPONDENCE command, 195
LISTWISE (keyword)
CATREG command, 181
LOADINGS (keyword)
OVERALS command, 212–213
PRINCALS command, 221, 221–223

MATRIX (subcommand)
ANACOR command, 168–169
HOMALS command, 205
OVERALS command, 214–215
PRINCALS command, 224–225
with SAVE subcommand, 204, 214, 224
MAX (keyword)
ANACOR command, 168
CORRESPONDENCE command, 194
HOMALS command, 203
OVERALS command, 213
PRINCALS command, 223
MAXITER (subcommand)
CATREG command, 179, 181
HOMALS command, 201
OVERALS command, 211
PRINCALS command, 220
MEASURE (subcommand)
CORRESPONDENCE command, 191
MISSING (subcommand)
CATREG command, 179, 181
missing values
with OVERALS command, 208
with PRINCALS command, 218
MNOM (keyword)
OVERALS command, 209
PRINCALS command, 219
MODEIMPU (keyword)
CATREG command, 182

NDIM (keyword)
ANACOR command, 168
CORRESPONDENCE command, 194
HOMALS command, 203
OVERALS command, 212–213
PRINCALS command, 223

NOBSERVATIONS (subcommand)
HOMALS command, 201
OVERALS command, 210
PRINCALS command, 220
NOMI (keyword)
CATREG command, 180
NONE (keyword)
ANACOR command, 167, 167–168
CATREG command, 182
CORRESPONDENCE command, 193
HOMALS command, 202
OVERALS command, 211, 212–213
PRINCALS command, 221, 222–223
NORMALIZATION (subcommand)
ANACOR command, 165–166, 171
CORRESPONDENCE command, 191
with PLOT subcommand, 167
NUME (keyword)
CATREG command, 180
OVERALS command, 209
PRINCALS command, 220
NUMERICAL (keyword)
CATREG command, 181
OVERALS command, 210–211

OBJECT (keyword)
HOMALS command, 202
OVERALS command, 211, 212–213
PRINCALS command, 221, 221–223
OCORR (keyword)
CATREG command, 182
ORDI (keyword)
CATREG command, 180
OVERALS command, 209
PRINCALS command, 220
OUT (keyword)
ANACOR command, 168
HOMALS command, 205
OUTFILE (subcommand)
CATREG command, 179, 184
CORRESPONDENCE command, 194
OVERALS (command), 206–215
active variables, 209
ANALYSIS subcommand, 209
compared to HOMALS, 209
compared to PRINCALS, 209
CONVERGENCE subcommand, 211
DIMENSION subcommand, 210

INITIAL subcommand, 210–211
MATRIX subcommand, 214–215
MAXITER subcommand, 211
NOBSERVATIONS subcommand, 210
passive variables, 209
PLOT subcommand, 212–213
PRINT subcommand, 211
SAVE subcommand, 213–214
SETS subcommand, 209–210
value labels, 212–213
variable labels, 212–213
VARIABLES subcommand, 208–209
with AUTORECODE command, 208
with RECODE command, 208

PERMUTATION (keyword)
ANACOR command, 167
CORRESPONDENCE command, 193
PLOT (subcommand)
ANACOR command, 167–168, 171
CATREG command, 179, 183
CORRESPONDENCE command, 193
HOMALS command, 202
OVERALS command, 212–213
PRINCALS command, 94, 221–223
with NORMALIZATION subcommand, 167
PRINCALS (command), 216
ANALYSIS subcommand, 219–220
compared to OVERALS, 209
DIMENSION subcommand, 220
MATRIX subcommand, 224–225
MAXITER subcommand, 220
NOBSERVATIONS subcommand, 220
PLOT subcommand, 94, 221–223
PRINT subcommand, 221
SAVE subcommand, 223–224
value labels, 222–223
variable labels, 222–223
VARIABLES subcommand, 218–219
with AUTORECODE command, 218, 218–219
with RECODE command, 218, 218–219
PRINCIPAL (keyword)
ANACOR command, 166
CORRESPONDENCE command, 192
PRINT (subcommand)
ANACOR command, 166–167, 171
CATREG command, 179, 182
CORRESPONDENCE command, 192

HOMALS command, 201
OVERALS command, 211
PRINCALS command, 221
PROFILES (keyword)
ANACOR command, 167

QUANT (keyword)
CATREG command, 182, 183
HOMALS command, 202
OVERALS command, 211, 212–213
PRINCALS command, 221, 221–223

R (keyword)
CATREG command, 182
RANDOM (keyword)
CATREG command, 181
OVERALS command, 210–211
RCMEAN (keyword)
CORRESPONDENCE command, 191
RCONF (keyword)
CORRESPONDENCE command, 193
RECODE (command)
with HOMALS command, 198
with OVERALS command, 208
with PRINCALS command, 218, 218–219
RMEAN (keyword)
CORRESPONDENCE command, 191
ROWS (keyword)
ANACOR command, 166, 167–168
ROWTYPE_ variable
ANACOR command, 168–169
CORRESPONDENCE command, 195
HOMALS command, 205
OVERALS command, 214
PRINCALS command, 224
RPOINTS (keyword)
CORRESPONDENCE command, 192, 193
RPRINCIPAL (keyword)
ANACOR command, 166
CORRESPONDENCE command, 192
RPROFILES (keyword)
CORRESPONDENCE command, 192
RSUM (keyword)
CORRESPONDENCE command, 191

SAVE (subcommand)
  CATREG command, 179, 183
  HOMALS command, 204
  OVERALS command, 213–214
  PRINCALS command, 223–224
  with DIMENSION subcommand, 204, 213, 223–224
  with MATRIX subcommand, 204, 214, 224
SCORE (keyword)
  ANACOR command, 168–169
  CORRESPONDENCE command, 194
SCORE variable
  ANACOR command, 169
SCORE_ variable
  CORRESPONDENCE command, 195
SCORES (keyword)
  ANACOR command, 167
SET_ variable
  OVERALS command, 215
SETS (subcommand)
  OVERALS command, 209–210
  with ANALYSIS subcommand, 209–210
SINGULAR (keyword)
  ANACOR command, 166
SNOM (keyword)
  OVERALS command, 209
  PRINCALS command, 219
STANDARDIZE (subcommand)
  CORRESPONDENCE command, 191
SUPPLEMENTARY (subcommand)
  CORRESPONDENCE command, 189
SYMMETRICAL (keyword)
  CORRESPONDENCE command, 191

TABLE (keyword)
  ANACOR command, 166
  CORRESPONDENCE command, 192
TABLE (subcommand)
  ANACOR command, 164–165, 171
  casewise data, 164
  CORRESPONDENCE command, 187
  table data, 164–165
TRANS (keyword)
  CATREG command, 182
  OVERALS command, 212–213
TRCOLUMNS (keyword)
  ANACOR command, 167–168
  CORRESPONDENCE command, 193

TRROWS (keyword)
  ANACOR command, 167–168
  CORRESPONDENCE command, 193

value labels
  ANACOR command, 167
VALUE LABELS (command)
  with ANACOR command, 170–171
VARIABLES (subcommand)
  CATREG command, 179, 180
  HOMALS command, 199
  OVERALS command, 208–209
  PRINCALS command, 218–219
  with ANALYSIS subcommand, 200, 209
VARIANCE (keyword)
  ANACOR command, 169
  CORRESPONDENCE command, 194
VARIANCES (subcommand)
  ANACOR command, 166
VARNAME_ variable
  ANACOR command, 169
  CORRESPONDENCE command, 195
  HOMALS command, 205
  OVERALS command, 214
  PRINCALS command, 224
VARTYPE_ variable
  OVERALS command, 214
  PRINCALS command, 225

WEIGHT (command)
  with ANACOR command, 169–170
  with CORRESPONDENCE command, 195
WEIGHTS (keyword)
  OVERALS command, 211

ISBN: 1-56827-211-1

9 781568 272115   90000

13263 001